Modal Music Composition

Stephen M. Cormier

Modal Music Composition

!A

Inman & Artz Publishers

Arlington, VA

Modal Music Composition (Fourth Edition) © 2004 - 2020 by
Stephen M. Cormier. All rights reserved. Published by Inman
& Artz Publishers. Printed in the USA by Signature Book
Printing. No part of this book or associated audio files
may be used or reproduced in any manner whatsoever
without written permission from the publisher except for
brief quotations in reviews or books. Inquiries are welcomed.
For information, address Inman & Artz Publishers, P.O. Box
2346, Arlington, VA 22202 or by email to
info@inmanartz.com. Visit www.inmanartz.com for downloads,
information and materials related to this book.

Fourth Edition: First U.S. Printing

ISBN: 978-0-975431849
Library of Congress Control Number: 2020912397

Preface

Modal Music Composition is intended to serve two functions. First, it is a reference source for composers and songwriters with an interest in modal musical scales. Numerous tables and examples provide basic information on modal melodic and harmonic properties in an easily accessible manner. Second, a fresh, systematic approach to the use of modal melody and harmony is presented to specifically compensate for the weaker harmonic stability of the modal scales, compared with the major scale used in tonal compositions. Thus, it may prove useful to those composers and songwriters still working largely within the major-minor tonal system who, nevertheless, feel the weight of its 400 hundred or so years of well-known compositional styles on their musical expression. The book has an even division between a discussion of necessary concepts and practical guidance. I assume that the reader has at least some familiarity with the most basic concepts and practice of tonal harmony such as major, minor and diminished triads, seventh chords, dominant harmonies, modulation and tonal voice leading. However, no specific knowledge of diatonic or other modal scales or music is required or taken for granted. I also describe some cognitive processes that are useful to consider in composition.

This book has had a long, meandering genesis, but if a beginning must be assigned to it, I would place it at the time when I first heard on the radio a harpsichord suite by Jean-Henri d'Anglebert, played by Gustav Leonhardt. Although I didn't know it at the time, the thing that grabbed my ear, apart from the music itself, was the mean-tone tuning used in place of equal temperament. Mean-tone tuning permitted keyboard music to incorporate a few chromatic notes in a key, but still maintained so-called key color, since each key had a distinct set of chromatic tuned intervals. Of course, equal temperament later equalized the scale intervals, thereby eliminating key color, but permitting all chromatic notes to be used freely.

The richness and tang of the mean-tone tuning resonated with me and a few years later, I also became acquainted with the modal music of the Middle Ages and Renaissance. In a different way, this also sounded more varied and subtle, despite blander harmonies. Having these alternatives to the tonal system (and its partner equal temperament) so readily available made the sameness of tonal relations more apparent. Thus, I was prodded to find ways apart from well-worn tonal progressions to add internal variety to music. Atonal (or post-tonal) music, while gripping and beautiful at its best, has difficulty in expressing the brighter emotions of romance, humor and happiness with the same adeptness as the darker, more serious emotions.

Quite a few 20th century jazz or classical works used modality in various ways, sometimes quite abstractly. Almost always, however, modal and tonal progressions are mixed rather than maintaining true modality. The weaker harmonic structure of the modes makes them susceptible to absorption into tonality. A few years ago, however, I came up with some thoughts on how to maintain the harmonic stability of the modes against tonal (major-minor scales) pressures. This book contains the fuller development and explication of those ideas. (Additional materials are available in the Library section of the publisher's website, www.inmanartz.com.)

I would like to thank Dr. Yo Tomita for the use of his very convenient Bach font for musical text. The music examples were created and printed with Sibelius® music notation software (Sibelius Software Ltd.) Thanks also to Lenore Fauliso for assistance and persistence well above the norm in locating and arranging auditions of most of the audio equipment used in recording the audio CD. Barbara Bickley-Stephens has graciously provided the apt and evocative illustration 'Harmony of Space' on the cover. I greatly appreciate Dr. Mark Cook (Catholic University of America Dept. of Music) taking the time from his more than busy schedule to provide a thorough and very useful review of an earlier draft of this book. Above all, I wish to express my appreciation to Dr. John Stephens, composer and conductor, for many years of friendship and for his conducting of the Study Composition 3. Needless to say, the responsibility for the ideas expressed and in particular, any errors of commission or omission are mine alone.

About the Author

Stephen M. Cormier has long pursued twin interests in science and music. He studied cognitive and neuro-psychology as well as music theory and history at the George Washington University where he received a doctorate in Cognitive Psychology. He has a particular interest in the association of cognition and information processing with emotion, as seen in his extended monograph, *Basic processes of learning, cognition and motivation*. Dr. Cormier has also served as Editor and written book chapters and articles in the field of human learning. With respect to music, he has studied violin, composed chamber and vocal music, made arrangements and has an active interest in audiophile recording techniques.

About the Audio Files*

Track Listing continued

[23] **Ex. 23: Lydian Modulation**
a. F – C   b. F - G
[24] **Ex. 24: Mixolydian Modulation**
a. G – C   b. G - D
[25] **Ex. 25: Aeolian Modulation**
a. A – E   b. A - D
[26] **Ex. 26: Locrian Modulation**
a. B - F♯   b. B - A
[27] **Ex. 27: Ionian Augmented Chords**
a. Augmented Tonic   b. Augmented Subdominant
c. Augmented Dominant   d. Augmented six-four   e. Augmented six-five
[28] **Ex. 28: Modal Augmented Fifth Chords**
a. Lydian Augmented Dominant   b. Lydian Augmented Tonic
c. Locrian Augmented Dominant   d. Mixolydian Augmented Subdominant   e.
Mixolydian Augmented Tonic   f. Mixolydian Augmented Dominant
g. Dorian Augmented Subdominant   h. Dorian Augmented Tonic
i. Dorian Augmented Dominant   j. Phrygian Augmented Tonic
k. Phrygian Augmented Subdominant   l. Aeolian Augmented Dominant
m. Aeolian Augmented Tonic
[29] **Ex. 29: Modal Augmented Six-four and Six-five Progressions**
a. Ionian six-four   b. Ionian six-five   c. Dorian six-four   d. Dorian six-five
e. Phrygian six-four   f. Phrygian six-five   g. Lydian six-four
h. Lydian six-five   i. Mixolydian six-four   j. Mixolydian six-five
k. Aeolian six-four   l. Aeolian six-five   m. Locrian six-four
n. Locrian six-five
[30] **Ex. 30: Dominant Inversions and Root Progressions**
[31] **Ex. 31: Myxolydian Progressions with Inversions**
a. Root Position   b. Non-dominant inversions   c. Dominant inversions
[32] **Ex. 32: Lydian Progressions with Inversions**
a. Root Position   b. First Inversions   c. Second Inversions
*Omitted [33] Ex. 33: Aeolian Progressions Compared to Dorian Progressions
[34] **Ex. 34: Secondary Dominant Progressions**
a. Ionian   b. Aeolian   c. Mixolydian   d. Phrygian   e. Lydian   f. Dorian
[35] **Ex. 35: Modulation between Major and Minor**
a. A minor to A major   b. A Aeolian to A Ionian
* Omitted [36] Ex 36:   Parenthetic Progressions of the Modal Dyads
[37] **Ex. 37: Parenthetic Progressions Only to Modal Steps in Agreement**
a. Lydian   b. Dorian   c. Mixolydian   d. Phrygian
* Omitted [38] Ex 38:   Tonal Degrees of the Modes
[39] **Ex. 39: Diatonic Cadences**
a. Ionian   b. Dorian   c. Phrygian   d. Lydian   e. Mixolydian   f. Aeolian
g. Locrian
[40] **Ex. 40: Dissonant Cadences**
a. Diatonic   b. Modal Chromatic   c. Unprepared Chromatic   d. Chromatic

Track Listing continued

---

* Audio Files available for download at www.inmanartz.com in the Library or contact Inman & Artz Publishers at info@inmanartz.com

Musicians

Examples for keyboard: Tracks 1 - 46

       Piano: Professor Steven Strunk (late)

Study Song Composition 1: Tracks 48
Study Composition 1 and 2: Tracks 49-50

       Sibelius® Music Notation program v.6 with Kontakt Player Gold (Native Instruments)

Study Composition 3: Track 51

       Conductor: Dr. John Stephens (late)
       American Symphonic Clarinet Choir:
           Leader: Michael Kelly
           E♭ Clarinet: Ben Redwine
           B♭ Clarinet 1: Nancy Genovese
           B♭ Clarinet 2: Jean-Francois Bescond
           Basset-horn: Michael Kelly
           Bass Clarinet 1: Charlene Critcher McDaniel
           Bass Clarinet 2: Denis Malloy
           (E♭ ContraAlto Clarinet: Robbie Robinson)

Equipment

Microphones: Earthworks QTC-1 Omni matched pair
           Schoeps M222 with MK41 capsule (for voice)
Microphone preamp: Millennia Media, Inc. M-2b Tube
Jecklin disk
PS Audio™ Ultimate Outlets™

Recording

Preamp direct to Analog-Digital Converter (no console)
Analog - Digital conversion: 88.2k, 24 bit

Producer: Stephen Cormier
Engineers: Archie Moore & Kimo van Gieson
Studio: Omega Recording Studios, Rockville, MD

Table of Contents

1

Introduction

As with other things of ancient origin, modal music receives a certain respect on one hand, and on the other is regarded as an incomplete or somewhat misshapen ancestor of its modern successor, the major-minor tonal system. The noted tonal theorist, Heinrich Schenker, commented upon the occasional use of modally based passages in the works of Beethoven and Brahms as somewhat delusional exercises, since the passages in question could be analyzed in tonal terms. Naturally, the analysis proved the insufficiency of the modal forms to express tonal concepts as lucidly as the major-minor scale. Of course, the same kind of reasoning could lead to the criticism that the flute is an insufficient wind instrument because it can't play fanfares as well as a trumpet.

Here, modal forms are accepted for the characteristics and properties that they possess. If such properties are sought, either as the basis of the composition or as a salutary modification and expansion of the still largely current tonal system, then modal forms can prove useful (see Jones). Actually, composers have intuitively felt this, since modal passages are often found scattered throughout the works of the most determinedly 19th century tonal composers. However, for the most part, they used modal scales and melodies in a haphazard and loosely integrated fashion, usually as a spot of 'local color' in otherwise firmly tonal works, or as with Fauré, to blur tonal progressions. This form of usage carried over to the more recent folk-tune based styles of popular and classical music. In the 20th century, due to the increased enthusiasm for musical styles devoid of ripe tonal harmonies, composers sometimes adapted medieval and Renaissance musical forms, which were based on modal practice. Of course, more recently jazz has made use of modal scales extensively as the framework for improvisation.

Neither art nor history stands still in an active society and it would be futile and anachronistic to attempt to reinstate the modal art as practiced in the Middle Ages into 21st century music compositions. Nevertheless, I believe that the potentialities inherent in the modal forms were not exhausted by composers of that period, if only because of the overwhelming conservatism of music linked to liturgical functions. On that premise, the modal scales have unexploited melodic and harmonic capabilities, which can be revealed with some modifications and added techniques applied to the original modal style. An analogy could be made with the use of the major and minor scales in the early stages of their development in the 16th and 17th centuries compared to their use by classical and Romantic composers. The scales basically remained the same, but the forms and musical interrelations inherent in them were more fully realized through changes in musical procedures and techniques.

Thus, this book contains a fresh approach to the procedures and methods needed to have a viable modal system for contemporary composers and songwriters. It is recognized that such an approach has to be well organized and detailed to compete with the tonal system. The modified modal system, if viable, should be able to work in varied circumstances, whether used instead of traditional major-minor tonality or alternating with it in a musical work. Of course, in the latter case especially, this updated modal system has to possess a certain correspondence with major-minor tonality so that the seams between the two are not awkwardly obvious. Whether this result can be achieved without hopelessly compromising modal qualities, I have to let readers judge on the basis of their own compositions. But it is important to note that the procedures that have characterized the major-minor scales can also be modified somewhat in the direction of modality, thereby lessening the gulf that needs to be bridged. To put it another way, modality and tonality can be viewed as two ends of the same basic continuum. As with most ends, they are more restrictive (monolithic) in their properties and form than the middle of the continuum. This book tries to show that the hitherto largely unexploited middle offers a greater sense of variety and amplitude while supporting a coherent compositional practice.

Although modal musical practice is often pictured as far removed from tonality, this division is at least somewhat based on historical facts, which can govern musical styles as much or more than purely musical considerations do. Certainly, in absolute terms, the similarities outweigh the differences inasmuch as the major-minor scales are direct descendants of the medieval modes. But major distinctions of style can hinge on relatively subtle differences in the rules governing musical form and content. Medieval modal music not only developed from a specific vocal melodic form (chant), but also for a specific purpose in liturgical services.

2

Naturally, this restriction in use, however much it gradually loosened, fostered a similar restraint in melodic and harmonic expressiveness.

Tonal music evolved in a period of increasing freedom for the composer and may well have been inseparable from that circumstance. Therefore, such composers could more systematically develop or even overdevelop the harmonic characteristics that formed the basis of its particular appeal. This is not to criticize tonality as a system (which would be ridiculous in light of the supreme masterpieces composed with it), but the reaction of 20th century composers to reduce the controlling force of harmony over rhythm and melody, either through atonality or a turn to a freer, diatonic form, was quite predictable. (Although paradoxically, atonality 'simplified' harmonic progressions by making them equally complex rather than equally simpler.)

Parallel circumstances at the end of the 14th and 16th centuries also created a reaction which paved the way for new styles of music. In the 14th century, the innovations in notating rhythm and note duration by de Muris and de Vitry led to works of extreme metrical complexity and part writing unequaled before the 20th century. Within a generation, however, English and Italian composers introduced a more lyrical melodic and harmonic style based on simple inversions of triads. Similarly, the mannered sophistication of madrigal composers at the end of the 16th century led to Monteverdi's operas and a simpler dramatic style a few decades later.

What perhaps sets the contemporary crisis of tonality apart from these earlier stylistic revolutions is the length of time that has passed without any clear successor. Indeed, to some extent, the reactions to tonality have come and gone and left the tonal system like a sandcastle miraculously standing with most of the foundation washed away. This is unprecedented I should think when one considers that a hundred years have passed in the meantime. It is possible that the tonal system has been preserved mostly due to the increasing influence of popular culture on art. And yet even popular music has shown a decided reluctance in recent decades to cling too closely to conventional major-minor forms. For example, the Beatles' use of modal scales in their songs has been well documented and popular music in general often displays an avoidance of clear tonic cadences at the close.

In times past, when a musical style became overly refined and stylized, composers would often borrow from popular or folk music to create a new, simplified, but also more direct expression. Composers in the 1920's and 30's did incorporate jazz elements occasionally and often made use of folk music from their own or other cultures, ironically at the

3

same time that these folk music styles were themselves fading away. Yet American popular music, and by extension much of world popular music, was derived from Hollywood or Broadway which itself was diluted classical music rather than an authentic and direct folk style.

Oddly enough, classical composers almost never employed the most resilient folk style, the blues, except very indirectly through jazz. It must also be admitted that, unless the influence is subtle, most such jazz-influenced classical compositions sound dated today. (This is in contrast to jazz compositions themselves, which often effectively integrate blues styles.) The blues and its associated modal scales had a strong influence on rock and related popular styles later in the 20th century, but seldom developed much beyond the early electric guitar blues of performers such as Muddy Waters or T-Bone Walker. Part of the problem for the jazz-influenced classical compositions lay in the strong rhythmic emphasis of these popular styles, which classically trained musicians find difficult to emulate. Classical music almost never requires that kind of rhythmic swing and timing, particularly at the level of the ensemble.

Thus, at the start of the 21st century, classical music (or formal music, which is perhaps a better term for music that requires notation to be created or performed), finds itself uneasily split along the fault line set by the definitive work of the past century, Le Sacre du Printemps. One camp relies on tonal and quasi-modal melodies typically based on folk or other relatively straightforward styles, while the other holds to chromatic or occasionally a noise-based atonality. In my view, although the latter post-tonal approach has much to recommend it, its acceptance by the public audience remains limited and it may remain as a style for connoisseurs. And it seems unlikely that the public will ever totally forsake a vocal melody-based musical style.

The search for a melodic style neither anachronistic nor abrasive continues to be perhaps the central issue perplexing composers of formal music. It might be asked how an approach founded on the medieval modes can avoid the peril of datedness. Clearly, an approach must be adopted which doesn't bind itself to the rules and restrictions typical of pre-tonal music.

To some extent, Romantic and some later composers did use modal passages in a non-modal context. A modal progression in these works might display occasional seventh and ninth chords and have a mildly complex melodic pattern, while retaining diatonic harmony. However, tonal forms quickly reassert themselves after a few measures. This indicates that the main purpose was to provide a momentary relief from the tonal cadential progressions and formulas. The modes fell out of favor due to their relative lack of harmonic clarity compared to the major-minor tonalities. Yet the increase in harmonic clarity in tonality led to a more and more frantic search for something to obscure that harmonic clarity.

We come to the startling conclusion that people want their cake and to eat it too. They want the structure and direction that tonal harmony can provide, but without the melodic and rhythmic straightjacket that accompanies it. The tonal dominant cadences have an effect similar to simple, direct sentences in literature. Neither one leave you in much doubt where you are. This effect can be heard in strikingly clear form in early Baroque keyboard or lute pieces when comparing the tonal dance music such as the courantes and minuets with works in the older passacaglia or rondeau form.

As we will see, the modes have an inherent disadvantage in expressing this kind of tonal organization due to their scalar structure. This relative harmonic weakness makes it difficult for music written in a diatonic mode to avoid slipping into a quasi-major scale or at least be interpreted by the listener as a slightly odd major scale or sometimes a melodic minor scale.

Actually, the early minor scale itself was transformed into a counterpart of the major scale by the addition of the leading tone, which also necessitated the augmented sixth degree. The harmonic limitations (characteristics) of the modes do permit a freer, more relaxed melodic expression and a corresponding rhythmic freedom. Melody and rhythm display a direct relationship with each other and an inverse relation to harmony. Where harmonic phrasing is strongest, melody and rhythm are most constrained.

If we follow this line of thought, the modes require some approach or procedures which will give them greater harmonic definition and stability without unduly compromising their melodic freedom. As with most things, the devil is in the details. I present in this book one approach without thinking that there are no others. I have striven to introduce enough method that the reader can assess it both for its internal logic and more importantly for its compositional efficacy. It is certainly not radical in its origins or its substance, not that any modal scalar system could be at this point.

However, I have tried to devise a system that is informed by the cognitive capabilities of the listener. By that, I mean the listener, far more than the score reader, is governed by the capabilities and constraints of the mind in recognizing and recalling and interpreting a stream of auditory information. The past century, in common with the early

Medieval period, has been replete with musical systems based on mathematical, symbolic or other rational schemes, which are independent of human cognitive capabilities in processing serially presented information such as music.

In Chapter 2, the diatonic modal scales and their scalar structure will be presented. Relationships are described in detail and summarized in tables. Since each mode has a unique intervallic structure, chordal relationships necessarily vary between them to a greater or lesser extent. The locations of the melodic tritone and the step with the diminished triad in the scale (formed on the seventh step in the major scale, of course) play a strong role in determining the basic character of the mode. A few additional modes used by 20th century composers are touched upon as a point of comparison. Since modern composers and songwriters are likely to be more familiar with the interrelationships of the major-minor scale compared with the modes, considerable attention is paid to presenting and describing modal chordal relationships.

In Chapter 3, comparisons are made between the modal and tonal systems. Topics of discussion include the transformation of the minor scale from its modal origins to a close counterpart of the major scale, the use of equal temperament to allow complete unification of the major-minor keys, cadential formulas and the distinction of defining vs. incidental differences that separate modal and tonal practice.

In Chapter 4, the new proposed approach to forming a coherent modal compositional practice is set forth. A fuller presentation is made of the major and minor forms of the modes and the dyadic relationships between modes that form a correspondence with the major-minor scale. The basis for the three modal scalar dyads or complements, the Lydian-Dorian, the Mixolydian-Phrygian and Ionian-Aeolian, is explained within the context of a modern modal system. (The term 'scalar dyad' should be distinguished from dyads related to pitches.) The correspondence of harmonic scale properties between the Ionian and Aeolian modes led to their pairing in the major-minor scale. Similar correspondences are shown to exist between the Lydian and Dorian modes as well as the Mixolydian and Phrygian modes.

Chapter 5 presents more specific stylistic issues in composing with the modes such as maintaining the mode harmonically, use of inversions, seventh and ninth chords, non-triadic modal harmony, melodic outline, bass melody and instrumentation, within-set dissonance and outer-set dissonance, use of within and outer-set dissonances as a substitute for the cadence pause, rhythmic considerations and their notation.

In addition, some more general human information processing concepts are touched upon, including short-term memory constraints and limitations in the number of scale notes, the role of recognition and recall in perception of formal relationships and the use of the full set or subsets of scalar elements as a determinant of style and complexity.

Chapter 6 presents a Modal Study Song using a typical form of verse, chorus and bridge. The Study Song is presented in the Ionian-Aeolian Dyad since these scales are most familiar to readers and they can more directly identify the similarities and differences in the Study Song with standard tonal system practice. The instrumentation is a B♭ Clarinet and Piano. The Study Song is set in a standard melody and accompaniment form where the Piano goes solo only in the Intro, Outro and Break. The chapter has an accompanying analysis, which describes the progressions, melodic motives and modal characteristics and procedures of the Clarinet and Piano parts.

Chapters 7, 8 and 9 present more extended Study Compositions for each of the modal dyads, the Mixolydian-Phrygian, the Lydian-Dorian and the Ionian-Aeolian respectively, along with accompanying analyses. The analyses for each of the Study Compositions describe the particular ways that musical features discussed in this book are used in the piece. The analyses also discuss some of the compositional decisions that should be considered in writing modal music.

They are not intended to provide a rigorous musicological description. Each of these three Chapters has a study composition scored for a clarinet choir in the modal scalar dyad in question. The study compositions illustrate particular concepts, procedures and relationships relevant to composing in that scalar dyad presented in the exposition of the modern modal system. Particular attention is paid to the use of parenthetic harmonies and melodic voice leading to support the modal identity and the harmonic relationships of each modal scalar dyad.

The study compositions, although they necessarily present particular ways of realizing the modal system, are not intended to define or restrict the use of the modern modal system by composers, but are offered simply as helpful examples. Their purpose is pedagogical rather than as a regular musical opus. More generally, they favor ways of implementing the approach that differ from the more customary practices of modal and tonal practice. The assumption is that composers and songwriters already have a wealth of material and experience with these customary procedures (for example, canon or sequences) and are best served by seeing the compositional efficacy (or lack thereof) of something less familiar.

Appendices 1, 2, and 3 describe the characteristics of the modal scalar dyads, Mixolydian-Phrygian, Lydian-Dorian and the Ionian-Aeolian, respectively in a reference format by presenting detailed information about their melodic and harmonic properties such as cadences, parenthetic harmonies and modulation within the scalar dyad and with the other 2 scalar dyads. These 3 Appendices are meant to be consulted as a handy summary reference when songwriting and composing, saving the reader from having to work out this information on their own. Typically, when a student is learning the tonal major-minor system they are forced to memorize or write down such basic relationships and formulae. Here where there are 6 modes and three dyads it can become a bit too much to keep track of by students. Thus, these Appendices can function as look up tables to quickly find a necessary bit of information while songwriting or composing.

The musical examples and tables (as well as Appendices 4 and 5, which present triadic progressions and parenthetic harmonies for each modal key respectively) were designed to present the most useful information in a practical compositional sense. The book is meant to provide composers with a comprehensive and in-depth reference source for modal harmonic and melodic properties regardless of their compositional practices. These reference materials are equally useful in aiding composition in accordance with the methods presented in Chapters 4 and 5.

2

The Modal Scales

The Diatonic Modes

Although the Greeks first mention the diatonic modes, the particular arrangement of modes familiar to us today developed gradually during the Middle Ages and Renaissance. Their initial use in plainchant was almost purely melodic, with harmony restricted to parallel octaves and fifths. In Example 1, the melodic scales of the seven current modes are presented as rationalized in the 16th century.

The Ionian mode, the first scale in Ex. 1 (showing the C Major scale), is the basis of the major scale. The Dorian mode starts on **D** or the second note of the corresponding major scale. The Phrygian starts on the third note, **E**, the Lydian on the fourth note, **F**, and the Mixolydian on the fifth note, **G**. The Aeolian mode starts on the sixth note, **A**, and corresponds to the natural minor scale. The Locrian mode starts on the seventh note **B**. (As the Medieval period progressed and polyphony achieved dominance, Dorian, Phrygian and Mixolydian came to be favored.)

Three main characteristics distinguish the standard melodic forms of the modal scales from each other: the initial tone of the scale, also known as the Final; the location of the two half-steps; the location of the tritone. We should note for the sake of completeness that in chant and in parts moving within the octave, a variant form of each mode existed in which the Final was the fourth degree from the lowermost note of the scale. These are the plagal modes, which have no meaning anymore, since music is not contained strictly within a single octave. The last scale in Ex. 1 displays the plagal form of the Ionian scale called HypoIonian. (They will not be mentioned further.)

Ex.1: Modal Scales

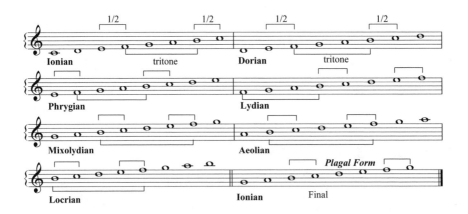

Let's examine each characteristic by itself first and then in relation to the others. The Final represented the ending note and often the first note of a chant or a melody, since it is the initial note of the scale and presumably first in importance. Yet if considered by itself, the Final appears as a weak distinguishing factor. If a melody starts on **C** but then ends on **D**, for example, have we used the Ionian or Dorian scale? This is not hypothetical since even the troubadour melodies from the Middle Ages often did this. If a melody or chant is very short, we might notice the discrepancy between the two notes, but the more intervening notes, the less noticeable the effect. If the Final is used more often in the melody, then its salience (prominence) can increase, but we could do the same thing by playing the note fortissimo. In other words, secondary operations on the Final can make it more definitive than it seems to be inherently.

The position of the two half-steps (melodic minor second) has a stronger organizing effect on the mode than the Final. The half-step constitutes what can be called a 'leading-tone' melodic relationship. The basis of this melodic tendency probably has some connection to the relative infrequency of half-steps to whole-steps (melodic major seconds) in the modal or diatonic scales. Since movement by whole-

10

step occurs more frequently, the half-step has the character of a subdivision of the norm (unlike in the chromatic scale). In the Ionian scale, the half-steps appear between the third and fourth scale degrees and between the seventh scale degree and Final **C**. The arrangement of these half-steps, particularly the leading-tone to the tonic, was one factor that led to the Ionian mode forming the basis for the major key in tonality. The leading-tone to the fourth scale degree is less remarked upon, but it gains significance by emphasizing the note lying a fifth below the Final.

From Ex. 1, we see that the Dorian mode has the half-steps between the second and third scale degrees and between the sixth and seventh scale degrees, the Phrygian between the first and second scale degrees and fifth and sixth scale degrees, the Lydian between the fourth and fifth scale degrees and the seventh scale degree and Final, the Mixolydian between the third and fourth scale degrees and sixth and seventh scale degrees, the Aeolian between the second and third scale degrees and the fifth and sixth scale degrees, and the Locrian between the first and second scale degrees and the fourth and fifth scale degrees.

Some partial overlaps exist between the modes:

Leading-Tone to Final	Ionian and Lydian
Half-step to 5th (Dominant)	Lydian and Locrian
Half-step to 4th	Ionian and Mixolydian
Half-step to 2nd	Phrygian and Locrian
Half-step to 3rd	Aeolian and Dorian
Half-step to 6th	Phrygian and Aeolian
Half-step to 7th	Dorian and Mixolydian

and presented alternatively that overlap on the half-step locations exists between the

Ionian	and the Lydian and Mixolydian
Dorian	and the Mixolydian and Aeolian
Phrygian	and the Aeolian and Locrian
Lydian	and the Ionian and Locrian
Mixolydian	and the Ionian and Dorian
Aeolian	and the Dorian and Phrygian
Locrian	and the Phrygian and Lydian

and also the half-step (ascending) arrangement in the

Ionian	emphasizes the Final and the 4th scale degrees

Ionian   emphasizes the Final and the 4th scale degrees
Dorian   emphasizes the 3rd and the 7th scale degrees
Phrygian   emphasizes the 2nd and the 6th scale degrees
Lydian   emphasizes the Final and the 5th scale degrees
Mixolydian   emphasizes the 4th and 7th scale degrees
Aeolian   emphasizes the 3rd and the 6th scale degrees
Locrian   emphasizes the 2nd and the 5th scale degrees

The half-step descending relationship is functionally weaker than the ascending relationship, but it has been used to emphasize the Final in the Phrygian mode and could be so used in the Locrian. The half-step descends to the

Final   in the Phrygian and Locrian
Dominant   in the Phrygian and Aeolian
4th scale degree in the Lydian and Locrian

The descending half-steps to the remaining scale degrees would appear to be too weak and tangential to be useful in providing a characteristic organization to their modes.

    The third distinguishing characteristic is the location of the melodic tritone (augmented fourth/diminished fifth) in the scale. There are two forms of the tritone in C Ionian and its counterpart modes: **F** to **B** and **B** to **F**. The difference is based on the absence of any half-steps in the **F** to **B** tritone and the presence of both half-steps in the **B** to **F** tritone. Three whole-steps create a more audible melodic tritone than two whole-steps and two half-steps. Assuming that we remain within the scale octave, the **F** to **B** tritone appears in the Ionian, Dorian, Phrygian and Lydian modes while the **B** to **F** tritone appears in the Mixolydian, Aeolian and Locrian modes.

    The location of the **F** to **B** tritone in the

Ionian   lies between the 4th and 7th scale degrees
Dorian   lies between the 3rd and 6th scale degrees
Phrygian   lies between the 2nd and 5th scale degrees
Lydian   lies between the Final and 4th scale degrees

The location of the **B** to **F** tritone in the

Mixolydian	lies between the 3rd and 7th scale degrees
Aeolian	lies between the 2nd and 6th scale degrees
Locrian	lies between the Final and 5th scale degrees

Admittedly, this effect will depend on the melodic activity lying between the Finals rather than straddling between two octaves. However, even with contemporary tonal or modal music, it is possible that melodies are statistically somewhat more likely to remain between the Finals an octave apart for any short given passage. In any event, the melodic position of the tritone should have a particular effect on approaches to cadences on the Final.

Some modes have the tritone on more prominent scale degrees than other modes. The Phrygian and Lydian have the **F** to **B** tritone between the second and fifth scale degrees and the Final and fourth scale degrees respectively. On the other hand, the Dorian and Ionian have it on the third and sixth scale degrees and fourth and seventh scale degrees respectively. Although the **B** to **F** tritone is somewhat less noticeable, the Locrian mode has it between the Final and fifth scale degree, the most prominent degrees of the scale, whereas in both the Mixolydian and Aeolian modes, that tritone does not rest on the Final, dominant or fourth scale degree.

Melodic Characteristics Distinguishing Each Mode

At this point, it is useful to consider these characteristics as they jointly define each mode.

Ionian

The Ionian mode has the Final on **C** (no sharps or flats), ascending half-steps to the Final and fourth degree, no significant descending relations of half-steps and the **F** to **B** melodic tritone between the fourth and seventh scale degrees. This mode has the tritone out of the way of melodic cadences. It is rare for a melodic part to move up from the fourth scale degree through the seventh scale degree to the Final. Even if this were to happen, the resulting instability would be resolved in natural fashion by the Final. The half-step on the seventh scale degree emphasizes the Final while the other emphasizes the fourth scale degree, which is also an important scale degree. The only side effect is that the fourth scale degree now becomes a slight competitor to the Final. The lack of significant half-step descending relationships does give more prominence to the ascending movement of the leading-tone of the mode.

Dorian

The Dorian mode has the Final on **D** (no sharps or flats), ascending half-steps to the third and seventh scale degrees, no significant descending arrangements of half-steps and the **F** to **B** melodic tritone between the third and sixth scale degrees. This mode has the tritone out of the way of melodic cadences since it rests on neither the Final, dominant nor fourth scale degrees. The ascending half-steps to the third and seventh scale degrees, however, also emphasize less important scale degrees. The lack of significant ascending or descending relationships does produce reduced melodic tension in this mode.

Phrygian

The Phrygian mode has the Final on **E** (no sharps or flats), ascending half-steps to the second and sixth scale degrees, descending half-steps to the Final and dominant and the **F** to **B** melodic tritone between the second and fifth scale degrees. This mode has the tritone prominently positioned on the dominant and on the second scale degree, which happens to be the dominant of the dominant (i.e., the second scale degree is also the fifth scale degree above the dominant). Melodic cadences have to be carefully constructed to avoid the tritone. The ascending half-steps to the second and sixth scale degrees are basically neutral. The Final would have no particular tendency to ascend to the second scale degree nor would the dominant to the sixth scale degree. The mode does have one of the strongest descending half-step relationships from the second scale degree to the Final. This descent was often used during the modal period. The half-step descent to the dominant is also relatively strong. The prominent tritone and descending half-steps combined with the lack of prominent ascending relations produce a mode with strong downward tendencies. These Phrygian mode characteristics present a contrast to both the Ionian and Dorian modes. The Ionian has ascending movement and a non-prominent tritone and the Dorian has neither a prominent tritone nor strong ascending or descending tendencies.

Lydian

The Lydian mode has the Final on **F** (no sharps or flats), ascending half-steps to the Final and dominant, descending half-step to the fourth scale degree and the **F** to **B** melodic tritone between the Final and fourth scale degree. This mode has the tritone prominently positioned, therefore. Melodic cadences have to be carefully constructed to avoid the tritone (if that is sought). The ascending half-steps to the Final and dominant are very strong, but end up competing with each other more than in the Ionian mode, where a half-step leads to the fourth scale degree and Final. In the Lydian mode, the existence of the tritone between the Final and fourth scale degree combined with the ascending half-step to the dominant means that the influence of the dominant (and Ionian mode) can easily exceed the Final if care isn't taken. (In the Lydian scale on **F**, the dominant represents the Final **C** of the Ionian mode.) The mode does have a prominent descending half-step relationship of the dominant to the fourth scale degree (but the diminished triad built on it lessens its utility). The prominent tritone and ascending half-step to the Final combined with the lack of prominent descending relations produce a mode with strong upward (leading-tone) tendencies. These Lydian mode characteristics present partial similarity to the Ionian and the Phrygian modes and a strong contrast with the Dorian mode. The points of similarity are the ascending movement of the Ionian mode and a prominent tritone in the Phrygian. Of course, the differences are significant too since the Ionian has a non-prominent tritone and the Phrygian has stronger downward tendencies than upward. The Dorian has no correspondence with the Lydian on any of these characteristics.

Mixolydian

The Mixolydian mode has the Final on **G** (no sharps or flats), ascending half-steps to the fourth and seventh scale degrees, no significant descending arrangements of half-steps and the **B** to **F** melodic tritone between the third and seventh scale degrees. The tritone doesn't have a major effect on melodic cadences. It is rare for a melodic part to move up from the third scale degree through the seventh scale degree to the Final. The half-step to the fourth scale degree emphasizes the scale degree a fifth below the Final. The only side effect is that the fourth scale degree now becomes a competitor to the Final as in the Ionian mode. The difference is that the ascending half-step to the seventh scale degree in the Mixolydian mode has little strength compared to the Ionian leading-tone to the Final. Thus, the Mixolydian fourth scale degree, without a counterpoise, becomes a greater threat to the Final.

Aeolian

The Aeolian mode has the Final on **A** (no sharps or flats), ascending half-steps to the third and sixth scale degrees, a descending half-step from the sixth scale degree to the dominant and the **B** to **F** melodic tritone between the second and sixth scale degrees. This mode has the tritone out of the way of melodic cadences since it rests on neither the Final, dominant nor fourth scale degree. The ascending half-steps to the third and sixth scale degrees also emphasize less important scale degrees producing weak leading-tone effects. The descending half-step relationship to the dominant has relative strength. The Aeolian mode has slightly more melodic downward tendency than the Dorian mode.

Locrian

The Locrian mode has the Final on **B** (no sharps or flats), ascending half-steps to the second and dominant, descending half-steps to the Final and fourth scale degrees and the **B** to **F** melodic tritone between the Final and fifth scale degree. This mode has the milder tritone very prominently positioned between the Final and the dominant. Melodic cadences can't easily avoid the tritone. The ascending half-step to the dominant is mixed in its effect since it moves from a perfect fourth to the diminished fifth. The Final has a strong tendency to ascend to the second scale degree The Locrian mode has a similar mixed effect from the descending half-step relationships from the second to the Final, and a somewhat stronger descent from the diminished dominant to the fourth scale degree The prominent tritone and descending half-step to the fourth scale degree and Final combined with the prominent contrary ascending relation to the second scale degree (Ionian) produces a mode with both upward leading-tone and downward melodic tendencies. These Locrian mode features produce similarities to the Phrygian and Lydian modes.

Modal Melody Examples

Before moving on to the harmonic implications of these modal scales, it is worthwhile to assess more directly their melodic differences. Below (Ex. 2) is a conventional diatonic melody in the Ionian (major scale), which is then set in the other modes diatonically. In other words, the original intervals are modified by a half-step in either direction if they cannot otherwise be kept within the diatonic modal scale. Thus the intervallic structure is changed, as it does if a major key melody is transposed diatonically to its relative minor key, but not when transposed between the various major keys. A leap of a fourth was avoided since that would result in a tritone leap for one of the other modes. As for the melody in this example and the other non-attributed music in this book, they are by Anonymous, because my name doesn't even rhyme with Schubert.

As can be seen and heard (in the audio files), a reasonably extended melody written for Ionian (major) does not sound the same when it is transposed diatonically in the other modes. Obviously, modal transposition is fundamentally different from key transposition within a mode due to the different position of the melodic tritone and the two half-steps (minor seconds). The notes in the modes other than Ionian that depart from the intervallic relationships of the C Ionian melody are indicated with a crosshead in

17

the Dorian and Phrygian transpositions. Maintaining the same intervallic relationships would create a noticeably chromatic melody in the other modes.

In Examples 3 & 4, diatonic variants of the C Ionian melody better suited to the Dorian and Phrygian modes are shown. Changed notes in the revised modal versions are indicated by the diamond noteheads. The reader is strongly encouraged to make their own variants on this or other Ionian melodies suited to each of the other modes.

The point of these examples is to demonstrate that the melodic use of the modes offers a significant departure from tonal melodic writing. Melodies written for one mode do not fit seamlessly into another except by happenstance or careful artifice. Thus, the insight of the composers who employed modal melodies occasionally to contrast tonal melody is confirmed again. Conversely, melodic writing must be carefully considered for each mode; one size or kind does not fit all. This seemingly obvious conclusion has been obscured by the prevailing practice of tonal composers to use major and minor keys almost interchangeably.

Ex.2: Melody in C Ionian and Diatonic Transposition to Other Modes

(Ex.2 continued): Melody in C Ionian and Diatonic Transposition

Ex. 3: Rewritten C Ionian Melody for the Dorian mode

Ex. 4: Rewritten C Ionian Melody for the Phrygian mode

Modal Melodic Practices

It would be nice to have an extended section on how to write outstanding modal melodies, however, the absence of any equivalent text in the history of music does give me pause. On the bright side, great music does not require the finest melodies, but it does require an absence of bad melodies. Studying the works of composers who were great melody writers is entertaining, but not terribly productive unless you're trying to ape their style. For one thing, unlike harmony, melody seems to be as much a talent as a learned skill. Composers without some native gift do not often learn to write great melodies in quantity, although there are a few exceptions such as Beethoven or Richard Strauss. For another, melody tends to be interwoven with a composer's rhythmic and harmonic propensities.

However, the example of Beethoven does offer some insight. His struggles with his musical material were legendary, but never aimless. He incessantly combined and recombined music cells and phrases until he found some promising lead, which he then refined carefully. The use of more than one mode, whether diatonic or modern, does put an increased emphasis on melody and rhythm, since harmonic direction is not as strong as with the major-minor scales. Therefore, modal music requires increased sensitivity to melodic nuances to be compelling. For this type of writing to succeed, composers and songwriters need to shape the melody to the characteristics of the mode. In extended works, it isn't necessary to create the most distinctive, beautiful melodies, since usually these would have an undue prominence. But music involving different modes, to be clearly audible to the listener and to impart some purpose to their use, must involve distinguishable and appropriate melodic practice between them.

The first thing that should be pointed out is that while a noticeable difference exists between melodies used in tonal works and modal melodies, the gap is not a huge one. Often times, tonal composers would make use of folk song tunes, which in many cases betray a modal flavor. The later 19th century composers such as Grieg or Bizet would sometimes modify a basically tonal melody to give it a modal coloring. Second, each of the keys in the modes has a relative counterpart in the major (Ionian) scale. D Dorian, E Phrygian and so on are relatives to C Ionian, which means of course that there is no chromatic difference between them. The difference is purely in the relative hierarchy and interrelationships of the scale degrees and the harmonies that are constructed on them. Third, tonal harmony has a greater constraint on melody than modal harmony since vertical coincidence of parts is more essential to its effects. Conversely, modal harmony allows melody to move more freely and compels it to act more forcefully at cadences and climaxes.

While it is not possible to provide the technique to write great modal melodies, there are some qualities that generally differentiate acceptable melodies from poor melodies. These qualities are a sense of direction (sometimes through intermediate stops) towards a melodic goal, a balance between convention and surprise in phrasing, some thematic integration and conformance to the characteristics of the mode. Lest the reader misunderstand, these are qualities to be respected unless one has something else specifically in mind that requires the melody to be directionless or unbalanced or totally conventional etc.

Melodic Direction

To take these points in turn, a sense of melodic direction stems from a hierarchy of the scale notes, temporary or more fixed, during a particular passage. The note towards which the melody is tending must necessarily be perceived as the most important note in that context. Modality of course assumes that there is a relatively fixed hierarchy for a given mode and fixed notes for keys in that mode. In Ionian it is reasonable to assume that the fourth and fifth scale degrees have the most prominence next to the Final with the third, second, seventh and sixth scale degrees following in roughly that order. The other modes have somewhat different hierarchies, in part based on the melodic characteristics discussed above, but as we will see, from the modes' harmonic properties in addition. Generally, the fixed hierarchy predominates, but it is possible for a melodic tendency to occur in a particular passage that is not in alignment with that hierarchy. Most often that would imply a modulation or temporary influence of a different mode, but it could also stem from the particular form that the melody takes. Looking at Example 2, it is evident that the **C** in measure 5 is a melodic goal of the preceding phrase. However, the **D** at the end of the same measure also has some properties as a temporary melodic goal. Notice that the ascending scale fragments spanning a fifth, beginning with the **E** at the end of measure 2, lead to the **D** as a subsidiary tendency. This slight conflict in melodic tendency keeps the melody moving until the **D** occurs again at the end of the next measure. This time though it merely serves as an upbeat to the fifth of the scale, **G**, at which point the melody does come to a semi-pause.

24

The altered Dorian mode melody (Ex. 3) has a slightly different melodic structure. Bear in mind that this melody and the altered Phrygian melody stem from an Ionian melody rather than being specifically devised for the Dorian and Phrygian modes. In addition, the changes were kept to the minimum necessary to create a reasonable modal version by leaving the rhythmic values mostly unchanged. Two particular obstacles present themselves in trying to transform the Ionian melody into Dorian: the differing locations of the melodic tritone and the weaker cadences in the minor Dorian mode. The tritone presents itself in the second measure of the unmodified transposition in a way which affects the melodic flow. To avoid that, it was necessary to reverse the motion of the turn downwards. While helpful, there is still a weaker melodic impetus in measure 3 (at least to my ears), perhaps due to the major third between the A and F in measure 2. This reduces somewhat the interplay of melodic tendencies between the D and E in measure 5 compared with the Ionian. An alternative version with a syncopation is presented in the ossia (small staff). This definitely creates greater drive all the way through to the half cadence on A. For comparison, see it in the Ionian version, in which circumstance it sounds excessive or at least unnecessary. In measure 6 the lead-in to the half cadence sounds weaker in the diatonic transposed Dorian version, due to the change in the melodic intervals. The altered version restores some of the missing momentum and incidentally reinforces the tonic D. The tritone created by transposition in measure 10 necessitated some slight changes in the melody in that and the following measure. Somewhat more change was needed to create a compelling Dorian final cadence. The A was reinforced in its role as the dominant by the addition of the C and second E in the final two measures. Modal cadences often benefit from added emphasis and increased motion.

Readers are invited to analyze the altered Phrygian melody presented in Ex. 4 to form an opinion as to why the changes were made and whether they create an acceptable Phrygian melody. They might also make their own modifications to these altered melodies and judge the difference.

Melodic direction (momentum) is affected by a number of controllable factors. Tonal music theorists often focus on the melodic line's structural tones to study the melodic structure in a more defined way. These structural tones are usually identified on the basis of their metrical position and harmonic basis. To offer a simplistic example, a melodic tone which is part of a root position tonic or dominant chord, placed on a strong beat, with a longer duration would typically have a higher structural position than a melodic tone which is an added tone to an inversion on a weak beat. The determination of the structural melodic line often involves detailed analysis, particularly in chromatic tonal works and a variety of scholarly texts can be consulted for the methods. For our purposes here, modal melodies and cadences can benefit from attention paid to ascending and descending structural lines and especially from convergences where an ascending lower line and descending top voice meet.

Most often, melodic goals in a tonal (major-minor scale) environment arise because of the tonal harmonic syntax or the specific melodic pattern or form at a given point (see Meyer). In the former case, the melody in a sense realizes the implications of the harmonic progressions. Tension is built up when an expected resolution is delayed, for example. In the latter case, the melodic form usually has some unrealized or incomplete aspect, which the listener expects to melodically resolve. A very common example is the gap-fill melody. In these cases, a melodic skip larger than a perfect fourth creates a gap, which the listener expects to be filled in as the melody progresses. Delaying the occurrence of an expected melodic tone that has been skipped over provides a melodic tendency at least on a local level.

These kinds of analyses of tonal melodies certainly have relevance to modal melodic construction, but caution is needed to avoid an uncritical application of them in the modal system. Modal harmony, as will be seen, has important differences from the major-minor scales and anyway each mode has some unique properties. In particular, the basis for structural melodic tones will not be exactly as it is with the major-minor tonal system. It is a goal here to provide the reader with enough information so that they will be able to assess modal melodies by adapting these techniques.

Conventional and Unconventional Melodic Progression

The definition of melodic balance is extraordinarily complex. As listeners, we know when we hear it, but there is no simple formula or set relationship that guarantees it. In this section, though, balance refers to the more limited area of conventional and unconventional melodic elements. 'Unconventional' is perhaps too strong a word as would be 'surprise'; the best melodies often have a balance between totally conventional areas and other areas where the progression follows a route other than the most likely or direct one. The departure from the most typical progression may be quite mild, remaining within the general style and range of normal possibilities that the preceding passages have established. That 'surprise' is not the essential factor is demonstrated by the continuing affect induced by a well-known melody as it is with a suspense movie seen for the third time. The listener experiences the music, as with the movie, in real time each time it is played since the listener finds it hard to step outside of the listening experience and survey it from above as would occur reading a score.

The variable melodic elements at issue here involve the melodic shape, its tonal (modal) implication, the rhythmic values and the relation of melodic rhythm with the established meter. There are myriad ways in which these factors can be used to enhance the melodic line, which makes a study of melodies difficult. Since there is not space here for a compendium and the reader will have the opportunity to study modal melodies in actual study compositions in later chapters, we will look specifically only at Examples 2 and 3 here for the last two factors. As noted, the same melodic line was retained to the extent possible for the modal variants and each example is modal specific, so the examples are not useful for the first two factors of shape and tonal implication. Melodic shape changes would have to deal with the position of the tritone and also the influence of the modal scalar structure on the cadences to the Final and fifth scale degree. The modal implications of a melody would be relevant if, for example, the Ionian melody took a turn into Dorian.

Composers and songwriters often vary the rhythmic basis of the melodic line in refrains or rondeau forms, but rhythmic variation can also be introduced within a melody. In Ex. 2, measure 10 introduces a syncopation right before the cadence, which accentuates, in my opinion, the feeling of closure in the more regular rhythm of the following measure. In the ossia to the melody mentioned above, there is another rhythmic displacement in measure 3 which the reader can directly assess for the different effect with the more regular rhythm in the same measure in the standard version.

Thematic Integration

Thematic integration is the practice of basing a work's melodic material on a small number of themes, motives, or melodies. Thematic integration has been a favored practice of later 19th and 20th century composers and, coincidentally or not, by composers of the modal period as well, although obviously the thematic integration took different forms in the respective periods. Thematic integration is a favored technique when harmonic organization becomes weaker or less straightforward. Less used in the Classical era, it gained favor in the increasingly chromatic compositions of Liszt and Wagner. In the modal practice of the 15th and 16th centuries, composers made frequent use of the techniques of augmentation, diminution and melodic inversion. Augmentation and diminution refer to increases or decreases in the relative durations of the notes compared to the original theme. Thus, in doubled augmentation all quarter notes become half notes, all half notes become whole notes and so on, but the melodic intervals remain the same. Medieval composers frequently had an entire melody in counterpoint with its augmented or diminished self. Earlier in the modal period, composers had made use of rhythmic integration of melodies by keeping the melodic note durations the same but varying the melodic line (isorhythm).

As the tonal system became more complex towards the end of the 19th century, an interest in thematic integration re-emerged, although entire melodies were less often used as its basis. More typically, a short theme or motif, perhaps only 4 or 5 notes in length, would be incorporated into various themes and melodies throughout a movement or even an entire work. In the 20th century, the degree of such motivic integration reached an extreme degree, not only with the 12-tone serial method, but even with neo-classical or folktune-based compositions.

Thematic integration is a useful technique in a modal context since the modal melody usually doesn't have the same tonal harmony to support and define its relationships. In the tonal system, a melody gains significance from the particular role it plays in the harmonic scheme more than from its intrinsic melodic shape, if only because composers were influenced or controlled in their thinking mainly by harmonic considerations. Modal music does not have the same restrictions on melody since their harmonic progressions, as we will see, don't constrain melody to nearly the same degree and the melodic rhythm does not have to conform to tonal harmonic rhythm.

In the Ex. 2 melody, we can find some degree of thematic integration. The last beat of measure 5 up to the 3rd beat of measure 6 is quite similar to measure 2 since they are rhythmically identical and have only minor interval differences. The major thematic integration is based on a scale fragment spanning a fifth. The first instance starts on the last beat of measure 2 followed by a rhythmic variant on the **D** in measure 3. There are overlapping variants starting on the **G** in measure 4 and the **A** in measure 5. In measure 8 we have an inversion of the scale fragment and arguably two more instances in measures 9 and 11. Note the relative freedom of the thematic occurrences, sometimes moving across the barline, sometimes staying within, with all of them having some unique aspect from the others. This metrical variety is generally not found in traditional tonal melodies.

Conformance to the Mode

As we see in the above melodic examples, modal transposition of melodies is not a mechanical process as it is with key transposition in the major-minor system. In particular, modal transposition to the parallel key of a different mode (e.g. **C** Ionian to **C** Lydian) almost involves rethinking the melodic line. This differentiation is a particular property of a modal system and greatly aids in restoring much needed variety to melodic and harmonic composition. It does place more importance on creating an appropriate fit between the melodic line and the mode. As can be seen in the examples, melodic phrasing has to be more carefully judged when using different modes and particular care needs to be shown when using different modes within the same composition. The scalar properties enumerated above and the harmonic properties of the modes presented throughout this book will be thoroughly examined to assist in this process of creating modally differentiated music.

Harmonic Implications of the Modal Scales

Since Western music has a vertical, harmonic dimension along with the horizontal flow of melody, we must now examine the harmonic implications of the modal scales. At the outset, we will limit ourselves to triadic harmony, chords based on the superposition of major or minor thirds within the diatonic mode. Of course, the distinction between major and minor modes is based on the structure of the Final or tonic triad. (The term Tonic will be used henceforth since the harmonic implications of the modes are now recognized.) The C Major triad has the major third, C - E, while a minor has the minor third, a - c. Thus, the Major modes are:

> Ionian
> Lydian
> Mixolydian

and the Minor modes are:

> Dorian
> Phrygian
> Aeolian
> (Locrian)*

*two minor thirds = diminished fifth

Earlier, we saw the overlapping relations between modes on their half-step locations. It is interesting to see how these relate to the major or minor key implications of each mode.

Ionian overlaps   Lydian and Mixolydian (Major/Major)
Dorian overlaps   Mixolydian and Aeolian (Major/Minor)
Phrygian overlaps   Aeolian and Locrian (Minor/Minor)
Lydian overlaps   Ionian and Locrian (Major/Minor)
Mixolydian overlaps Ionian and Dorian (Major/Minor)
Aeolian overlaps   Dorian and Phrygian (Minor/Minor)
Locrian overlaps   Phrygian and Lydian (Minor/Major)

From this, we see that Ionian is the only mode which has overlap on its half-step locations with the other two major modes, the

Lydian and Mixolydian. Lydian overlaps the Locrian (the most dissonant mode, as defined by the location of the diminished triad) and Mixolydian overlaps the Dorian. As for the minor modes, both the Aeolian and the Phrygian overlap two other minor mode scales. The remaining minor modes, the Dorian and Locrian, have overlap with both major and minor modes. As one would expect, the Locrian overlaps the most dissonant major mode (Lydian) and the most dissonant minor mode (Phrygian) apart from itself. The Dorian has the mildest relatives in the Aeolian and Mixolydian modes.

Although the mode can be designated major or minor, the scale degrees can have the same sonority or a different sonority as the tonic triad (Table 1). The Ionian mode has major triads on the tonic (Final), fourth scale degree and dominant. Conversely, the Aeolian mode has minor triads on the tonic, fourth scale degree and dominant. These are the only modes with consistent sonority on all three of the most significant degrees of the scale and clearly show why they were chosen as the basis of the major and minor keys. The diminished triad falls on the fourth scale degree (subdominant) in the Lydian mode, the fifth scale degree (dominant) of the Phrygian mode and the tonic of the Locrian mode. These are the more dissonant modes due to the prominent placement of the melodic tritone and diminished triad.

Table 1: Arrangement of Major (M), Minor (m) and Diminished (D) triads for each mode

I	II	III	IV	V	VI	VII	Mode
M	m	m	M	M	m	D	Ionian
m	m	M	M	m	D	M	Dorian
m	M	M	m	D	M	m	Phrygian
M	M	m	D	M	m	m	Lydian
M	m	D	M	m	m	M	Mixolydian
m	D	M	m	m	M	M	Aeolian
D	M	m	m	M	M	m	Locrian

Table 2: Arrangement of Major (M), Minor (m) and Diminished (D)* Seventh Chords

I	II	III	IV	V	VI	VII	Mode
M	m	m	M	m	m	D	Ionian
m	m	M	m	m	D	M	Dorian
m	M	m	m	D	M	m	Phrygian
M	m	m	D	M	m	m	Lydian
m	m	D	M	m	m	M	Mixolydian
m	D	M	m	m	M	m	Aeolian
D	M	m	m	M	m	m	Locrian

In this table diminished refers to the triad the seventh is added to, as in the leading-tone triad in the major scale (**b/d/f/a**), rather than the diminished seventh chord of dominant harmony (**b/d/f/a♭**).

Since modern music routinely uses seventh and ninth chords, built with one or two additional triads above the fifth, these are also given by mode in Tables 2 and 3. The Tables refer to the interval of the seventh or ninth over the tonic, not to the exact composition of all the component triads.

Table 3: Arrangement of Major (M), Minor (m) and Diminished (D)* Ninth Chords

I	II	III	IV	V	VI	VII	Mode
M	M	m	M	M	M	D	Ionian
M	m	M	M	M	D	M	Dorian
m	M	M	M	D	M	M	Phrygian
M	M	M	D	M	M	m	Lydian
M	M	D	M	M	m	M	Mixolydian
M	D	M	M	m	M	M	Aeolian
D	M	M	m	M	M	M	Locrian

*In this table diminished refers to the triad the ninth is added to, as in the leading-tone triad in the major scale (b/d/f/a/c).

The Keys and their Modes

Although up to now we have discussed only the modal keys equivalent to C major (Ionian), the other keys available in the major-minor system all have corresponding keys in each of the modes. Since the Aeolian mode is the basis for the modern minor key, we are already familiar with its corresponding keys, e.g., **a** minor (**C** major), **e** minor (**G** Major), **c** minor (**E♭** major).

Table 4: Table of Keys for the 7 Modes

Ionian	Dorian	Phrygian	Lydian	Mixoly.	Aeolian	Locrian
C	d	e	F	G	a	b
G	a	b	C	D	e	f♯
D	e	f♯	G	A	b	c♯
A	b	c♯	D	E	f♯	g♯
E	f♯	g♯	A	B	c♯	d♯
B	c♯	d♯	E	F♯	g♯	a♯
F	g	a	B♭	C	d	e
B♭	c	d	E♭	F	g	a
E♭	f	g	A♭	B♭	c	d
A♭	b♭	c	D♭	E♭	f	g
D♭	e♭	f	G♭	A♭	b♭	c
G♭	a♭	b♭	C♭	D♭	e♭	f

Table 4 presents the basic set of corresponding modal keys to all major (Ionian) keys without listing enharmonic equivalents. One easy way of remembering this set of keys is to memorize the sequence of modes in the order given (Ionian, Dorian etc.). Then one simply needs to remember the scales for each major (Ionian) key (the rows in Table 4) to identify the equivalent modal key. For example, the E major scale is E, F♯, G♯, A, B, C♯, D♯. Therefore, the 4th mode in order, the Lydian, must have the 4th note of the E major scale, A, as its key for four sharps.

Modern Symmetric Modes

Although the medieval modes have been used most frequently, some 20th century composers employed other types of scales. These often had scale intervals based on symmetrical relationships rather than the cycle of fifths. The three most common types of symmetric scales are the Chromatic Scale, the Whole Tone Scale and the Octatonic Scale.

The Chromatic Scale obviously contains all twelve tones in the major-minor system and indeed in the vast majority of Western music. Thus, it has only one form (Ex. 5), characterized by semitone (minor second) intervals between all notes.

Ex.5: Chromatic Scale

The scale has symmetry because each scale point is separated by the same interval, the tritone evenly divides the scale points and also six minor seconds equal a tritone interval. The Chromatic Scale formed the basis of the 12-tone or serial method, but it has been used more freely by Schoenberg in earlier compositions (*Pierrot Lunaire*, for example) and many other composers. It can be distinguished from highly chromatic tonal music based on the nature of the voice leading and whether symmetry or hierarchical relationships predominate in the use of scale degrees.

The Whole Tone Scale was made famous by its inclusion in Liszt's and Debussy's works among others, but is much less widely found than the Chromatic Scale. The scale has six notes each separated by a major second. Each represents 6 of the possible 12 pitches, therefore, there are thus two possible forms of the scale a semitone apart (Ex. 6).

Ex.6: Whole Tone Scales

Whole Tone Scale 1   Whole Tone Scale 2

The Whole Tone Scale has symmetry because each scale point is separated by the same interval and the tritone evenly divides the scale, since three major seconds equal a tritone interval. The scale has harmonic attributes distinct from the major-minor system. Because the fifths are either diminished or augmented, the major or minor triad cannot be constructed from its intervals.

The Octatonic Scale (Ex. 7) has an alternating pattern of minor and major seconds and can be considered the superposition of two diminished seventh chords. There are three different forms of this scale, with **C, C♯,** and **D** the respective tonics. Again, the scale divides evenly at the tritone (5th scale point). Unlike the Whole Tone Scale, the interval of the perfect fifth can be formed on half of the scale points. However, in contrast to the diatonic modes, a tritone can be formed between all of the scale points within a given Octatonic Scale.

Ex.7: Octatonic Scales

Octatonic Scale 1   Octatonic Scale 2   Octatonic Scale 3

The symmetric scales displayed above possess an inherent tonal ambiguity because this symmetry produces equivalence between different scale points and chords rather than the hierarchy found in the diatonic modes and particularly the major-minor system. The diatonic modes are dependent on the perfect fifth which is, as Schoenberg once quipped, a little bit more than half an octave. The perfect fifth can be formed on all but one scale degrees and the tritone (diminished fifth) on only one scale point. In contrast, in the symmetrical scales, more than one melodic and harmonic tritone can be formed within the scale. Additionally, the symmetrical mode tonic has a direct tritone relationship with another scale degree instead of (or in addition to) the perfect fifth, a relationship only found in the Lydian and Locrian diatonic modes. The only diatonic mode with some symmetrical character is the Dorian mode. Referring back to Ex. 1, the Dorian mode has a symmetrical placement of the half-step within each tetrachord (sequence of four notes).

Twentieth century composers such as Bartok or Stravinsky have sometimes made use of octatonic modes in combination with the diatonic modes. This kind of mixed usage generally involved a partially atonal or at least highly chromatic context in which modal attributes are present notionally more than in easily recognizable form. The symmetric Dorian mode is often favored, but even here more in the form of tetrachords comprising musical motives or cells rather than in sustained modal passages (see Antokoletz).

Harmonic Progressions of the Diatonic Modes

In this section, we will set forth the various triadic relationships (including sevenths and ninths) that characterize each of the diatonic modes. Although many of these are found in the major-minor system, they are defined by different nomenclature and have a different status there, so we will generally not refer back to that role. For example, in the major-minor system the diminished triad is known as the leading-tone triad, but it serves as the subdominant of the Lydian mode and the dominant in the Phrygian mode.

Although each of the modes will be examined in turn, the Ionian mode will be dealt with summarily since it has the same scalar attributes as the current major scale. In contrast, the Aeolian mode is quite distinct from its non-diatonic descendant, the minor scale. It should be emphasized that the basic chordal relationships will be presented independent of stylistic judgments. At this point in the evolution of musical style, any chord can be followed by any other chord as long as the composer has an artistic justification in musical or dramatic terms.

Each mode's basic sonorities were shown above for triads and seventh chords on each scale point. Since the modes all share the same 12 tonics, for simplicity, we will use the C major (Ionian) scale as the exemplar and translate each of the basic chord relationships into the modal relative for C Ionian (i.e. D Dorian, E Phrygian etc.). For example, the triad on G represents the fifth in C Ionian, but the fourth in D Dorian, the third in E Phrygian and so on. Thus, the G major triad has a different functional relationship in each mode. Each triad and seventh chord will be presented in sequential relation to all the other such chords, both preceding and following it, for C Ionian (and the corresponding modes). For example, the root position C major triad would be shown preceding and following other diatonic triads and seventh chords first in root position and then in most inversions. The C major triad is shown in root position in Example 8. To save space here, the remaining chords in root position are shown in Appendix 4. Ninth and higher chords are not shown because the increased number of notes in the chord increases the flexibility of voice leading.

With respect to the chord sequences, the priorities were soprano (and bass) melody within the above severe constraints, avoidance of melodic repetition when feasible, contrapuntal voice leading and spacing in that order. Tritone relations between chord notes are also generally kept in inner or non-adjacent voices. (It should be noted, though, that the tritone is more prominent in the diatonic modes compared with major and minor scales because the major (Ionian) and minor (Aeolian) are the only tonic triads that do not contain either tritone note for any given key.) The reader is invited to improve upon the chord sequences, either melodically or contrapuntally, noting however, whether a modification in one aspect changes another for the worse.

As mentioned, modal composition requires a greater emphasis on melody and rhythm due to the looser harmonic organization of the modal scales. A major purpose in presenting the triads and seventh chords of the mode(s) in this way is to avoid the typical presentation of chords as cogs in the major-minor system of dominant harmony. Harmonic considerations are co-equal with melody and rhythm rather than pre-eminent in modal composition. Thus, chordal progressions that do not conform well to the logic of dominant harmony may still be useful in underlying modal melody.

The reader should refer back to Ex. 8 and Appendix 4 for the following discussions of the modal progressions. Tables 5 - 11 below show whether the triad agrees in mode with the tonic triad and whether the triad or seventh chord forms a tritone with other scale triads. The diminished Ionian VII triad and modal equivalents have an internal tritone so they are not considered in these tables.

Ionian Progressions

Ionian triadic progressions are basically those of the major keys in the major-minor system and are well covered in any tonal harmony text. As noted, the Ionian mode is only one of two modes that have no tritone relationships between the tonic triad and the other modal triads in the scale. Other modal values of its triads and their tritone relations are presented in Table 5. It should be emphasized that the last column describes the tritone relations of the added seventh note only and not those of the entire seventh chord.

Table 5 : Ionian Mode Triads

Scale Triad Degree	Agrees with Tonic Mode	Triad Has Tritone with Triad on	7th Has Tritone with Triad on
I	-	NONE	VII, IV, II
II	N	VII, V, III	NONE
III	N	VII, IV, II	NONE
IV	Y	VII, V, III	NONE
V	Y	VII, IV, II	VII, III
VI	N	NONE	NONE
VII	N	-	NONE

Ex.8: C Major (Ionian) Root Position Triad Progressions to the Other Triads and Seventh Chords

Table 6 : Dorian Mode Triads

Scale Triad Degree	Agrees with Tonic Mode	Triad Has Tritone with Triad on	7th Has Tritone with Triad on
I	-	VI, IV, II	NONE
II	Y	VI, III, I	NONE
III	N	VI, IV, II	NONE
IV	N	VI, III, I	VI, II
V	Y	NONE	NONE
VI	N	-	NONE
VII	N	NONE	VI, III, I

Dorian Progressions

The Dorian mode pattern of major and minor triads is displayed in Table 6 along with the triads and seventh chords which form the tritone between constituent tones. The modal Dorian I is the **d** minor triad. The triads on II and V agree in mode with the Dorian tonic triad (compared with IV and V in Ionian). The progressions of the Dorian triad and seventh chords are shown in Appendix 4.

Tonic.

The Dorian minor tonic has a tritone relationship with Dorian II, IV and the diminished VI. The added seventh does not create a tritone. Dorian IV is major and the tritone lies between the third of both I and IV while it occurs with the fifth of II. When both I and IV are in the first inversion, a tritone exists in the bass, logically enough (Appendix 4, staff D3). The lack of agreement between I and IV slightly diminishes the role of Dorian IV, but it also makes it less competition for the tonic than Ionian IV is to the Ionian tonic. (Since I stands as the dominant of IV for all the modes except Lydian, the modulation is easily accomplished, but particularly so when both are in agreement.) The tonic and Dorian V are in agreement.

II.

Dorian II has more importance in Dorian than Ionian since it agrees with the minor tonic. Because Dorian II and V are in agreement with Dorian I, the progressions between these triads stabilize the mode, as Ionian IV and V do even more powerfully in that mode. Dorian II has a tritone between its fifth and the third of I, the root of III and the diminished VI. (The seventh does not create another tritone, though.) The tritone is only moderately obtrusive with the tonic since II and I would have to be in second and first inversion respectively for it to appear in the bass. On the other hand, the root of III is in tritone relationship with the fifth of II (see staff E1/F6).

III.

This triad has a modest harmonic role in Dorian for several reasons. First, a typical Ionian progression III to VI is ineffective because Dorian VI is diminished. Second, as a major triad, it lacks agreement with the tonic. Third, its root forms a tritone with the fifth of II as well as the third of IV. However, this does not lessen the utility of the soft III - I cadence (see staff F5). It should be noted, however, that this cadence is slightly stronger than in the Ionian mode since major to minor is more definite than the reverse. As a neutral triad, it does not inhibit melodic flow either.

IV.

The Dorian subdominant lacks agreement with the Dorian tonal degrees and thus is less harmonically central than in Ionian. For the same reason, it is less of a threat to the tonic (see staff G3). Its third forms a tritone with the root of III and the third of I as noted, but this relation has only modest significance in voice leading. Although III - IV/IV - III are not customary Ionian progressions, they can have somewhat more utility in Dorian. Since it provides an alternative to the VII - IV progression, the III – IV progression gives some modal differentiation and keeps the Ionian C from assuming too much prominence (staff G6/G4). Unlike in Ionian, there is no tritone between Dorian IV and V. The added seventh does form a tritone with the fifth of II, however.

V.

The Dorian dominant is quite strong since it agrees with the tonic triad and has no tritone relation with it or any other triad, even as a seventh chord. This also makes the V - IV and IV - V progression more flexible (staff A6). However, the common Ionian V - VI progression becomes less useful due to the diminished VI (staff A1). The relation with VII is also altered compared with Ionian since Dorian VII is not a diminished triad and thus not able to act as a dominant substitute (staff C2).

VI.

This is the Dorian diminished triad. By extension, it could be used as a IV^7 substitute should that be useful (staff B6/B2). The relation between VI and VII is potentially disruptive to the Dorian mode since the root of VI could be interpreted as a leading-tone. As noted, the common Ionian progression with III is fundamentally changed.

VII.

A major triad, Dorian VII can be used in cadences with the tonic but does not function as an appendage to the minor dominant (staff C1/C5). Although the triad has no tritone relations, the added seventh forms a tritone with the third of I and the root of III. Its relationship with the major IV triad requires some caution since a prominent IV - VII progression would make VII compete somewhat with the Dorian tonic or at least disrupt the sound of a minor mode. Its neutrality makes it a useful underpinning to Dorian melody.

Phrygian Progressions

Table 7 displays the pattern of major and minor triads in the Phrygian mode and the triads and seventh chords which form the tritone between constituent tones.

Table 7: Phrygian Mode Triads

Scale Triad Degree	Agrees with Tonic Mode	Triad Has Tritone with Triad on	7th Has Tritone with Triad on
I	-	VII, V, II	NONE
II	N	V, III, I	NONE
III	N	VII, V, II	V, I
IV	Y	NONE	NONE
V	N	-	NONE
VI	N	NONE	VII, V, II
VII	Y	V, III, I	NONE

Tonic.

The minor Phrygian tonic has a tritone relationship with Phrygian II, VII and the diminished V (staff E1/E4/E6). The added seventh has no tritone relation. The tritone exists between the fifth of the tonic and the root of II, and the third of VII. Phrygian II is part of the typical cadence to the Phrygian tonic and VII is also harmonically significant to the mode. As for the dominant, the voice leading is affected by the tritone between the respective fifths as well as the diminished character of the triad on V.

II.

The Phrygian II is major and thus lacks agreement with the tonic. Because of the semitone relationship, Phrygian II often substitutes for the dominant in tonic cadences with the root of II descending to the tonic root (staff E1/F6). Harmonically, the Phrygian II may be the distant basis of the Baroque era's Phrygian half cadence used in chromatic cadences to the dominant. This half cadence led to the Neapolitan sixth chord (flattened second) in first inversion; it acted as a substitute for the subdominant. In Phrygian, however, this progression is less forceful because the dominant is diminished rather than a major triad (staff F3). This triad also has a tritone between its root and the third of III.

III.

This triad has a modest harmonic role due to its position and lack of agreement with the minor tonic. However, it can be used in III - I cadences although its effect is more similar to the Dorian III - I cadence than to the Ionian (staff G5). The tritone falls between the third of III and third of VII as well as more noticeably with the root of II. The added seventh also forms a tritone with I. As a neutral chord it can freely underlie Phrygian melody.

IV.

The Phrygian subdominant is a minor triad and thus has agreement with the Phrygian tonic (staff A3). It does not form a tritone with any other triad. This triad plays an important role in harmonically shaping the mode along with II, V and VII. Because of the diminished V, the Phrygian IV can be overused unless some care is taken to balance it with the triads more associated with the dominant (i.e. III, V and VII).

V.

The Phrygian dominant, despite being based on the diminished triad, is still important to the mode if only because the root does form the fifth with the tonic (staff B3). Obviously, tonic cadences utilizing V have somewhat reduced strength, but the (half) cadences on the dominant are even more affected. In principle, they are equivalent to Locrian tonic cadences (e.g. staff B3/A2/E4). The tonic cadences on the other hand approximate the common VII - III progression in Ionian major. Another common Ionian progression V - VI becomes a slight threat to the Phrygian tonic because of the leading-tone relationship, but the VI - V progression parallels the II - I descent (staff C6). The relation with VII is also altered compared with Ionian since Phrygian VII is not a diminished triad and thus does not have a dominant-like function (staff D5).

VI.

This is a major triad with a relatively strong descending relationship to the Phrygian dominant a half-step below (staff C6). It thus helps to reinforce the Phrygian dominant in parallel with the similar II - I progression. As with the subdominant, the triad has no tritone relationships but the added seventh does form a tritone with the root of II and the third of VII. The III - VI progression has the same functionality in Phrygian that it does in Ionian major (staff C4/G3).

VII.

A minor triad, Phrygian VII has agreement with the tonic and helps define the mode. The VII makes an effective and more relaxed alternative cadence with the tonic compared with II - I (staff D2). This triad does have a tritone between its third and the fifth of the tonic triad and the third of III.

Lydian Progressions

Table 8 displays the pattern of major and minor triads in the Lydian mode and the seventh chords that form the tritone between constituent tones.

Tonic.

The major Lydian tonic has a tritone relationship with Lydian II, VII and the diminished IV. The added seventh does not create a tritone relation. The tritone exists between the root of the tonic and the third of II and the fifth of VII. Lydian II can be used in the cadence to the Lydian tonic through V, but VII is not harmonically significant to the mode except as the leading-tone. As for the subdominant, the voice leading is strongly affected by the tritone between the roots as well as the diminished character of the triad on IV (staff F3).

II.

The Lydian II is major and has agreement with the tonic. Its third forms a tritone with the third of VI in addition to the tonic. The added seventh forms a tritone with VII. Half cadences with V, particularly with the added seventh, too firmly install the dominant as the (Ionian) tonic (staff G3). Since the Lydian subdominant does not form an effective counterweight to the dominant, it is difficult to clearly re-establish the Lydian mode. As we will see, secondary

46

dominant effects offer a solution for the use of the II - V cadence. Lydian II, acting as a substitute for the subdominant, can progress to the tonic (staff G6).

Table 8 : Lydian Mode Triads

Scale Triad Degree	Agrees with Tonic Mode	Triad Has Tritone with Triad on	7th Has Tritone with Triad on
I	-	VII, IV, II	NONE
II	Y	VI, IV, I	VII, IV
III	N	NONE	NONE
IV	N	-	NONE
V	Y	NONE	VI, IV, I
VI	N	VII, IV, II	NONE
VII	N	VI, IV, I	NONE

III.

This triad has a modest harmonic role due to its position and lack of agreement with the tonic. It can be used in soft III - I cadences as in the Ionian mode since the progression is also minor to major (staff A5). It has no tritone relationships and offers a useful progression with VI. As a neutral chord it can freely underlie Lydian melody.

IV.

The Lydian subdominant is a diminished triad. Because of the diminished IV, the Lydian V can be overused in tonic cadences and become a threat to the Lydian tonic in the process unless some care is taken to balance it with the triads associated with the subdominant (i.e. II, IV and VI). The root of IV does serve as a leading-tone to V, although this relation also has to be treated carefully.

V.

The Lydian dominant has agreement with the tonic and the triad has no tritone relationship. However, the added seventh creates a tritone with VI, IV and I. The V - I cadence is strong as one might expect (staff C4). Lydian V can also progress to VI. The relation with VII is altered compared with Ionian since Lydian VII is not a diminished triad and thus does not have a dominant-like function (staff E2).

VI.
This is a minor triad with tritone relations with II and VII. Lydian VI is a neutral chord which can progress to III, II, V and VII and freely underlie Lydian melody (staff D4/6).

VII.
A minor triad, Lydian VII does not have agreement with the tonic. The VII, although its root is the leading-tone to the tonic, has a somewhat weaker cadence with the tonic than in Ionian, possibly because of the tritone between the fifth of VII and the tonic root (staff E1). However, it does have a double leading-tone relationship with the tonic and the fifth of I, a characteristic that was fairly often used in medieval music in the final cadence, albeit chromatically in other modes. This triad also has a tritone with the third of VI. It can freely underlie Lydian melody.

Mixolydian Progressions

Table 9 displays the pattern of major and minor triads in the Mixolydian mode and the triads and seventh chords that form the tritone between constituent tones.

Tonic.
The major Mixolydian tonic triad has a tritone relationship with Mixolydian III, V and VII. The added seventh creates a tritone with VI as well. The tritone exists between the third of the tonic and the third of V and the root of VII (staff G4/D3/G6).

II.
The Mixolydian II is minor, lacking agreement with the tonic. It has no tritone relationships. Progressions to V, particularly with the added seventh, rather suggest the minor mode since both triads are minor in opposition to the tonic. The Mixolydian II relation to the

subdominant parallels the Ionian in its minor to major character (staff A3/A2).

Table 9 : Mixolydian Mode Triads

Scale Triad Degree	Agrees with Tonic Mode	Triad Has Tritone with Triad on	7th Has Tritone with Triad on
I	-	VII, V, III	VI, III
II	N	NONE	NONE
III	N	-	NONE
IV	Y	NONE	VII, V, III
V	N	VI, III, I	NONE
VI	N	VII, V, III	NONE
VII	Y	VI, III, I	NONE

III.

This triad is the Mixolydian diminished triad and due to its weak scalar position does not serve a significant harmonic function. It can progress to VI and may function in place of the tonic chord in some non-cadential contexts (staff B5).

IV.

The Mixolydian subdominant is a major triad and agrees with the tonic. The triad has no tritone relations, although the added seventh does make a tritone with V and VII. Because of the minor V, the Mixolydian IV can become a threat to the Mixolydian tonic particularly with prominent I - IV progressions, unless some care is taken to balance it with dominant effects. The IV - I cadence has more importance than in Ionian (staff C3/C4).

V.

The Mixolydian dominant does not have agreement with the tonic while the third of the triad has a tritone relationship with VI and the third of the tonic. The V - I cadence is not particularly forceful due to the minor - major progression. Mixolydian V can also progress to

VI. The relation with VII is altered compared with Ionian since Mixolydian VII is not a diminished triad (staff D3/D2/D1).

VI.
This is a minor triad with tritone relations between its fifth and the third of V and the root of VII. Mixolydian VI is a neutral chord that can progress to II, V and VII and freely underlie Mixolydian melody.

VII.
A major triad, Mixolydian VII has agreement with the tonic and helps define the mode. The VII makes an effective alternative cadence with the tonic compared with IV - I or V - I. This triad does have a tritone between its root and the third of the tonic triad and the fifth of VI.

Aeolian Progressions

Table 10 displays the pattern of major and minor triads in the Aeolian mode and the triads and seventh chords which form the tritone between constituent tones.

Table 10 : Aeolian Mode Triads

Scale Triad Degree	Agrees with Tonic Mode	Triad Has Tritone with Triad on	7th Has Tritone with Triad on
I	-	NONE	NONE
II	N	-	NONE
III	N	NONE	VI, IV, II
IV	Y	VII, V, II	NONE
V	Y	VI, IV, II	NONE
VI	N	VII, V, II	NONE
VII	N	VI, IV, II	V, II

Tonic.

The minor Aeolian tonic has no tritone relationships, the only mode sharing this property with the Ionian mode. Since the subdominant and dominant are both minor, the minor tonality is pronounced and predominantly consonant (staff A3/A4).

II.

The Aeolian II is diminished, but the II - I progression has some effectiveness. It can also progress to III or V (staff B1/B3).

III.

The Aeolian III is major and lacks agreement with the tonic. The triad has no tritone relations, however, the added seventh does make a tritone with the third of IV and the root of VI. It can progress to VI or sometimes to the tonic in a soft cadence similar to the Dorian (staff C3/C5).

IV.

The Aeolian subdominant is a minor triad and agrees with the tonic. The triad has tritone relations with the fifth of V and the third of VII. The IV - I cadence is relatively strong (staff D3/D4).

V.

The Aeolian dominant is minor and shares agreement with the tonic. The fifth of the triad has a tritone relationship with the root of VI and the third of IV. The V - I cadence is consonant and strong. The relation with VII is altered compared with Ionian since Aeolian VII is not a diminished triad (staff E4/E2).

VI.

This is a major triad with tritone relations between its root and the fifth of V and the third of VII. The Aeolian VI - III progression forms a parallel function with Ionian VI and III (staff F4). As a neutral chord, it can freely underlie Aeolian melody.

VII.

A major triad, Aeolian VII lacks agreement with the tonic. The VII makes an effective alternative cadence with the tonic compared with IV - I or V - I (staff G1). This triad does have a tritone between its third and the third of the subdominant triad and the root of VI.

Locrian Progressions

Table 11 displays the pattern of major and minor triads in this mode and the triads and seventh chords which form the tritone between constituent tones. The Locrian mode is viewed as minor since the minor third interval comprises the diminished tonic triad. Agreement with other minor triads is more a matter of degree than identity which should be borne in mind in the following discussion.

Table 11 : Locrian Mode Triads

Scale Triad Degree	Agrees with Tonic Mode	Triad Has Tritone with Triad on	7th Has Tritone with Triad on
I	-	-	NONE
II	N	NONE	V, III, I
III	Y*	VI, IV, I	NONE
IV	Y*	V, III, I	NONE
V	N	VI, IV, I	NONE
VI	N	V, III, I	IV, I
VII	Y*	NONE	NONE

Tonic.

The Locrian mode has the only diminished tonic. This makes the mode less stable than any of the others (staff B3/F3). The added seventh does not form another tritone with other triads and provides a perfect fifth between the third and seventh, making this chord somewhat more consonant than the triad (staff E4/F3). Although the dominant has sometimes been assigned to VI rather than V since the roots of the I and V are a tritone apart (a parallel with occasional Phrygian mode usage in the medieval period), this is still a weak harmonic cadence. The subdominant is a perfect fourth higher than the tonic however.

II.

The Locrian II is major and has no tritone relationships. It can progress to VI or V (staff C5/C4). It can also make a descent to the tonic as in the Phrygian mode (staff C6).

III.

The Locrian III is minor. The triad has tritone relations between its third and the third of VI and the fifth of IV. It can progress to VI or possibly to the tonic (staff D3/D5).

IV.

The Locrian subdominant is a minor triad and agrees with the tonic. The fifth of the triad has tritone relations with the root of V and the third of III. The IV - I cadence is stronger than the V - I progression (staff E3/E4). The VII - IV progression suggests the minor mode with IV as the tonic.

V.

The Locrian dominant is major but its root lies a tritone above the tonic, disrupting its dominant tendencies. The root of the triad has a tritone relationship with the third of VI and the fifth of IV. The V can progress to VI or downward to IV. The relation with VII is altered compared with Ionian since Locrian VII is not a diminished triad (staff F4/F2).

VI.

This is a major triad with tritone relations between its third and the root of V and the third of III. It is a neutral chord and can progress to II, III or IV (staff G3/G4/G5).

VII.

A minor triad, Locrian VII has no tritone relations. The VII makes an alternative cadence with the tonic compared with the II - I or IV – I progressions (staff A1).

This concludes the initial survey of modal melodic and triadic harmonic characteristics. Each of the modes displays some unique and some overlapping melodic and harmonic interrelationships. These modal differences are distinct from simple changes of key in the major-minor system since exact diatonic transpositions are not possible from one mode to another. A diatonic melody in one mode must be modally transposed with chromatic changes to maintain the same melodic intervals between notes. Each mode has different harmonic relationships between its scale elements as well. This attribute of the modes became obscured in the major-minor tonal system due to the distortion of the minor scale properties to more closely resemble the major scale, i.e. the harmonic and melodic minor scales. But even within the major-minor system, key transposition between minor scales preserved some essential modal differences from the major scale key transpositions. It's just that the modal character of these differences were obscured and half-forgotten. Modal composition thus requires sensitivity to these differences for proper expression.

3

The Relation of Modal to Tonal Scales

In this chapter, the modal melodic and harmonic characteristics already discussed will be compared with the major-minor system. The objective is to define the nature of the differences between these approaches rather than reiterate the compositional practice of major-minor tonality or even modal practice in past centuries. From an understanding of the essential differences, we can more clearly see what procedures can be modified to accommodate the other system's approach, what procedures cannot be changed without undermining that system and what compositional effect can be expected from maintaining a divide between the two. We will first examine the basic features of major-minor tonality, the tonal characteristics of the major scale, the natural minor and the harmonic minor. Then tonality is compared with modality, focusing on the distinction between inherent or fundamental features as opposed to modifiable (stylistic) features.

Major-Minor Tonality Properties

Major Scale

The modern major scale is equivalent to the Ionian mode (which actually evolved chromatically from Lydian usage). The Ionian mode has a unique assemblage of several characteristics that are only individually present in other modes. The first feature is the leading-tone to the tonic, an attribute shared only with the Lydian mode. The ascending semitone relation also exists in a harmonic context as with the Ionian V - I progression. The third of the V triad is of course the leading tone of the scale and typically moves to the root of I. This reinforces the movement by fifths in the roots (see McHose).

The leading-tone became a central organizing melodic and harmonic principle of the major scale and provided the impetus for many of the chromatic alterations introduced into progressions other than V - I. The V - I progression became the prototype for other progressions such as II - V, VI - II and so on. Since the other progressions did not possess the leading tone relationship to the second root, the third of the first chord was often chromatically altered to create the leading-tone to the following chord.

The second feature was the agreement of the major tonic triad with both the subdominant and dominant triads. The quality of the major scale was thus confirmed in its main harmonic structural elements. A third feature of the Ionian mode is the consonant relation of the tonic triad. The Ionian tonic triad does not form a tritone with any other diatonic chord of the mode. (The added seventh does form a tritone with IV and II, though.) The only other mode with a similarly consonant tonic is the Aeolian, the basis of the natural minor (as seen in Tables 5 - 11). This attribute makes voice leading more flexible and, given the ubiquity of the V - I progression, increased the overall consonant quality of tonal harmonies.

As noted, with the Ionian mode, the melodic tritone occurs between the third and seventh notes of the scale, rather innocuously placed for typical melodic constructions, especially compared with modes such as the Lydian, Phrygian and Locrian. Thus, the combined effect of the melodic placement of the tritone, the non-tritone forming tonic triad and the use of the V - I progression as the prototype for other tonal progressions created an even more consonant mode than the original diatonic Ionian, which allowed freer movement between the diatonic triads of the mode.

Of course, composers soon felt that they had created a surfeit of consonance and looked around for dissonant chords and progressions to increase the musical tension. The increase in progressions by fifths and chromatic dominant harmonies also compounded the decreased musical variety by restricting melodic flow. The constant movement of roots by fifths forced melody into similar recurring patterns to avoid obscuring the dominant movements. The introduction of too many melodic notes foreign to the dominant and

56

tonic chords would weaken the quality of the tonal progression. Tonal composers usually made such melodic notes 'passing' tones of brief duration or in non-salient position in the melody (i.e. not the high, low or repeated note). In addition, the dominant harmonies created their own pattern of strong and weak beats based on the harmonic role of the chord which restricted melodic and rhythmic elements.

One early and critical solution was the adoption of equal temperament in preference to earlier natural, Pythagorean or mean tone tuning. By standardizing the intervals of chromatic and diatonic notes, the restricted usability of keys remote from C major and a minor became moot. Now all keys, no matter how many sharps and flats, were alike in the intervals between their diatonic scale notes and all chromatic notes. This permitted composers not only increased flexibility in choosing keys for a work or individual movement, but also in creating temporary modulations to near or remote keys and in the chromatic alterations essential to dominant harmonies.

The usability of all 12 notes in the chromatic scale also provided a means for composers to chromatically enrich chords and progressions into the very consonant major scale. Chords such as the Neapolitan sixth, diminished seventh or the augmented sixth not only formed additional leading tones and chromatic notes, but also reintroduced the tritone at least in its harmonic form. The diminished seventh, for example, contained two tritones in its intervallic arrangement, **B/D/F/Ab**.

Finally, composers added additional notes to the triad. Seventh and ninth chords first became common in the dominant and leading-tone triads, but gradually were extended to non-dominant triads as well. Other notes such as appoggiaturas also increased the harmonic complexity of tonal chords. Although the major scale had originally evolved in the direction of greater consonance than the diatonic modes, by the end of the 19th century, the dissonance level of the major scale had become far greater than the modes.

Minor Scale

Natural Minor.

The development of the major key from the Ionian was paralleled by the development of the minor key from the Aeolian

57

mode. The tonic triad of Aeolian shares the Ionian feature of non-tritone relations with all other diatonic chords of the mode. The melodic tritone falls between the second and sixth note of the scale, slightly more prominent than Ionian but not as unavoidable as Lydian, Phrygian and Locrian. It also shares the agreement of the tonic triad with the subdominant and dominant triads. In this case, of course, all three are minor triads. Thus, the quality of the minor scale is confirmed in its main harmonic elements. These features are inherent to the Aeolian mode and what is termed the natural minor scale.

However, the leading-tone is conspicuous by its absence. Aeolian has a full step between VII and the tonic triad. This not only changes melodic voice leading, but also changes the nature of dominant progressions. In Aeolian (natural minor), the V - I progression has no leading tone between the third of V and the root of I, for example, **E/G/B** to **A/C/E**. Both **G** and **B** are a full step away from the tonic **A**. To stay within this pattern, the creation of other secondary dominant harmonies would also have to avoid the leading tone. If the progression was chromatically altered to make II a (Aeolian) dominant to V, the II chord (**B/D/F**) would have a raised <u>fifth</u>, F♯, resolving to the V (**E/G/B**). Notice that **D** and F♯ are a full step from **E**. Thus not only does the natural minor differ in agreement from the major scale, it also lacks the critical feature of the leading-tone.

Harmonic Minor.

Because of the importance of harmonic relationships in the major scale, composers felt a need to impose similar attributes on the minor scale. To deal with the issue of dominant harmony in minor keys, composers created a variant of the natural minor called the harmonic minor. In the harmonic minor, the VII step of the minor scale was chromatically raised to create a leading-tone. Thus, in **a** minor, the VII step **G** was raised to **G♯**. That made the V chord in minor equivalent to the major V. This chromatic VII, however, introduced a problem because of the odd interval of the augmented second between VI and VII, **F - G♯**. So the VI step had to be raised as well to F♯, although this alteration only worked harmonically or in melodic segments ascending to the tonic. Thus, G♯ had to go to A and F♯ to G♯. If some other progression was desired, then the harmonic minor had to revert to the natural minor with unraised **G** and **F**. Inevitably, major and minor scales began to merge since the harmonic difference between **a** minor and **A** major, for example, was limited to one note, **C** vs. **C♯** because **F♯** and **G♯** now existed in both scales.

The evolution of the major-minor system presents interesting paradoxes. Originally, the major and minor keys developed as simplifications of the seven modes in the direction of greater consonance and harmonic directness. Soon, however, variety was re-introduced in the form of chromaticism which was made possible by equal temperament. The use of chromaticism increased rapidly in the form of dominant harmonies, key modulations and added leading-tones which forced the minor scale to conform to the major scale. But these chromatic changes were almost always involved with the creation of dominant sounding harmonic progressions, even when the standard V – I cadence was avoided or delayed. Although these modifications had the original purpose of restoring some variety lost in the transition from the modal to the major-minor system, their increasing use fostered a uniformity which began to constrict its melodic and rhythmic elements and created a higher level predictability to these harmonic constructions.

Comparison With Modality

At this point, the modal and tonal systems can be compared with each other more precisely. However, the modal system needs to be distinguished from the particular stylistic practices of the Middle Ages (see Schubert; Owen). Even in the Middle Ages, stylistic factors as fundamental as dissonance treatment varied considerably from the early period of <u>organum</u> to the last phase of polyphonic <u>cantus firmus</u> masses (e.g. Palestrina). Melodic constructions also varied considerably from the early troubadours in the 12th century to the melodies of the 16th century madrigalists. Generally, the movement was in the direction of more metrically and modally regular melodies and more restricted dissonance treatment (see Aubrey).

This increasing modal melodic regularity and restricted voice leading actually paved the way for the development of the major-minor system. The greater regularity made the introduction of restrictive harmonic rules less noticeable. Conversely though, the harmonic rules made rhythmic and melodic deviations from the underlying harmony more difficult. In the tonal system, the regularity stems from the harmonic requirements of the system whereas in the modal system, it is a function of the particular style adopted by the composer.

Defining Differences between Modality and Tonality

This thought leads us into the distinction between defining properties of a system and freely modifiable, incidental properties. Due to the accidents of history, a confoundment often exists between the underlying musical structure and the particular uses that are made of that underlying structure. Composers at any given time generally exploit only some fraction of the possibilities inherent in the musical system. It is only over sufficient periods of time for stylistic variations to occur that the factors that are constant can be reliably distinguished from those that are changed without overthrowing the system.

Several factors in the major-minor system remained essentially constant over the period of its codification in the late 1600s until its loss of complete dominance in the early 1900s. The most decisive, clearly, was the preference for the V - I (V^7 - I) progression, with its extensions of II - V - I and IV - V - I. In the Ionian mode, the V - I also possessed the added inducement of the leading-tone. Most of the other factors stem from the desire to organize a composition around the dominant to tonic cadence. The use of chromatic leading tones in secondary dominant harmony emulated the Ionian V - I cadence; the restriction in backwards (retrogressive) and to a lesser extent non-dominant progressions prevented a loss of harmonic momentum to the cadence; metrical and rhythmic regularity fostered a chordal form of writing in which chord elements either began and ended together or were grouped with each other in tight arpeggiation. This had the concomitant effect of reflecting the harmony in the melody. The maintenance of intervallic relationships, particularly those of the major scale, while maintaining harmonic consistency, also forced the minor scale into that mold and removed the other modes that conflicted with it.

The centrality of the dominant to tonic cadence to the development of the major-minor system and tonality can be heard if one listens progressively to music of the 15th, 16th and 17th centuries. The use of the V - I cadence preceded many of the other attributes of the major-minor system mentioned above. Composers began to use it fitfully at first, in no small measure because the V - I cadence in the most favored modes did not have the compelling quality of the Ionian. (Dorian, Mixolydian, and Phrygian were most often used in the later Middle Ages and early Renaissance.) Two other inhibiting factors were the avoidance of the ascending leading-tone in the chant repertoire (for unknown stylistic reasons) and the similar avoidance of short regular phrases in religious and secular art music. Gradually though, the Ionian cadence became used often enough that it pulled the Ionian mode first into equality, then to preeminence. This process continued and accelerated through the 18th century when the V - I cadence reigned supreme.

These attributes stand in opposition more or less to modal practice. As noted, the most frequently used modes did not have as salient a form of the V - I cadence. Furthermore, Mixolydian and Phrygian have V triads that lack agreement with the tonic triad. The composers before the 16th century were certainly aware of the V - I cadence and used it occasionally, particularly in secular works, but did not view it as an organizing principle in a harmonic sense. The modal style viewed harmony as the avoidance of discord rather than something central to the organization of a musical work.

The constant attempts by modern theorists to show a harmonic master plan to the modal compositions of the Middle Ages and Renaissance only proves how effaced the memory of that style has become after centuries of major-minor tonality. The wellsprings of the modal style are melody and rhythm and it was the conceptualization and notation of rhythm that was the great theoretical insight of the period. The preoccupation of musical theorists and composers alike lay in the development and systematization of rhythmic schemes, which culminated in the isorhythmic compositions in which a rhythmic pattern controlled the interplay of all the parts. The greatest examples of isorhythm are the motets of John Dunstable and the *Mass* of Guillaume Machaut, but rhythmic concepts were central to the modal compositional process of this time (see Hoppin).

Of course, the relative inattention to harmonic considerations other than in the negative sense of controlling dissonance proved a weakness of the system. This harmonic lack of emphasis made the harmonic strength of the V - I cadence a refreshing novelty and eventually undermined the system. The histories of tonality and

61

modality both show that if you throw a family member out the front door, they are sure to re-enter through the back door, the family members in question being melody, rhythm and harmony.

The attributes of the major-minor system mentioned above as consequences of the V - I cadence used as an organizing device are absent or reduced in the modal period. Chordal movement was diatonic but made more equal use of scale steps. Pitch dyads (two note harmonies) were as prevalent as triads even late in the period. Progressions would be present in both forwards and backwards sequences (V - I, I - V, I - IV, IV - I, V - II, II - V etc.). The leading tone was occasionally used at the most important sectional cadences as a chromatic alteration but functioned purely as a natural melodic intensification rather than a harmonic structural device.

In keeping with the importance of melody and rhythm, the part writing often involved contrasting rhythms called <u>hemiola</u> (e.g. 6/8 in one part and 3/4 in another) and general metrical looseness compared to tonality. Composers created melodies keeping firmly in mind the characteristics of the mode employed. The *Missa cuiusvis toni* by Ockeghem provides a striking confirmation of this through its overtly proclaimed capability of being transposable and performable through various modes. This was regarded as a singular tour de force by contemporaries. Such an attitude would be hard to understand if mode was not a determiner of melodic construction. No tonal composer would state proudly that one of their pieces could be transposed and performed in a different key. In fact, as we saw in the previous chapter, melodies created in one mode are not usually directly transposable to other modes.

Incidental Differences between Modality and Tonality

Although many differences exist between historical modal and tonal compositions, not all of them should be seen as central to the distinction between them. Such features as the use of seventh and ninth chords, dissonance treatment, voice leading, and modulation should be viewed as incidental rather than defining features of each approach.

Seventh or ninth chords or any other diatonic chord for that matter are not incompatible with modality, although they only appear sporadically in medieval compositions. Neo-modal compositions in the

20th century often used such chords. Actually, tonality is more restrictive with such chords, limiting them almost entirely to dominant harmonies. Non-dominant seventh and ninth chords had a slow acceptance and were not really common until the end of the 19th century.

Similarly, dissonance treatment per se is not a defining difference between modality and tonality since tonally organized music was quite consonant in its early manifestations and modality is not disturbed by diatonic dissonance. Chromatic harmony when used mainly in conventional secondary dominant harmonies can strengthen a tonality, but conceptually there doesn't seem to be a reason why it wouldn't have a similar effect in a modal composition. Of course, at some level chromaticism weakens tonality and modality. The related issue of voice leading presents a clear difference in historical practice since the modal compositions of the past had rather strict rules in resolving suspensions and chromatic notes, but again voice leading does not by itself stand as a defining difference between modal and tonal systems. A wide range of voice leading practice exists in both modal and tonal compositions.

Modulation became a favorite practice of tonal composers partly to insert chromaticism and thus some necessary variety into the restrictive major-minor system. Modulation did occur even in the old modal compositions, but was not a prime characteristic for a variety of reasons. First, many compositions were written in the modal equivalent of (Ionian) C major; thus, Dorian mode basically meant **D** Dorian and so on. Second, with the variety provided by different modes, there was less urge to modulate between keys within a mode. Third, in keeping with the interest in rhythmic schemes, variety often was sought by changes in meter (modus, tempus and prolation in medieval terminology). Fourth, the lack of equal temperament made most keys with more than a couple flats or sharps seriously out of tune. Nevertheless, with equal temperament, modulation to different keys within a mode (e.g. **D** Dorian to **F♯** Dorian) can be accomplished quite as well as in tonality. However, the different modes would have their own modulatory schemes and requirements because of the particular harmonic relationships of each mode.

In summary, the modal system developed in the Middle Ages exploited certain of its potentials such as rhythmic variations, but for a variety of reasons such as liturgical doctrine and issues of tuning never fully developed its harmonic and to a lesser extent its melodic possibilities. The major-minor tonal system, since it came about in an era of increasing freedom, was far more thoroughly developed and exploited by later composers. This suggests that the medieval modal system may have potential for musical expression untapped by composers prior to 1600.

4

A Modern Modal System

Having covered some of the fundamental melodic and harmonic characteristics of the individual diatonic modes and briefly compared modal with tonal practice, it is worth exploring whether a modal system can be formulated which represents a worthwhile alternative to the major-minor system. Prior modal practice has either been in concordance with the medieval modal system, used to insert different chords or progressions into tonal music or used as scales for jazz improvisation. While effective on their own terms, these various approaches don't have the organizational logic of the tonal system, nor do they have a systematic process for maintaining modal stability in more chromatic or harmonically complex situations.

As argued, the decisive difference between the modal and tonal systems was the adoption of the Ionian V - I cadence in all its ramifications produced by tonal thinking. But an essential part of that process was the elimination of all conflicting tendencies present in the other modes. Therefore, simply maintaining the integrity of the different modes provides an effective barrier to the major-minor system, even if the incidental attributes such as dissonance treatment or seventh and ninth chords linked to it in tonal compositions are maintained in the modal system.

However, the necessary harmonic control and structure in a modal system are not maintained by adding harmonic extensions to chords. Although the modes differ in their harmonic tendencies, they are both weaker in harmonic organization and have substantial overlap with more other modes than does the major-minor system. Some reduction of harmonic control is desirable in my view, but the modes vary quite a bit in the degree of reduction, or to put it another way, some modes pose more obstacles to audible harmonic organization than others.

The overlap in the melodic and harmonic attributes of the modes also poses a problem in maintaining the integrity of a mode. As we saw in the previous chapters, although each mode has a unique collection of melodic and harmonic attributes, most individual attributes are shared with at least one other mode. For example, both the Lydian and Ionian mode have a half-step between VII and I. Conceptually, this issue is similar in form to the distinction between closely related keys. **C** and **G** Ionian or **E** and **B** Phrygian differ by only one sharp note while **D** and **G** Dorian or **F** and **B♭** Lydian differ by just one flat note. The problem with modality is compounded though, since not only the key but also the mode have to be distinguished from plausible modal alternatives.

A modern modal system can be expected to accord a more prominent role to melodic and rhythmic flow, but after the experience of a developed and systematic harmony, it is not a compelling solution to return full circle to the harmonic laxness of the earlier modal compositions, particularly when the strictures of voice leading and chordal formation found there are not also followed. Therefore, the modal system proposed here does present some possible ways to increase harmonic organization without reducing all modes to one standard. The degree to which procedures are followed is obviously a stylistic question in this or any system, but no mandates will be pronounced.

Relation of Major and Minor Modes in the Modal System

We can all agree on one fact about the major-minor tonal system: it is composed of a major scale and a minor scale. The Ionian major became linked to the Aeolian minor in the early stages of the development of tonality in all probability for the two reasons already mentioned, a tonic triad with consonant relations to the other diatonic triads and the agreement between the tonic, subdominant and dominant in the minor (Ex. 9).

Ex.9: Ionian and Aeolian Triads

This major-minor linkage assumed a critical role in tonal harmonic organization because, as we saw previously, each mode already contains a mixture of major and minor triads. Thus, Ionian (or the major scale) has major triads on I, IV and V and minor triads on II, III and VI. All the other modes, whether major or minor, have the same composition of triads, varying only in their relative positions. The association of a major scale (mode) with a minor scale (mode) then simply provides an external confirmation of an internal property of a mode.

The benefit of this linkage is profound, however, since the resulting harmonic organization permits a systematic approach to modulation as well as the introduction of chromatic chords (as will be seen). The immediate question, therefore, is whether the proposed modal system can take advantage of this relationship as well.

We saw that Ionian isn't the only major mode and Aeolian isn't the only minor mode. Since Ionian and Aeolian were thought to form a pair of similar modes despite the other contrasting qualities between them (more so initially), we can ask whether the other modes have mutual affinities. If we maintain the correspondence associated with the Ionian and Aeolian modes, we should seek modal pairs with similar tonic triad relations and similar agreement between the tonic triad and other scale steps.

Looking back at the Tables in Chapter 2, let's start with the Lydian major mode (Table 8). The tonic triad has a tritone relation with II, IV and VII. The steps in agreement with the tonic triad are II and V. If we look at the other Tables, we cannot find another tonic triad with an exact match of tritone relationships as the Lydian, however, the Dorian and the Phrygian both overlap on 2 of the 3 steps and both are minor modes. The Dorian tonic triad (Table 6) has

67

tritone relationships with steps II, IV and VI while the Phrygian (Table 7) has tritone relations with II, V and VII. However, if we look at the agreement of the tonic triad, we see that only the Dorian also has agreement of II and V with the tonic minor. Thus, the Dorian minor mode has the closest correspondence with the Lydian major mode (Ex. 10).

Ex.10: Lydian and Dorian Triads

Turning to the remaining major mode, the Mixolydian, we see from Table 9 that the tonic triad forms a tritone with steps III, V and VII. The tonic triad is in agreement with steps IV and VII. We saw that the Phrygian mode has a tonic triad that overlaps on 2 of the 3 scale steps forming the tritone, namely, V and VII, while differing only on II. Furthermore, its tonic triad is in agreement with steps IV and VII, in keeping with the Mixolydian. Thus, the Phrygian minor mode has the closest correspondence with the Mixolydian major mode (Ex. 11).

Ex.11: Mixolydian and Phrygian Triads

The only remaining mode is the Locrian, which has the diminished tonic triad. Obviously, its tonic triad forms a tritone with all of the scale steps but two. Since it is the only diminished triad, it is strictly speaking not in agreement with any other scale steps. However, since it does have the minor third in the tonic triad, the Locrian is typically grouped among the minor modes. In that case, it is in agreement with steps III, IV and VII. The Mixolydian is the only major mode with overlap on even 2 of the steps. However, if **B** Locrian has a relative major, it should be a minor third above the Locrian tonic which would be **D**. (Note that Ionian is a minor third above its relative minor, **A** - **C**, as are Lydian to Dorian, **D** - **F**, and Mixolydian to Phrygian, **E** - **G**.) However, **G** Mixolydian has the same key signature as **B** Locrian. It seems clear that Locrian doesn't have a major scale counterpart since it would have to be a major scale based on **D** with no sharps and flats. The closest scale is **D** Mixolydian with one sharp. The diminished Locrian tonic induces this asymmetry (Ex. 12).

Ex.12: Locrian Triads and False Major Triads

Although the two factors noted seem to be the only identifiable reasons why the Aeolian became paired with the Ionian as opposed to another minor mode, the predominant factor must be the correspondence in the agreement between the tonic triad and specific other steps. The commonality facilitates similar chordal movement in both modes, the main difference being the location of the diminished triad. Of course, in the Aeolian mode, step II forms the diminished triad instead of the VII of the Ionian mode.

In summary, three pairs of modal major-minor scalar dyads can be identified based on tonic triad tritone relations and agreement with other scale steps: the Ionian - Aeolian, the Lydian - Dorian and the Mixolydian - Phrygian. The diminished Locrian stands apart. The agreement of the tonic triad with particular scale steps seems more important than the tritone relationships in determining mutual affinity.

Parenthetic Harmonies

Parenthetic harmonies is a term most often applied to secondary dominant chords, but it really has a more general sense of any transient chromatic progression which doesn't disturb the existing key. We will first examine the secondary dominant effect, since this is by far the most common use of parenthetic harmonies in the tonal music of the past, before examining the concept in the fullest sense.

Major-Minor System Secondary Dominants

One of the signal developments of the major-minor system was the compositional practice of parenthetic or secondary dominants. Every triad of a given mode or key has another triad a fifth above it (with unmodified root) except for the diminished triad (Ex. 13). The Ionian V - I relation is the most obvious example, but the same relation exists between VI - II, VII - III, I - IV, II - V and III - VI. The lone exception, the Ionian IV - VII involves the tritone and diminished VII.)

Ex.13: Dominant-Like Ionian Progressions

The other modes have the same property except for the location of the tritone. The Dorian mode III - VI progression has the same tritone relation as Ionian IV - VII, as do the Phrygian mode II -

V, the Lydian mode I - IV, the Mixolydian VII - III, the Aeolian VI - II and the Locrian V - I.

The prominence of the Ionian V - I progression fostered the use of other progressions involving roots a perfect fifth apart within the Ionian mode. In this way, the musical flow had a strong sense of harmonic movement even when the dominant and tonic of the key were not present. The difference between music in the Ionian mode and the major scale lies mainly in the emphasis or lack thereof of progressions between chords with roots a fifth apart. In other words, the difference between the two is functional rather than inherent.

Although movement by fifths within the Ionian mode can be accomplished diatonically on other steps, the particularly emphatic quality of the Ionian V - I progression is not present due to the lack of a leading-tone relationship, except in the I - IV progression. However, this latter movement is somewhat of a threat to the tonic as mentioned. Once equal temperament became established, the introduction of chromatic notes became freed from all tuning restrictions. This permitted the restoration of a leading-tone to all the progressions by fifths, although these were now chromatically altered triads. For example, the II chord in C Ionian is **D/F/A** which progresses by a fifth to V or **G/B/D**. To emulate the V - I progression, the **F** was raised to **F♯**, forming a **D** major triad. This altered chord now is the same as the actual dominant of the **G** major chord if it were the tonic chord (key of **G** major).

Similarly, triads other than the IV chord (and the diminished VII) can be chromatically altered to form the dominant of the triad a fifth below (Ex.14).

Ex.14: Secondary Dominant Major Scale (Ionian) Progressions

71

In the major-minor system, chords are valued to the extent that they advance the musical phrase through dominant progressions. If a chord does not do this in its original diatonic form, then it is chromatically altered. This process in a sense constitutes a transient modulation to the key of that triad, although harmonically it doesn't disturb the key due to its brevity, particularly if a diatonic chord follows this momentary disturbance. Of course, modulation tends to weaken a tonality, but through the clever trick of modulation through the dominant, the key strength was enhanced at the same time that notes foreign to the key were being introduced. Logically however, we can see that even here there is some point at which dominant harmonies begin to weaken more than they strengthen tonality. The latter stages of tonality showed this quite clearly.

Modal System Secondary Dominants

The development of the parenthetic or secondary dominant harmonies went hand in hand with the growth of the major-minor system, so it played no role in the medieval modal system. Strangely, it has not played much if any role in more recent neo-modal compositions. Perhaps it was viewed as too reminiscent of the major-minor system and too incompatible with a historical modal style. Yet, there is no logical barrier to parenthetic harmonies in the modal system. However, the other modes, since they lack the decisive quality of the Ionian V - I progression, will also have a different quality to secondary dominant effects. The Lydian mode is the one partial exception since it does have a leading-tone relationship between its V and I triads, but the V^7 - I progression is different than the Ionian because of the full step between the seventh and the third of the tonic triad. The leading-tones are to the tonic and fifth instead.

In fact, each of the modes has a different quality of secondary dominant harmonic relationships due to their differing scale structure. To mention the most obvious example, the Phrygian mode has the diminished V triad and therefore cannot support conventional secondary dominant effects. Since each mode has its own characteristics, it is useful to examine each in turn (Ex. 15).

Ex.15: Modal V - I Progressions: Ionian to Locrian

Ionian.

This is identical to the major scale and has the most emphatic V - I cadence and thus the same secondary dominant harmony effect. There are no tritone relations.

Dorian.

The Dorian V - I cadence involves two minor triads with no tritone relationship. The only (ascending) leading-tone relation occurs between the fifth of V and the third of I, not a particularly strong effect.

Phrygian.

The Phrygian V is diminished and the tonic is minor. The fifth of V forms a descending leading-tone to the root of I, somewhat intensifying the progression to the tonic. There is a tritone between the fifth of V and the fifth of I. The diatonic V cannot function in a secondary dominant harmony with II since either the {V of V} - V progression would be from diminished to diminished or the V would have to be chromatically altered to form a minor Phrygian I. For example, in **E** Phrygian, the V is **B/D/F**. But if V acts as a temporary tonic for II (V of V) then the progression would have to be {V of V} (**F♯/A/C**) to V (**B/D/F♯**). Thus V would now be outside the key of **E** Phrygian.

Lydian.

The Lydian V - I is similar to the Ionian since both V and I are major chords and there is an ascending leading-tone between the third of V and the root of I. There is a tritone only with the seventh of V and the root of I.

Mixolydian.

The Mixolydian V is a minor chord moving to the major tonic, which lessens the dominant effect. A tritone exists between the third of V and I. The minor V chord cannot be interpreted as a Mixolydian tonic. There are no leading-tone relations.

Aeolian.

The Aeolian V - I is similar to the Dorian since both are minor triads and there are no tritone relations. A weak ascending leading-tone relation does exist between the fifth of V and the third of I.

Locrian.

Since the Locrian I is diminished and the V is a tritone above the root, there is no conventional dominant effect. However, the V is a major chord so it can serve as a temporary tonic to II {V of V}, but obviously it cannot serve as a Locrian diminished tonic.

Parenthetic Tonal Harmonies

Although the major-minor system principally employed secondary dominants, they are only one part of the wider notion of parenthetic harmonies and transient modulation. Even if we restrict ourselves to the case of a diatonic triad acting as a temporary tonic, we can see that there must be six other triads in its diatonic key. For example, if we take the V of C major as a temporary tonic, then it acts as a G major tonic (Ex. 16). The dominant of the G major triad is the D major triad. However, if G major is now a transient key, it also possesses a II, III, IV, VI and VII step. Tonal composers made occasional use of such non-dominant parenthetic chords, whether or not one accepts that they have a specific harmonic effect (see Piston). Note however, that some of the triadic relationships (II, IV, VI) are not distinguishable from the key of the original tonic C. Adding a seventh would not change this ambiguity for the three such parenthetic progressions in the Ionian mode.

Ex.16: Parenthetic Ionian Harmonies to the Dominant

V of V V   II of V   III of V   IV of V   VI of V   VII of V

Chord progression could proceed from {III of V} or {VI of V} to V, for example, as well as from {V of V} to V. Generally, since tonal composers valued dominant sounding progressions, such non-dominant movement was not a prominent part of the musical style. Additionally, if one stays too long in the new key, it becomes less transient and more an actual modulation. Thus, such parenthetic modulations are usually defined as at most two or three chords in the new key before returning to the dominant of the original key (Ex. 17).

Ex.17: Extended Parenthetic Dominant Progressions

V of V   V of V   V   I   II of V   V of V   V   I
of V

For example, a parenthetic extended harmony might be {V of V of V} to {V of V} to V or {IV of V} to {V of V} to V, with a definite return to the original key after V. The sequence must terminate in the original key to make harmonic sense as a parenthetic harmony. In other words, not finishing with V in the above examples would make questionable the harmonic logic of the progressions at least in terms of the original key.

Of course, the dominant is not the only point of departure and return in a parenthetic harmony sequence (Ex. 18). For example, the subdominant could be the terminus of the progression {II of IV} to

{IV of IV} to IV or step III could be the terminus of the progression {IV of III} to {II of III} to III.

Ex.18: Parenthetic Ionian Harmonies to the Subdominant and Mediant

II of IV   IV of IV   IV   IV of III   II of III   III

The character of these progressions will not sound like secondary dominant progressions obviously, but will instead be equivalent to the same progression in a particular key. To the extent that the progression can be audibly interpreted to be in the key of the temporary tonic, the progression will solidify the prominence of that chord, if not as definitely as the dominant cadence. And if the temporary tonic is an integral part of the established key, then it will in turn support that key and its tonic.

The phrase used in the last paragraph 'audibly interpreted to be in the key of ...' is an important qualification. These kind of progressions can weaken tonality if they proceed to other chromatic chords, as occurred in late Romantic music, or can be ambiguous if the chords and progressions can be logically part of two or more keys. To take a simple example of the latter case, the Ionian tonic triad can stand as the dominant of its own IV triad. This makes the **C** major I - IV (**F** major V - I) progression ambiguous unless the seventh (**B**♭) is added to the tonic chord. The **B**♭ clarifies the key since **F** major is unambiguously demonstrated, transforming the tonic chord into a {V of IV} chord. Conversely, I⁷ - IV with a **B**♮ seventh confirms **C** major as the key of the progression.

Parenthetic Modal Harmonies

The general process of parenthetic harmonies involving dominant and non-dominant progressions outlined for tonal scales can be applied directly to the modal scales and has much greater applicability and utility. The reason for this lies with the varied harmonic relationships across the different modes which favor certain progressions for one mode but are less useful in the others. In addition, since the non-Ionian modes have a less emphatic harmonic structure, the parenthetic harmonies offer a means of supporting the mode that would be difficult to achieve diatonically (Ex. 19).

Ex.19: Lydian Parenthetic Harmonies

II of V   V   V⁷ of V   V   VI⁹ of II   II   VII of V   V

We can use the Lydian mode as a modal example. As noted in Chapter 2, the Lydian mode can be somewhat unstable due to the diminished IV which cannot counterbalance the strength of the V. Thus, prominent harmonic progressions involving the Lydian V can make it difficult for the Lydian I to assert itself as the tonic. However, chromatic progressions or chords can be used to mark the Lydian V as the dominant without establishing it as an apparent tonic (Ex. 20).

The example first shows a simple diatonic **F** Lydian progression with triads only, V – VI – II – V - I. The concluding I triad sounds like the start of a new progression or an afterthought to the preceding V (which sounds like Ionian I in this context). In 20b, we have the same progression but this time with a II⁷ chord before the V. This creates an even more definite cadence on the Lydian V (Ionian V⁷ - I). The next variation, 20c, has the II⁷ chord followed by a V⁷ chord, V - VI - II⁷ - V⁷ - I. The seventh on V slightly reduces the cadential feeling between II and V, but the I still doesn't compete successfully with V.

Ex.20: Alternative Lydian V -VI - II - V - I Progressions

V   VI   II   V   I   V   VI   II⁷   V   I

V   VI   II⁷   V⁷   I   V   VI   II   V⁷   I   VI   V   V⁷of V   V⁷   I

     The next variation returns II to a triad while leaving V as a seventh chord. This provides a slightly smoother sequence to I, since the dominant seventh chord creates an expectancy of a cadence, even though the Lydian I does not have the precise character expected. Furthermore, the lack of a seventh chord on the preceding II also reduces the strength of the cadence between II and V. The following variation 20e shows a parenthetic harmony, in this case, a secondary dominant. However, note that this is a <u>Lydian</u> parenthetic harmony on II {Lydian V of V}. If the V is set as a parenthetic Lydian tonic, the key would be C Lydian which has one sharp unlike C Ionian. Now the Ionian cadential sound of the II - V has been subdued. The **F** Lydian triad sounds much more integrated into the progression, if not exactly like an Ionian V - I cadence. But we don't seek an Ionian cadence in Lydian!

     In some cases, the non-dominant parenthetic progressions have greater utility than dominant progressions. Parenthetic dominant progressions have greater harmonic strength, but for that reason can be more difficult to string together without risking the stability of the existing key. If two or more secondary harmonies follow after another, the feeling of a new key becomes pronounced when the second such chord is reached. With non-dominant progressions, the danger of unplanned modulation is lessened because they have less harmonic strength and because the second such chord will not inexorably sound like a tonic.

As Schoenberg noted also, the perception of a cadence is established as much or more so by melody and rhythm than by harmony. In a composition, the cadential aspects of a progression can be manipulated through the use of inversions, arpeggiation, syncopation, orchestration and so on. Nevertheless, the harmonic ambiguities, more prominent tritone relations and milder harmonic progressions of the non-Ionian diatonic modes do create a constant resistant effect to these other manipulations. More care needs to be taken not only to control an unwanted sense of an Ionian cadence, but also to keep the mode distinct where there are seven possibilities rather than just the two of the major-minor system.

Defining and Maintaining the Mode Harmonically

Harmonic Ambiguity of the Modes

The point about harmonic ambiguity raised in the preceding section is an important issue because of the expanded possibilities of the modal system compared with the (mostly major) major-minor system. In the major-minor system, for example, a scale with no sharps and flats is either C major or a minor and occasionally both at the same time. In the modal system, it's anything from Ionian to Locrian.

This is a great strength of the modal system, since it permits a healthy variety of melodic and harmonic relationships, but with freedom comes increased responsibility. The major-minor system, by constantly intermingling the major and minor scales and by the concomitant imposition of major scale characteristics at all times, made the major-minor scale distinction so hard to decipher that even gifted tonal theorists such as Schenker had to base such distinctions on a detailed analysis of melodic lines rather than the harmonies.

The same process applied to the modal system ultimately leads to the chromatic scale and amodality, if not outright abandonment of hierarchical relations with respect to scale degrees (atonality). These approaches are outside the scope of this book, not to mention, well-known and the subject of prior books and the basis of thousands of 20th century compositions. Having said that, it is also fair to note that there are a number of intermediate steps along the path to amodality and different styles may lodge themselves at different points. For example, one approach might strictly preserve the differences between all seven modal scales, another might merge the scalar dyadic pairs identified earlier in this chapter. In other words, there could be a merger of characteristics between the Mixolydian and the Phrygian scales, the Lydian and Dorian scales and the Ionian and Aeolian pair in a modal approximation to the major-minor system (which would presumably result in harmonic minor scales in each scalar dyad). The Locrian would still be standing apart. This would leave three different systems as opposed to the solitary major-minor system and would still impart some needed melodic and harmonic variety, although less than the first approach obviously.

If the goal is to preserve modal distinctions, then progressions and melodies have to make use of relationships that more uniquely define the mode and control the occurrence of ambiguous elements to those situations where modulation or ambiguity is sought. Modulation and chordal overlap in the modal context can either be between keys within the mode (e.g. **D** Dorian to **F** Dorian), the relative major or minor (e.g. **A** Dorian to **C** Lydian), the parallel major or minor (e.g. **E** Mixolydian to **E** Phrygian), the cross-modal relative or parallel key (e.g. **D** Ionian to **A** Mixolydian) or between keys across modes (**D** Dorian to **C** Mixolydian).

The complete set of overlapping diatonic chords will be presented later in the chapters on the 3 modal dyads, but some discussion is useful here. As an initial example, let's take the **A** major triad, **A/C♯/E** (Table 12). This triad represented as a capital A in the table is present in three keys in the Ionian scale: **D**, **A** and **E** Ionian. If we look at the corresponding modal scales to the Ionian, we can see that the triad occurs in 3 keys in each of the remaining 6 modes for a total of 21 keys in seven modes.

Table 12: Occurrence of the A major Triad in Modal Scales

Ionian	Dorian	Phrygian	Lydian	Mixoly.	Aeolian	Locrian
D	e	f♯	G	A	b	c♯
E	f♯	g♯	A	B	c♯	d
A	b	c♯	D	E	f♯	g♯

Logically, the quickest way to avoid harmonic ambiguity should be to clearly establish and maintain the mode. By itself, this eliminates all but three possibilities. Unfortunately, modal distinction is not as simple a task as key definition. Establishing the key (sharps/flats) by itself leaves 7 possibilities. (On the other hand, it clearly isn't a problem to find some other mode and key to modulate to if that's what you want to do.)

Since a single triad or even seventh chord is contained in more than one key, two or more chords are needed to uniquely specify the key assuming the mode has been established. In the major-minor system (or Ionian-Aeolian here) certain dominant two-chord progressions were found most useful, IV - V or II - V, in order to specify the key. The V step was more important than the tonic in this process. The other modes have different combinations. Dorian mode has no useful two-chord dominant progressions that define the key; however, Dorian IV - I is unique to a key. Phrygian mode has a unique V - IV progression but it does involve the diminished triad. The II - I progression involving the descending semitone tonic cadence is also key specific. Lydian mode has no useful 2-chord progressions that define the key apart from the diminished IV. The Mixolydian V - I is key specific as is VII - I. Aeolian VI - V is key specific. The Locrian mode has easily defined keys since any progression involving the tonic is unique as is the IV - V progression. There are many 3-chord triadic progressions unique to a key, if not a mode, as are more complex or irregular chords.

Harmonic Definition of the Mode

Distinguishing modes as opposed to keys requires more effort for two reasons: there are more modes than keys to confuse in categorizing a short chord sequence and the modes have overlapping characteristics which favor harmonically more stable modes. However, here also chromatic elements can help define and maintain a mode far better than could be achieved through a strictly diatonic approach. Several harmonic methods of enhancing modal definition and stability will be presented here, although readers are encouraged to discover additional methods.

Modulation.

Modulation from one key to another within a mode introduces chromatic elements from the standpoint of the original key at least. This is not necessarily true between modes because of relative keys, e.g. **a** minor to **C** major or **G** Mixolydian to **E** Phrygian. In principle, modulation between keys within the modes is no different than modulation within the major-minor system. Modulation can be prepared or unprepared, although as Piston notes, these are relative terms. Generally, preparation involves movement to a key directly by way of shared chords (pivot chords), or indirectly through related keys. In the latter case, more chromatic chords are typically employed as the pivot chords. As the tonal style progressed, more distantly related keys were used in modulating passages. The term 'unprepared modulation' is typically restricted now to cases where close or distant key progression is not governed by any particular scheme and all (triadic) chords are free to follow one another in any movement between keys.

Modulation within the modes can follow any of these particular styles of modulation. What does change are the particular procedures and chord progressions that would be used, at least with prepared modulation and its pivot chords. Since each mode has different harmonic and melodic characteristics, the textbook examples given for major-minor tonality do not necessarily work well. It is useful to examine each mode by itself to see how modal modulation might work in a relatively straightforward setting using shared triads. Note that the examples are kept relatively simple, but with some attention paid to both soprano and bass melodic line. In addition, the modal cadences are milder and less conclusive than the conventional V^7 - I major-minor (Ionian) cadence. In a modal modulation in an actual musical work, the establishment of the new key after modulation generally requires more emphasis and repetition than is seen in these brief examples.

Ionian Mode Modulation.

Since Ionian is covered in texts of tonal harmony, we will not linger over it, although we will use the Ionian mode (major scale) as a reference point. One issue that deserves some comment is the role of the dominant in modulations. In the major-minor system, the dominant is not a good pivot chord because it defines the key and the effect would be overly abrupt and confusing. By having a few preparatory chords before the appearance of the dominant progression, particularly the key defining progressions mentioned above, the new key can secure its place more effectively. The situation with the other modes is not as clear cut, because of the reduced dominant effect in them. We will examine whether V can easily be used as a pivot on a mode by mode basis.

Dorian Mode Modulation.

The Dorian mode scale degrees in agreement with the tonic are II and V while VI is the diminished triad. Dorian prepared modulation to diatonically related keys can occur through steps I, II, V and VII most readily depending on which steps overlap between the two keys. Dorian III is slightly awkward as a modulation pivot since the typical III - VI progression involves the diminished triad, but is not unusable. In Dorian mode, it is the IV - I progression that is unique to a key rather than customary progressions involving V. For this reason, using V as a pivot does not have the same drawback as it does in Ionian since other chords would be needed to be included to define the key sequence anyway. On the other hand, if IV - I is to be used to define the key, then it would be best not to use IV as the pivot chord unless it moves to other chords than the tonic. The remaining steps can be used as pivots if they fit within the particular modulatory progression. Some examples of simple modulations to Dorian keys closely related to **D** Dorian are shown in Ex. 21.

83

Ex.21: Dorian Modulation

Phrygian Mode Modulation.

The Phrygian mode triads in agreement with the tonic are IV and VII while V is the diminished triad. Phrygian prepared modulation to diatonically related keys can be accomplished through I, III, IV, VI and VII. Phrygian II is not the best choice for a pivot chord due to its importance to the Phrygian tonic cadence while V is diminished. Since II - I and V - IV are unique to a key in Phrygian, the most neutral pivot chords are generally III, VI and VII, while I and IV are usable in some cases. Some examples of modulations to closely related Phrygian keys from E Phrygian are shown in Ex. 22.

Lydian Mode Modulation.

The Lydian mode triads in agreement with the tonic are II and V while IV is the diminished triad. Lydian modulation can be accomplished most easily through I, II, III, VI and VII. Lydian V is not the most favored choice for a pivot chord due to its importance to the Lydian tonic cadence while IV is the diminished triad. However, with care the V can be used in a repetitive sequence with the tonic. Lydian has no useful 2-chord progressions that define the key, so all the pivot chords are usable depending on the modulatory progression. Some examples of modulations to closely related Lydian keys from F Lydian are shown in Ex. 23, including the use of Lydian V as pivot in the first sequence.

Ex.22: Phrygian Modulation

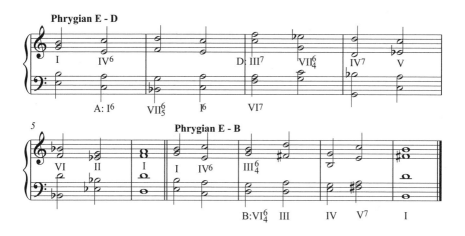

Ex.23: Lydian Modulation

Mixolydian Mode Modulation.

The Mixolydian mode triads in agreement with the tonic are IV and VII, while III is the diminished triad. Mixolydian prepared modulation can be accomplished most easily through I, II, VI and VII as the pivot chords. Mixolydian IV is not the best choice for a pivot chord due to its relative strength against the tonic, which is greater than even the Ionian IV possesses. In addition, modulations to the key of the Mixolydian IV can have an overly facile character if made too directly. Mixolydian has a useful 2-chord progression in V - I that defines the key, but the problems in using V for the pivot are less severe than with the subdominant. Some examples of modulations to closely related Mixolydian keys from **G** Mixolydian are shown in Ex. 24.

Ex.24: Mixolydian Modulation

Aeolian Mode Modulation.

The Aeolian mode triads in agreement with the tonic are IV and V while II is the diminished triad. Aeolian modulation can be most easily accomplished through I, III, IV, VI and VII. Aeolian V is not the best choice for a pivot chord due to its importance to the Aeolian tonic cadence while II is diminished. Since IV - V and V - VI are unique to a key in Aeolian, the most neutral pivot chords are III, VI and VII, while I and IV are usable in some cases. Some examples of modulations to closely related Aeolian keys from **A** Aeolian are shown in Ex. 25.

Ex.25: Aeolian Modulation

Locrian Mode Modulation.

The Locrian mode, if considered as a minor mode, has III, IV and VII in agreement with the tonic triad while I is also the diminished chord. This makes modulation in the Locrian mode both easier and trickier than with the other modes. It is easier because the I, II and V progressions are key unique and trickier because of the omnipresent tritone interval. Pivot chords should probably be limited to the minor triads III, IV and VII or the major triad on VI. Some examples of modulations to closely related Locrian keys to **B** Locrian are shown in Ex. 26.

Augmented chords of the fifth and sixth.

These chords became more common with Wagner and later tonal composers, but occasionally show up as early as Bach and Mozart. Their function was to provide additional impetus to tonic and dominant progressions (Ex. 27). The augmented fifth chord is generally a major triad with a raised fifth (Ex. 27a) and therefore based on the (Ionian) scale degrees with major triads, that is, I and V (and less often IV) in the major scale. (If constructed on a minor triad, then the third and fifth are raised, but this was less frequently used.) Since these chords are used to establish or re-establish the (Ionian) dominant, the augmented I progresses to IV while the augmented V progresses to I. The augmented IV usually goes to II presumably because VII forms the tritone.

Ex.26: Locrian Modulation

The various augmented sixth chords evolved from minor key passing tones and suspensions. These chords are based on II or IV and have the raised fourth scale degree and a lowered (minor) sixth scale degree (Ex. 27b-c). They typically proceed to V. The chords came about through melodic considerations with chromatic leading-tones to the tonic or dominant triads. In the early days of tonality, when key relationships were relatively clear-cut, there was less need for their services, so to speak. Later on, as tonal harmony became highly chromatic and key stability and definition declined, stronger means were needed to restore a tonic or key.

In the current context, modal stability is inherently somewhat weaker than in the major-minor system, so these augmented chords (or their melodic leading-tone equivalents) can play a useful role in certain situations in shoring up a mode harmonically. Of course, other forms of melodic voice leading can achieve a similar effect in situations where such chords are too out of place.

Ex.27a-c: Ionian Augmented Chords

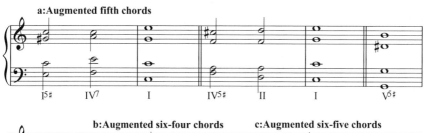

These chords have different implications depending on the mode, however. With respect to the augmented fifth, it is built on a major triad to create the characteristic intervals of 2 major thirds. Each mode has a different arrangement of the major triads. Only Lydian and Locrian (apart from Ionian) have major triads on V; Mixolydian and Lydian have major triads on I and Dorian and Mixolydian have major triads on IV. (Note however that the Lydian progression from the augmented I to IV involves the tritone between the roots.) The standard Ionian progressions transposed to these modes are shown in Ex. 28.

To use the augmented triad in minor, the third and fifth must be raised. The double augmentation does present a more noticeable chromatic alteration and its acceptability will be more dependent on the prevailing style. Since the basic progressions remain the same, further examples are not necessary.

In the typical pattern of the Ionian (major) scale, the augmented fifth on I and V progresses to another major triad. This progression also occurs with the V - I in Lydian and the I - IV in Mixolydian. The IV - II Ionian progression progresses to a minor triad as does the Mixolydian and Dorian. A progression to a diminished triad occurs with Lydian I⁵♯ - IV and Locrian V⁵♯ - I.

The augmented sixth chords have more generality across the modes since they can be derived from major or minor triads and in fact the six-five-three is an enharmonic variant of dominant seventh chords.

Ex.28: Modal Augmented Fifth Chords

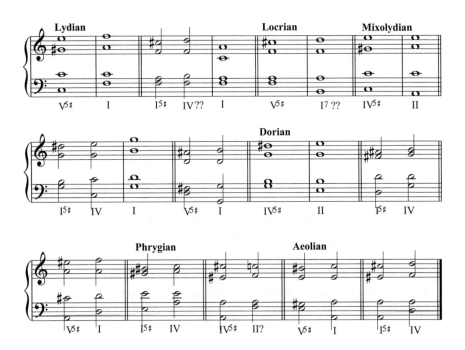

The resolution of the augmented interval signals the difference with the seventh chord since the augmented note resolves upwards while the seventh resolves downward typically. The augmented sixth chords usually progress to V whether based on II or IV, but can also go to I or III (Ex. 29).

Ex.29: Modal Augmented Six-four and Six-five Progressions

Note that the Dorian progression involves the minor V and has one whole-step relation rather than all half-steps as in the Ionian augmented sixth progression to V, while in the progression to Dorian III (major) there is now a repeated tone that in the Ionian mode moves by half-step. The Phrygian progressions are similar to the Dorian except that the progression to V involves a diminished triad. The Lydian mode already has the augmented fourth on the IV step, so the chromatic alterations would involve the flattened sixth scale degree (and seventh in the six-five-three chord). The voice leading is similar to the Ionian since Lydian V is major and III is minor. The reader should compare the sound of the regular Lydian IV - V - I progression with the six-five-three substituted for IV.

The Mixolydian mode has a minor to minor six-four-three progression and a major to minor six-five-three progression to V, but Mixolydian III is diminished. The Aeolian has the minor to minor six-five-three to V progression, but the six-four three chord is built on the diminished Aeolian II. The progression to III is similar to the Dorian. The Locrian progressions to V and III are similar to other modes but of course the tonic triad is diminished. The augmented sixth chords do provide a bit more momentum to the Locrian V - I progression.

The advantage of the augmented sixth chord is that it can be produced via melodic considerations more variedly than the typical dominant seventh chord and it can therefore operate in modes not conducive to the formation of such secondary dominants (e.g. Phrygian). In the major-minor system, the uniformity of the harmonic organization led to the inclusion of remotely related chords to provide some variety, particularly in the cadences. In the modal system, melodic and harmonic variety stem more directly from the scales, but result in less tightly wound harmonic structures. Thus, these augmented chords or their voice leading equivalents can buttress a dominant or tonic without forcing the mode into the major-minor system.

Obviously, exclusive reliance on such techniques could end up as restrictive as tonality, but this is no different with any musical system. Tonal composers had to balance the various tonalities in a work and make more ambiguous an overly definite key and more clearly define a wavering key to maintain a pleasing musical flow. Modal composers similarly have to balance the various methods of modulation and modal key definition. Harmonic methods should not render one mode indistinguishable from another nor is there the same need to import features of other modes to enrich a mode as existed in major-minor tonality. Melodies and harmonies which constantly shift across all the modes produce the modal equivalent of shifting tonalities and really fall outside the modal system into amodality.

This is not the same as having several different modes in a composition and modulating between them, since the integrity of an established mode or key is not diminished retroactively by modulations from it. Don't misunderstand. Its role and significance in the organization of the entire work or movement will be affected, but this will not change its stability in the passages where it does appear. For example, Mahler's *Symphony 9* begins in the key of **D** and closes in **D♭**, but audiences never stand up at the end and ask what happened to the concluding movement in **D**.

In addition, such mongrelizing of modes would greatly impair the development and maintenance of modally sensitive melody. Inevitably, harmonically weaker modes will succumb or be absorbed by the stronger (i.e. the Ionian) or all will merge back into the chromatic scale. Although many great works remain to be written in the chromatic scale, they cannot possess the modal character sought here. In particular, that character should involve more distinctive and subtle melodic construction in keeping with the individual modes.

Inversions.

The ambiguity of seven modes coexisting within the same scale (key) that two existed in the major-minor system creates added problems for modal definition. Even two modes proved too much for the major-minor system as it turned out. The minor mode quickly became an appendage of the major and lost most of its Aeolian modal character. Logically, there are two approaches to managing the problem: first, we can use methods such as the augmented chords and other voice leading considerations to tighten the harmonic structure of a particular mode and second, we can minimize the obviousness (salience) of progressions and chords which might introduce ambiguity or disrupt the modal definition. The second approach is exemplified here by the procedure of chordal inversions.

Chords are evaluated, at least since Rameau, on the basis of their root. The principal difficulty with the system of root analysis arose with chordal inversions where the root note is in an upper voice and another note of the chord is in the bass (lowest note). Notationally, the chord is the same whatever note of the chord lies in the bass, e.g. V, V⁶, V² are all dominant chords and have the same functional role in the tonal system. However, from the listener's standpoint, and the composer's, they are not completely interchangeable. Chordal inversions are perceived as less stable or more ambiguous harmonically than so-called root position chords. Generally, the higher the chord note placed in the bass, the less stable the chord. Thus, a V² chord with the seventh in the bass (third inversion) sounds considerably less stable than the same chord with the third in the bass (first inversion).

Tonal composers took advantage of this effect to vary the intensity and salience of the ubiquitous dominant progressions. A V - I progression with both chords in first inversion perceptibly reduces the cadential sound and the composer would use other nonharmonic means to reduce the obtrusiveness of such 'interior' dominant progressions. For example, the orchestration or rhythm or melody would work against the cadential progression. Obviously, at the end of a phrase or movement, the opposite process would be employed of maximizing the salience of the cadence (Ex. 30).

Ex.30: Dominant Inversions and Root Progressions

Harmonic cadences usually require help from other aspects of the music to be convincing. This fact is usually glossed over in most harmony texts since it is more difficult to analyze and present the melodic, rhythmic and instrumentation attributes of a passage and their relative role compared with the harmonic attributes. Nevertheless, such cadences can exert a positive influence in defining and maintaining modal definition. By emphasizing chordal progressions that define the mode and reducing the salience of chordal progressions that suggest alternative modes, modal stability can be enhanced without drastic restrictions in chordal movement. This is a significant issue in a modal system where melodic considerations have a more equal footing with the harmonic aspects.

Composers employed inversions in order to smooth out bass lines and improve melodic voice leading in the upper voices. Root position chords generate disjunct motion and particularly so in dominant progressions. However, tonal composers generally restricted triadic inversion to the first inversion with the third in the bass. The second inversion (fifth in the bass) was mostly restricted to the I triad and used mainly in the cadence before V. Seventh chord inversions were more freely employed even with the fifth and seventh in the bass.

Although inversions place an upper tone in the bass, once there the note takes on a harmonic significance it did not possess as an upper voice. There is no definite theoretical explanation of why this happens other than an appeal to the overtone series. Schoenberg offered the explanation that the overtones of the bass note in inversions conflicted with the overtones of the displaced root. The bass note in general, because it is lower, often has more audible overtones than a higher note.

In a modal system, there is no need to observe the restricted use of the six-four chord or any other with inversions. But it is useful to note the harmonic significance that bass notes assume simply as a result of being in the bass. This has important implications for modal chord progressions and melodic voice leading, both in the bass and other voices. Although we will see this factor specifically used in the study compositions for the modal dyads presented in later chapters, some general discussion is warranted here.

In the tonal system, composers made use of the more ambiguous inversions to create harmonic substitutes for root position chords. For example, a II triad in first inversion now has the fourth scale degree as the bass note. Composers, in fact, would often use a II^6 triad in place of a IV chord in a progression, particularly where they did not want a strong cadence. Inversions of seventh chords were quite common as well with concomitant substitutions, except perhaps for the V² chord. The seventh in the bass forms a stronger dissonance and downward impetus.

The same principle can be applied with even greater utility to the modal system. Each mode has scale step relations and progressions which distinguish it from other modes in the same way that certain progressions defined the key in the tonal system. Conversely, there are progressions which weaken a mode by suggesting a competing mode or modes. To take one example, we noted the competition of the Mixolydian IV (Ionian I) with the Mixolydian I for the tonic role. This makes Mixolydian I - IV and to a lesser extent VII - IV progressions problematic for the maintenance of the modal identity. Avoidance of such progressions could handle the problem; however, it turns out that the IV and VII triads are precisely those in agreement with the major Mixolydian tonic. Through the use of inversions, however, the effect of the progression can be softened, either by inversions of the IV and VII themselves or the inversion of appropriate alternatives that put the fourth or seventh scale degrees of the scale in the bass (Ex. 31).

Ex.31: Myxolydian Progressions with Inversions

$$\text{VII} \quad \text{IV} \quad \text{V} \quad \text{I} \quad \text{VII}^6 \quad \text{IV}^6_4 \quad \text{V} \quad \text{I} \quad \text{V}^6_5 \quad \text{II}^6 \quad \text{V}^7 \quad \text{I}$$

In the first sequence, the root progression favors IV as the tonic over the Mixolydian I. The second sequence softens the cadential feeling so that IV (or the VII - IV progression) is no longer competing with I. The third sequence mildly restores the impetus of the VII - IV progression by placing the roots of these triads in the bass (of inverted chords) but still does not threaten Mixolydian I.

96

Some additional examples are shown in several modes of the difference provided by inversions in controlling modal definition, while keeping other factors relatively constant (Exx. 32 and 33). Each additional attribute could increase or decrease the effect of the inversions.

Ex.32: Lydian Progressions with Inversions

Ex.33: Aeolian Progressions Compared to Dorian Progressions

In Ex. 32, the Lydian progression in the first sequence shows the competition between Lydian V and I. In the second sequence, the II^7 and V are in first inversion while the third sequence has the diminished IV and II in second inversion. The inversions reduce the relative strength of the Lydian V to the point where it does not oppose the I triad.

In Ex. 33, the Aeolian progression in the first sequence has almost equal justification as a Dorian progression. In the remaining sequences, a few inversions on chords indicative of Dorian greatly alters the relative impetus to the Aeolian tonic and also increases or reduces the plausible interpretation of the mode. Of course, inversions can be combined with other techniques such as parenthetic harmonies or the leading-tones and augmented chords to further define the mode.

Seventh and ninth chords.

Tonal composers gradually increased their usage of seventh and ninth chords, although the great majority of them were dominant or secondary dominant chords. Non-dominant seventh and ninth chords became more frequent at the end of the 19th century and early 20th century when the tonal system began to break down. Seventh chords were rare in the medieval modal system and the seventh was very strictly handled as a passing tone or suspension with downward resolution by step.

Interestingly, modern jazz compositions are more likely to employ such complex chords as ninths, elevenths and thirteenths, whether tonally or modally derived. In these jazz compositions, modally derived chords, often chromatically embellished, are mostly used in a tonal framework to provide colorful or unusual progressions rather than as a separate system from the major-minor system (see Miller). In a modern modal system in which harmonic control must compete more with melody and rhythm, extended diatonic chords (diatonic seconds/ninths, fourths/elevenths and sixths/thirteenths) would often arise through melodic considerations. In the modal system as well as the tonal system, these added diatonic notes can be used to control harmonic definition by limiting the ambiguity of triads. Since more notes of the scale are present, the possibilities are narrowed as to the key. The added tones can be diatonic to the original key or to the key of the (parenthetic) tonic. However, chromatic embellishments common in jazz need to be more carefully considered here where tonal system scaffolding is less used.

Dyadic relationships between modes compared with the major-minor scales

One of the most crucial underpinnings of the tonal system was the scalar dyadic relationship established between the major and minor scales. This relationship evolved over time and had several separable elements. The first element was a correspondence of tonal triads between the two scales, the second element was the use of secondary dominants of non-agreeing triads derived from the corresponding mode's keys and the third element was the modification of the minor mode scale in the direction of the major scale with the raised sixth and seventh scale degrees. The third element rather goes against the rationale for the modal system so we will not discuss it, but the first two elements have great utility in the development of a coherent harmonic basis for the modes.

The agreement of modal triads with the tonic triad has already been discussed in previous chapters. The correspondence between the Ionian and Aeolian modes on the location of their 'tonal' degrees made it easier to create parallel progressions and move between them in modulations. A similar correspondence exists between the Lydian and Dorian modes and between the Mixolydian and Phrygian modes. Linking these pairs into major-minor dyads permits a greater harmonic coherence without <u>requiring</u> a fundamental alteration of their modal differences.

Creating a parallelism of progressions between a major and minor mode provides a relatively weak justification for such linkages. The stronger reason is the opportunity to make a logical use of parenthetic harmonies and secondary dominants on the scale degrees of the paired modes. Since a mode, whether the tonic triad is major or minor, has both types of triads formed on its scale degrees, it is necessary to create opposite mode parenthetic harmonies at least occasionally. Modal coherence further requires that these opposite mode harmonies be based on a specific mode.

In the Ionian-Aeolian (or major-minor scale) dyad, each mode necessarily draws upon the other's chordal and key relationships when forming parenthetic harmonies. For example, in the C Ionian major scale, the II forms a minor triad not in agreement with the major mode

99

while V forms a major triad. A secondary dominant based on V would have a **D** major (Ionian) triad progressing to the **G** major (Ionian) triad. A secondary dominant of II would be an **a** minor (Aeolian) triad progressing to a (Aeolian) **d** minor triad. However, the major-minor system, desiring the leading-tone relation of the Ionian V - I progression, altered the minor secondary dominant to create the leading-tone. Thus an **A** major triad progressed to the **d** minor triad. This transformation formed the third element of the dyadic relationship between major and minor scale.

In a modal system, the major key dominant progression has a different character in Mixolydian compared with Ionian and Lydian. Mixolydian has a minor V triad rather than the major triad found in Ionian and Lydian. This creates part of the harmonic variety of the mode. If the purpose is to encourage such harmonic variety, then the characteristics of the modes should not be bent to one standard. A modal Ionian-Aeolian dyad would preserve Aeolian characteristics in the formation of parenthetic harmonies. The secondary dominant of the **d** minor Aeolian triad would therefore be an **a** minor triad. Similarly, an **e** minor triad formed on **C** Ionian III would have a secondary dominant of **b** minor rather than **B** major in the major-minor system.

This process is reversed in Aeolian where the major triads have secondary dominants based on Ionian. Aeolian VI would have a secondary dominant of a **C** major triad progressing to an **F** major triad while Aeolian VII would have a **D** major triad progressing to a **G** major triad. In some cases, the secondary dominant is harmonically ambiguous as it is identical to a triad in the original relative mode. The key of **A** Aeolian already has a **C** major triad on III. The secondary dominant on Aeolian VI has to be in the form of a seventh chord with an added **B♭** to depart from **A** Aeolian. Conversely, the secondary dominant on VII with the **F♯** is already outside **A** Aeolian. Ex. 34 displays the respective {V of V} triads for each of the modes. As can be seen, not all involve a chromatic change from the current key.

Ex.34: Secondary Dominant Progressions

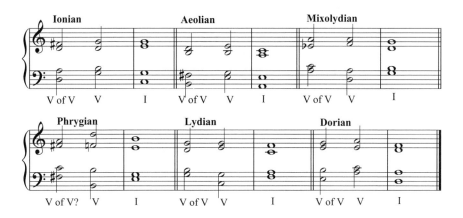

Table 13 shows a summary of the chromatic relation of secondary dominant {V of V} to dominant in the modes: the Ionian has an altered third in {V of V}, the Dorian an altered ninth (second), Phrygian an altered root, Lydian an altered seventh, Aeolian an altered fifth and Locrian an altered eleventh (fourth). Mixolydian is the only major mode with V not in agreement with the tonic. A {V of V} would be based on the Phrygian mode with altered fifth and ninth.

Certainly, the dominant progression is more definite with Ionian than with most of the other modes except perhaps for Lydian. And the Phrygian mode has a very marginal dominant progression. But the differences help define the modes harmonically and maintain them in the face of competition from other modes. In the modal system, the secondary dominants in agreement with the tonic confirm the mode while the secondary dominants not in agreement confirm its complement. This permits modulation between the pairs of a dyad that has been anticipated in the internal relations of each mode (key) individually.

Table 13: Chromatic Relation of Secondary Dominant {V of V} to Original Key

MODE	V of V Chord Note with Chromatic Alteration
IONIAN	3rd
DORIAN	9th (2nd)
PHRYGIAN	root
LYDIAN	7th
MIXOLYDIAN*	5th and 9th
AEOLIAN	5th
LOCRIAN	11th (4th)

* Mixolydian V is minor and not in agreement (Phrygian mode)

Conversely, it puts into sharper relief the modulations between the 3 modal scalar dyads since these are unconfirmed within each dyad. Therefore, the modal system has two areas of difference from the major-minor scale system: first, the secondary dominants of minor or major triads remain in agreement with the temporary tonic and second, three different scalar dyads exist (plus the Locrian mode) rather than just the one (semi) dyad of the major-minor system.

Although the tonal system relied almost exclusively on secondary dominant progressions rather than the full range of parenthetic progressions, the modal system has a larger role for parenthetic harmonies because of the variation in dominant progressions across modes. Some modes have important non-dominant progressions and variable strength dominant progressions. The wider framework of parenthetic harmonies permit the shaping of these varied progressions in a direct way. Although the obviousness of the relation is not as great with non-dominant parenthetic harmonies, a definite and specific relation does exist between them and the temporary tonic. If they are used in a modally consistent manner, then the modal harmonic organization should be enhanced without erasing the modal differences.

In summary, the modern modal system has a more even balance between unity and variety than the major-minor system. With respect to unity, the parenthetic harmonies, scalar dyadic intra-relations and the diatonic scale provide coherence; with respect to variety, major and minor modes and different dyads provide distinctive differences. Unlike the chromatic scale, the listener does have certain consistent hierarchical relations within a mode and scalar dyad. Unlike the mostly major - slightly minor system, the same harmonic relationship is not repeated in each mode and key.

Overview of Modal Scalar Dyad Characteristics

It is worthwhile to provide an overview here as a means of integrating the concepts of the previous discussions. The modal dyads are major and minor modes paired on the basis of the corresponding position of the tonic triad and the other triads in agreement with it. The Ionian-Aeolian scalar dyad (and major - natural minor scales) has IV and V in triadic agreement with their respective tonics. The major-minor system altered this relationship when they converted the natural minor V triad to a major triad for the sake of the major scale V - I progression. (In the remaining discussions of the modal scalar dyads, the Ionian-Aeolian scalar dyad will <u>not</u> be synonymous with the major-minor scale here. No harmonic or melodic modification of the natural Aeolian mode scale degrees to fit the Ionian major mode is assumed.)

With respect to the other modes, the Lydian-Dorian scalar dyad has II and V in triadic agreement with their respective tonics while the Mixolydian-Phrygian scalar dyad has IV and VII in triadic agreement with the tonic. Locrian has no counterpart major mode due to the diminished character of its tonic.

Ionian-Aeolian Scalar Dyad

Since the Ionian-Aeolian scalar dyad has greater familiarity to readers and because there is potential confusion due to its close relation to the major-minor scale, it makes a good place to start. The Ionian and Aeolian modes have an exact correspondence only in the position of the triads in agreement with the tonic, however, there isn't an exact correspondence in the position of the triads not in agreement with the tonic due to the differing locations of the diminished triad. The Aeolian mode has a diminished triad on II (Ionian minor triad) in contrast with the diminished VII in Ionian (Aeolian major triad). Conversely, the triads on III and VI in both modes are in non-agreement with their tonic triads. In summary, all scale degrees except for II and VII have a similar relation to the tonic triad in both Ionian and Aeolian.

The tonal system usefully divided the triads of the major scale (and minor) into dominant-related and subdominant-related chords (see Schoenberg). The I triad serves as the tonic for V, but serves as the dominant for IV; thus, a harmonic tension is created between the dominant and subdominant in their relations to the tonic. The dominant-related triads were III and VII in addition to V, while the subdominant related triads were II and VI in addition to IV. The relationship was based presumably on the overlap of chord elements and the concomitant similarity in chordal progressions of the triads. Thus, III shares 2 notes with V and one note with VII, V shares 2 notes with VII and so on. Seventh chords based on these triads would contain all 3 notes of the triad above. Similarly, II shares 2 notes with IV and so on. As we saw with inversions, related triads were substituted rather freely with inverted triads with the same note in the bass, e.g. II^6 and IV.

Looking at the triads not in correspondence, II and VII, they are balanced between the dominant and subdominant sides. The Ionian VII is conveniently placed below the tonic where it can function as a leading-tone. The diminished Aeolian II is somewhat more intrusive on the subdominant side, but with IV in agreement with the tonic, this does not create a significant issue for subdominant progressions in this mode. Dominant progressions are somewhat more affected by the absence of a leading-tone in the Aeolian V - I progression (as opposed to the harmonic minor scale). However, the modal consistency of Aeolian as a minor mode is correspondingly enhanced since V remains a minor triad in agreement with the I.

Since the minor Aeolian mode is not harmonically modified to make it a twin of the major Ionian, the distinction between the two members of the scalar dyad is greater than with the major-minor scale. This has significant compositional implications. First, the interchangeability of major and minor keys built on the same tonic note is severely restricted. Obviously it is possible to modulate back and forth between, say, **A** Ionian and **A** Aeolian, but it will feel more like a modulation between keys and mode than a similar movement within the major-minor tonal system (Ex. 35).

Ex.35a-b: Modulation between Major and Minor

In major-minor tonality, the minor key has the augmented sixth and seventh scale notes, so there remains but one note harmonically different between the major and minor parallel keys. The key of **a** minor has F♯ and G♯ as does **A** major, the only difference thus is C versus C♯. Tonal composers often switched between the two keys (modes) from measure to measure or even within a measure. As mentioned, the distinction became so blurred that very careful analysis became necessary sometimes to figure out whether a later tonal passage was in a minor or major key.

The Ionian and Aeolian modes, on the other hand, have three altered notes separating each of the parallel keys. **A** Ionian has three sharps and **A** Aeolian has no sharps or flats so the harmonic and melodic differences make themselves felt in nearly every progression. In contrast, the relative major and minor mode keys have somewhat closer relations in the modal system than in the tonal system. For example, **A** major and **f**♯ minor have more different steps than **A** Ionian and F♯ Aeolian. In **f**♯ minor, the augmented sixth and seventh scale degrees, **D**♯ and **E**♯, are not harmonically present in **F**♯ Aeolian or in **A** Ionian for that matter.

The Ionian-Aeolian scalar dyad has more disparate harmonic tendencies than its major-minor counterpart. From this stems the greater melodic and harmonic variety and freedom of the modal system. What then holds the modal pair together so that we can legitimately call it a scalar dyad? Similarity of progressions and cross-relationships of the modes' internal structure by parenthetic harmonies (and as with any tonal piece, good compositional practice) distinguish each modal dyad from the other.

Remember that distinguishing keys within a mode is relatively easy compared with maintaining modal identity between six (or seven) alternatives. The scalar dyadic relation actually helps this latter problem since the forms of the parenthetic harmonies are unique to a dyad (Ex. 36).

In the example, we see examples of parenthetic progressions to each scale degree of the major mode in each scalar dyad, starting with the Ionian modes followed by the corresponding progressions in the Lydian scalar dyad and the Mixolydian scalar dyad. The Ionian mode progressions are based on the progressions in agreement with the mode, either IV - I or V - I.

Two things stand out in this example: the varying pattern of chromatic alterations in the {V of x} and {IV of x} triads and the questionable {V of VII} on VII. The relation of various parenthetic harmonies to the original key and mode necessarily varies. The issue of parenthetic harmonies on the diminished triad turns on the willingness to use the Locrian mode, but it does seem to offer small benefit posed against the complications of its use within a dyad balanced between major and minor modes.

Looking at the examples for the other two dyads based on the same parenthetic progressions, there is no exact correspondence. In the Lydian mode, while {V of x} is similar to the Ionian, the {IV of x} has the diminished triad progressing to the Lydian diatonic triad. With its Dorian partner, the {V of x} fits the Aeolian pattern, but the {IV of x} is a major triad in contrast to the Aeolian minor IV. In the Mixolydian mode, the {V of x} is a minor triad unlike the Ionian or Lydian modes while {IV of x} is a major triad similar to Ionian but contrasting with the diminished Lydian. The Phrygian {V of x} is of course a

106

diminished triad while the {IV of x} is a minor triad like the Aeolian but in contrast to the major Dorian {IV of x}.

Ex.36: Parenthetic Progressions of the Modal Dyads (Major)

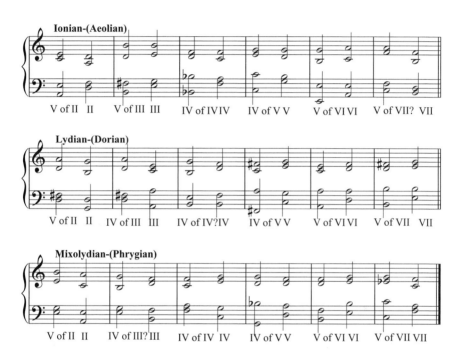

Applying the same logic to the other two scalar dyads as done with the Ionian-Aeolian, we would have the progressions of Ex. 37. In other words, we will have the parenthetic progressions based on those triads that are in agreement with the tonic triad. In Ex. 37a, we see Lydian and Dorian progressions based on II and V while the Mixolydian and Phrygian progressions in Ex. 37b are based on IV and

VII. Now in all cases the progressions maintain the modal identity whether major or minor. The reader should compare the sounds of these different progressions. Unless the intent is to revert to the practice of the major-minor scale, the distinction between the major and minor modes even within a dyad need to be confirmed by the use of these triads in agreement.

Ex.37a-b: Parenthetic Progressions Only to Modal Steps in Agreement

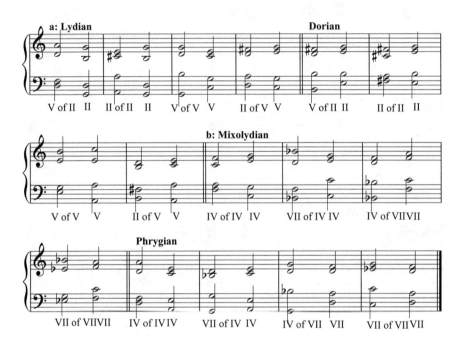

What if the reader in fact wants to emulate the practice of the major-minor system with the 3 modal scalar dyads? By this, we would mean that the minor scale would be put into conformance with its counterpart major. In the case of the Aeolian mode, there is no need to discuss it since all conventional harmony texts describe in detail the use of the minor scale and the effect of its harmonic modifications.

However, the situation with the other minor modes is not considered in such discussions.

In the Lydian-Dorian scalar dyad, if we modify the Dorian mode harmonically using the same procedures as transformed the Aeolian mode into the minor scale, we would have to give it more Lydian features. First, this would involve creating a major triad on Dorian V. Lydian also has the leading-tone to the tonic but modification of Dorian V would produce that. The Lydian mode also has the diminished IV, but it is doubtful that we would seek to emulate that within the modified Dorian mode. If we make the minor Dorian V a major triad, we need to augment the VII scale degree or the third of the V triad. For example, in modified **D** Dorian we would have a **C♯** instead of the C♮. Since the Dorian sixth scale degree is a half-step (minor second) below the seventh scale degree, the augmentation of the seventh scale degree creates a whole-step with the sixth scale degree. Thus, the sixth scale degree would <u>not</u> also require augmentation. At this point, we have a nearly exact counterpart to the minor scale in the major-minor system since **d** minor has the augmented sixth scale degree and the C♯. The only slight difference is that in Dorian, the sixth scale degree would remain unaltered from its normal B♮. Therefore Dorian VI♭ would not reappear in non-cadential passages as it does in **d** minor.

If we modify Phrygian in the direction of its major scale counterpart, Mixolydian, the diminished V would have to be altered to a minor V by raising the fifth of the triad. This would be the second scale degree of the scale. Thus **E** Phrygian would have the scale note **F** augmented to an **F♯**. However, this makes it nearly an exact duplicate of **e** minor, the main difference being the leading-tone (**D♯**) in **e** minor cadences which would be out of place here. Mixolydian has no leading-tone relationship between its VII and the tonic triad.

From this analysis, we can see that there is not much justification for trying to emulate the major-minor system in the formation of the other two modal scalar dyads. Mixolydian does not have a forceful harmonic structure compared to Ionian or even Lydian. Lydian for its part has a pronounced dominant tilt that would be further unbalanced by mimicry in its dyadic partner, the Dorian mode. The use of the modal system, therefore, seems to require the maintenance of the harmonic difference between the modes even when they are members of the same dyad.

Lydian-Dorian Scalar Dyad

The major Lydian and minor Dorian modes have an exact correspondence in the position of the triads in agreement with the tonic, however, there is not an exact correspondence in the position of the triads in <u>non-agreement</u> with the tonic due to the differing locations of the diminished triad. The Dorian mode has a diminished triad on VI (Lydian minor triad) in contrast with the diminished IV in Lydian (Dorian major triad). Conversely, the triads on III and VII in both modes are in non-agreement with their tonic triads. In summary, all scale degrees except for IV and VI have a similar relation to the tonic triad in both Lydian and Dorian.

Looking at the steps not in correspondence due to the diminished triad, IV and VI, they are both on the subdominant side, creating a dominant tilt to the dyad. In other words, progressions on the dominant side proceed more freely than subdominant-related progressions. The diminished Lydian IV triad cannot function easily as the tonic for I and counterbalance V, while the V - I progression has a strong leading-tone relationship and modal agreement between the two triads. Less obtrusively, the Dorian diminished VI has a slight negative influence on subdominant influence and the IV - I progression lacks modal agreement, while the V - I progression possesses modal agreement without a leading-tone relation.

Mixolydian-Phrygian Scalar Dyad

The major Mixolydian and minor Phrygian modes have an exact correspondence in the position of the triads in agreement with the tonic, however there is not an exact correspondence in the position of the triads in non-agreement with the tonic due to the differing locations of the diminished triad. The Phrygian mode has a diminished triad on V (Mixolydian minor triad) in contrast with the diminished III in Mixolydian (Phrygian major triad). Conversely, the triads on II and VI in both modes are in non-agreement with their tonic triads. In summary, all steps except for III and V have a similar relation to the tonic triad in both Mixolydian and Phrygian.

Looking at the steps not in correspondence due to the diminished triad, III and V, they are both on the dominant side, creating a subdominant tilt to the dyad. In other words, progressions

110

on the subdominant side proceed more freely than dominant-related progressions. The diminished Phrygian V triad reduces the strength of the V - I progression while the IV - I progression has modal agreement between the two triads. In addition, the II - I progression is quite strong due to the descending leading-tone. Less obtrusively, the Mixolydian diminished III has a slight negative influence on dominant influence, weakening the alternative III - I cadence. Also, the V - I progression lacks modal agreement since V is a minor triad progressing to the major I. Conversely, the Mixolydian IV - I progression possesses modal agreement.

Summary

The modal scalar dyads have distinctive attributes not only in terms of the individual modes, but also as dyads. This introduces greater differentiation of harmonic and melodic characteristics than is found in the major-minor system. The modal system maintains a greater separation between major and minor modes due to the absence of harmonic modifications to the minor mode of the scalar dyad. This makes the Ionian-Aeolian dyad distinct from the major-minor system despite the overall similarity of keys. Emulating the harmonic modifications of the minor scale in the major-minor system are shown to have little utility in the modal system. Thus, the major and minor modes have to remain distinct within the modal system.

5

Stylistic and Cognitive Considerations for the Modal System

The attributes of the modal system discussed up to this point have stemmed from the inherent melodic and harmonic properties of the various modes. The position of the tritone, half- and whole-steps, major and minor triads and so on all vary from mode to mode. With the presentation of the modal dyads and their relationships, the growing complexity brings also more stylistic choices for the composer. In the tonal system, these compositional choices present themselves in the context of musical history as the evolution of tonal system style and practice. The difference between a piece by Mozart and one by Richard Wagner is audible to even the uninformed listener. Yet many techniques found in Wagner are found in Mozart, if not in the same frequency or exact manner. Similarly, medieval composers such as Guillaume de Machaut and Josquin DesPrez used the same modal system or modern composers such as Alban Berg and Anton von Webern used the 12-tone system, but their music is very different from the other. Thus, stylistic choices have almost as much influence as the inherent musical characteristics of the scales used by composers.

Although unborn styles cannot be predicted, stylistic variables within the modal system have parallels in tonal system practice such as dissonance treatment or modulation. These examples in historical practice can guide our speculations. The following discussion of stylistic variables is simply meant as a thought provoking exercise rather than dictates on how a modern modal system should be used nor is it intended as a comprehensive examination of them. The discussion is divided into harmonic, melodic, rhythmic and general issues.

Harmonic Stylistic Issues

The stylistic topics concerned with harmony that will be looked at here are diatonic versus chromatic dissonance, cadence treatment, and in more detail, modal modulations, whether within the mode, within the modal scalar dyads or between different dyads.

Diatonic and Chromatic Dissonance

Dissonance treatment is no longer governed by set rules, which are made to be broken anyway. However, the modal system does have significant differences from the tonal system familiar to most readers and this is the context for the current discussion. Diatonic dissonance (dissonance between notes within a key) was never a noted feature of the tonal system and had a very circumscribed role in it. Essentially, diatonic dissonance could be found in the dominant seventh chord and the occasional ninth chord. Non-dominant diatonic dissonance was scarce until the tonal system started to break down. The tonal system didn't have a place for chord notes not based on the triad such as the intervals of the fourth or sixth above the root. Even with the ninth chord, which obviously involves the interval of the second above the root placed an octave higher, composers regularly maintained the separation of the octave between the root and second rather than placing the ninth in inversion below the root.

The modal system, since it doesn't have the same stress on dominant harmonies, can allow a greater role for diatonic dissonance, which we will define as scale notes a second, a fourth and a sixth above the root (along with the interval of the seventh to a lesser extent). The Lydian-Dorian scalar dyad and the Mixolydian-Phrygian scalar dyad have their 'tonal' degrees on II and V or IV and VII respectively. To maintain their modal identity, these scale degrees and their triads do need to be prominently used in the dyadic progressions. But another way that the scale degrees themselves can be used is in non-triadic formations or added to triads (Ex. 38).

Ex.38: Tonal Degrees of the Modes Used in Chords

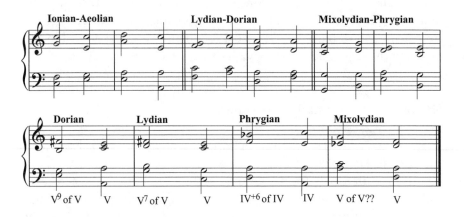

The Ionian-Aeolian sequence in Example 38 shows a non-triadic chord based on the tonal degrees of tonic, scale degree four and five. In the Lydian-Dorian progressions, a chord formed from the tonic, scale degree two and five appears. Similarly, in the Mixolydian-Phrygian progressions, non-triadic chords are formed from scale degrees four and seven. Triadic chords with added second, fourth or sixth can also be formed. Actually, the added (not augmented) sixth chord can occasionally be found in the tonal literature. Since scale degree two in the Lydian-Dorian dyad and scale degree four in the Mixolydian-Phrygian dyad are the roots of the triads in agreement with the tonic, their presence strengthens the mode and the key. The other diatonic notes do not have the same mode-defining status but obviously do confirm the key.

The parenthetic harmonies afford another use for these 'tonal' degrees in the different modes. As shown in Table 13 (in Chapter 4), the position of the chromatic note of secondary dominant chords (to the original key) varies by mode. Ionian, Aeolian and Phrygian have chromatic alteration of the triad but the other modes have the chromatic note in higher positions. To avoid the ambiguity of a secondary dominant chord that contains only scale degrees of the original key, composers generally add the chromatic note to the triad. Tonal composers for example in using the {V of IV} chord (i.e. the tonic triad) would add the seventh to the triad since that contained the chromatically altered note. Similarly, clarification of the secondary dominant chord in the Lydian, Mixolydian, Dorian, and Locrian modes requires adding the appropriate dominant scale degree to the chord or sounding it in the melody. The same principle can be extended to non-dominant parenthetic harmonies.

Chromatic notes are more complexly related to the key and mode. If they arise due to a parenthetic harmony, then they at least have an immediate relation to the key. Some of these harmonies can also confirm the mode, but this would have to be examined on a case by case basis. Other chromatic notes can arise through voice leading to the tonic, dominant, subdominant or locally important chords as we saw with the augmented fifth and sixth chords. Naturally, too many such notes begin to break down the modal system and replace it with the chromatic scale, but this is no different than with the major-minor system.

Cadences

The tonal system developed the strongest diatonic progression, the V^7 - I, and kept it through every change of style until its (somewhat) dissolution in the early 20th century. The modes do not have the harmonic structure to support this kind of cadential autocracy and it would diminish the advantages of the modal system to try and force it into a rigid harmonic mold. The cadential progressions will necessarily vary from mode to mode or at the very least from scalar dyad to dyad given the melodic and harmonic differences between them.

Consonant.

The most typical diatonic cadences for each mode are noted in Ex. 39 although they were mentioned in Chapter 2 as well. The Ionian mode is well-known in its guise as the major scale. The Aeolian mode, unlike the minor scale, has no leading tone, but IV and V do agree with I. Aeolian cadences include V - I (minor-minor), II - I (diminished-minor) and VII - I (major-minor).

115

Ex.39: Diatonic Cadences

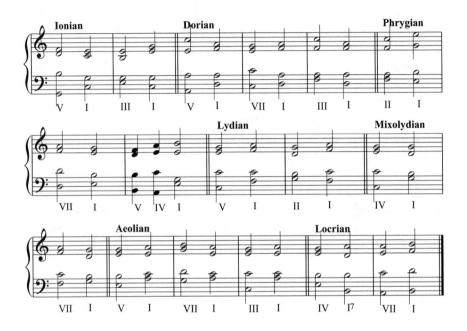

The Dorian mode has the V - I (minor-minor) and the III - I/VII - I (major-minor) cadences while the Lydian has the II - I (major-major) and the strong V - I (major-major). The Mixolydian mode has weaker cadential progressions. The V - I is a minor to major progression and III - I is an awkward dissonant to major progression, but VII - I and IV - I can be used. The Phrygian mode has the strong II - I (major-minor with leading tone) cadence with a weaker VII - I (minor-minor) cadence. The V - I cadence is complicated by the diminished V but still possible as a substitute III⁷ - I progression or possibly used in a V - IV - I progression. The Locrian mode has the dissonant tonic which severely affects cadences. The II - I and VII - I are possibilities but even they are more convincing with a I⁷ or I⁹ with omitted fifth.

Dissonant.

The use of dissonant (or chromatic) chords in creating a cadential pause is another possibility; that is, a chord which is dissonant in relation to the preceding musical passage or context, but not necessarily dissonant in itself. This has not been generally considered before for a variety of reasons. In the initial modal period, the system had its basis in octaves and fifths (organum) and in almost all styles carefully introduced and quickly resolved non-triadic harmonies. In the development of the tonal system, the controlling cadence was V - I and another type of cadence which strongly conflicted with it would have been disruptive to the tonal system. Additionally, the more chromatic and dissonant the tonal system became, the more necessary a relatively consonant cadential pause also became, until the arrival of the chromatic scale and atonality. In contrast, the current modal system, even allowing for stylistic variations, is considerably more harmonically consonant than is typically found in music of the past century.

This is a consequence of two things: the need to maintain some degree of modal identity and the associated balancing of melody and rhythm with harmony. Even the average listener of pop music or film goer has become accustomed to a higher level of dissonance or even atonality (as long as it is in an otherwise musically simple context or associated with video). In other words, although the music public has not welcomed undiluted serial or melodic atonality, the emancipation of the dissonance has been considerably more accepted.

Dissonant chords therefore stand out more in the modal system, particularly if they are not part of an ongoing counterpoint, i.e. passing harmonies. The reverse happened in atonal music or even chromatic tonal music where the diatonic or curtly constructed melody stood out against the dissonant norm. This latter phenomenon, like many things, can be heard in Beethoven, such as in the late string quartets. The modal cadences have greater variety and plasticity than the tonal dominant progression, but they do not have greater strength and consequent capacity to demarcate (pause) a progression or passage.

Of course, dissonance is usually thought of as motion-inducing in the sense of propelling the music forward to a resolving chord. As noted though, the dissonance really has become more emancipated and the typical resolutions of the tonal (or old modal system for that matter) can seem almost trite unless disguised or embellished in some way. Even such non-abrasive modern composers as Ravel show a lack of concern in the resolution of dissonant chords or use them coloristically. Although the use of diatonic or chromatic dissonance to form a cadence or cadence-like stop has sometimes been a feature in modern formal music (e.g. Ives' final chord in his *Symphony 2* or the a♭ triad terminating the rising C scale at the beginning of Sibelius' *Symphony 7*), it has more often shown up in informal music. Sudden dissonant chords have been used effectively to end popular songs, e.g. *Rejoyce* by the Jefferson Airplane. The jazz pianist Thelonious Monk often used a dissonant chord, sometimes repeated several times in succession, or a short dissonant chordal progression to stop a musical phrase and begin another (e.g. *Rootie Tootie*).

If a dissonant or chromatic chord is used as a cadential figure, it would generally have to have a longer duration (note value) than the preceding notes or be otherwise set apart in some fashion, or it will assume a more conventional role, e.g. an appoggiatura. This is not much different than any other cadential sequence in the tonal or medieval modal system. The cadential quality is obviously heightened by rhythmic and melodic figuration as well.

Several kinds of dissonant chord cadences can be distinguished depending on the preceding and subsequent progressions using the Ionian mode as an example (Ex. 40). The first case shows a short progression to a diatonically dissonant (added fourth) chord, the second case to a chromatic but consonant chord (parenthetic harmony), the third case to a chromatically dissonant chord. Each has a different effect and obviously the cadential quality is also dependent on the subsequent musical passage. In the first case, the dissonance is relatively mild, albeit unresolved, and stands out somewhat only because of the bland preceding harmonies. A conventional G major triad could be substituted to gauge the effect of the dissonance. The melodic tritone formed between the F and B in the dissonant chord also contributes slightly to its dissonant relation with the first 2 measures. More pungent diatonic dissonances could of course be employed such as tone clusters.

The degree of dissonance will obviously be assessed in relation to the context of the chord. The second case substitutes a consonant chord with a chromatic relation (parenthetic harmony) to the prevailing key. The pausing quality of this chord is somewhat greater despite the perfect fifth now between the **F** and **B♭**. In the third case, a chromatic dissonant chord creates a pronounced pause to the motion. The effect is exaggerated because of the preceding purely diatonic measures. The fourth case shows its use in a more typical chromatic context.

Ex.40a-d : Dissonant Cadences

Since the effect of the dissonant cadence can be quite strong, in some ways the same as a full cadential V^7-I progression in root position, it has to be used sparingly or be an integral part of the musical style. The effect of each type of cadence cannot be adequately captured with a few examples since almost every aspect of the music and scoring will affect the strength and quality of the cadential effect. However, the same can be said of the dominant cadence in the tonal system despite its far greater uniformity.

In short, the use of dissonant cadences provides the modal system with a useful resource given the greater variety, but reduced strength of its cadential progressions. Increased emancipation of the dissonance permits their usage, as is evident in contemporary informal music which is still tonal in character. Although cadences will receive more detailed examination in the study compositions, all the possible uses of these progressions are only limited by the imagination of the composer.

Modulation

Modulation between keys was a prime characteristic of the tonal system and became an integral part of sonata form. Although modulation could occur between as well as within the major and minor scales, the increasing correspondence between the two made modulations between major and minor scales (modes) more conceptual than real. The medieval modal system for its part did admit the possibility of modulation between modes, even if composers seldom employed this technique in any consistent manner.

The techniques associated with modulations in the tonal system became quite elaborate as composers began to modulate to more and more distant keys. Modulations to closely related keys, i.e. keys with one flat or sharp more or less, can be easily accomplished through shared chords, as explained in elementary harmony texts. Modulations to the relative minor or major were handled through a simple adjustment of progressions in the same key when they weren't dealt with more directly and offhandedly. With respect to parallel major and minor keys, their virtual correspondence in the tonal system made this a useful avenue to more distant progressions. For example, a modulation from C major to A♭ major could be accomplished by moving through c minor. C major goes to c minor and progressions using the non-cadential c minor scale's 3 flats only need to move one step to the 4 flats of A♭ major or f minor. (Schoenberg discusses in detail a variety of sophisticated tonal modulation techniques in his *Harmony* treatise.)

The frequent use of the major-minor correspondence to effect distant modulations is not as workable within the modal system because of the more pronounced distinctiveness between major and minor modes even within a modal dyad. To take the previous example, since the C Ionian and C Aeolian modes do not have a common V triad as in the major-minor system, the directness of a modulation between them is reduced. The number of shared chords is reduced rather drastically actually to zero. Of course, modulations can be accomplished in abrupt fashion or slow, circuitous fashion and there is no modulation that is impossible due to the reduced viability of that particular modulatory technique.

In the major-minor tonal system, prepared modulations could be accomplished through shared diatonic chords or ambiguous chromatic chords. The shared diatonic chords are straightforward enough and are presented in the chapters on the modal dyads. The chromatic chords used by the tonal system fall into several categories: secondary dominants, diminished sevenths and other harmonic minor chords, augmented sixths and other chords capable of reinterpretation in a different key.

In the modal system, secondary dominants and augmented sixths (re-notated seventh chords) are freely available as the context permits. However, the chords derived from harmonically altered minor scales are not usable within the modal system for the reasons advanced in Chapter 4. More generally, the modal system, since it places more emphasis on the scale (mode) structure, can accommodate triadic and non-triadic chords. Thus, the degree of overlap is best viewed as between the two scales rather than particular chords.

For example, F Lydian has no sharps or flats while G Lydian has two sharps. There are only two triads in common, namely, G major and e minor, however, in terms of the scale notes, the overlap is 5 out of 7. D Lydian with three sharps has zero triads in common with F Lydian, yet 4 out of 7 notes are shared between the two. Whether the degree of melodic and non-triadic harmonic overlap is of value in modal modulation depends in large part on stylistic issues. If non-triadic (diatonic) chords form an integral part of the harmonic structure, then their usefulness as modulatory mechanisms would seem clear. If triadic constructions are prominent, though, the listener would probably have difficulty in perceiving the non-triadic chords as harmonically relevant.

This discussion raises the possibility of what might be termed melodically prepared modulation as opposed to harmonic preparation. For example, F Lydian has 4 notes or more in common with six other Lydian keys. By emphasizing common notes in modulatory passages, a temporal distance is instituted between the divergent notes in the initial and target keys, making the appearance of the altered notes less unprepared, one might surmise. Taking a modulation from F Lydian to D Lydian (3 sharps), one could have a melody which avoided F, C, and G and gradually introduced F♯, C♯ and G♯ in order to smooth the transition between keys, if smoothing of a harmonically unprepared modulation was sought.

In the modal system, three types of modulations can be distinguished: within a mode, within a scalar dyad and between scalar dyads. For the purpose of this discussion, abrupt or otherwise unprepared modulations will not be considered since these follow no set procedure. Also, we will consider the issues of modal modulation in the general sense here since the chapters on the dyads go into more specific details in the analysis of the study compositions. Within-mode modulations are straightforward if the two modal keys share diatonic chords. More distant modulations are slowed by the reduced similarity of the minor and major modes within a dyad. The characteristic progressions of the mode do not change from key to key, but since each mode differs in these progressions so the within-mode modulations will similarly vary by mode.

Within-mode modulation.
The within-mode prepared modulations that share one or more triads are handled the same way as in the tonal system, but we do have to consider the characteristic progressions of the mode. As an example, we will consider the modulation between D Dorian and A Dorian. A Dorian shares triads on I, III, V and VII with D Dorian. Some modulations from D to A Dorian are shown in Ex. 41a and b. The Dorian mode has a relatively strong V - I cadence so it is best not

to use the V as a pivot chord. The first case uses IV (VII) as the pivot and the second case uses VII (III).

Ex.41a-b: Dorian Within-mode Modulation from D to A

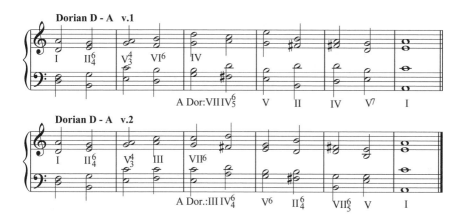

In the first case, note the use of inversions in the first 2 measures to create an anticipation in the bass of the II - V progression in Dorian seen (slightly extended) in the penultimate measure. The **E** and **B** are also the roots of the **A** Dorian 'tonal' triads and **E** is the soprano high note prior to the cadence.

A different example is provided for the Mixolydian modulation from **G** to **D** (Ex. 42). The Mixolydian mode has a weaker V - I progression so alternative cadences can be used including V - II - I and (V -) IV - I. In the first case, the V of **D** Mixolydian is used as the modulation pivot with the VII⁷ - I cadence. In the second case, the pivot is accomplished with the II of **D** Mixolydian (VI of **G**) with a V - IV - I cadence.

Ex.42a-b: Mixolydian Within- mode Modulation from G to D

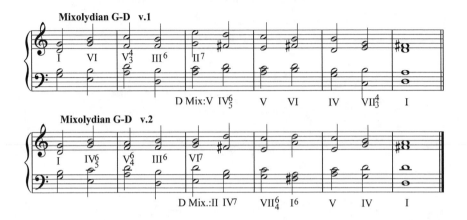

Within-dyad modulation.

A within-dyad modulation can involve modulating from the major mode to the minor mode or vice versa. It can also involve using keys from the other mode as intermediate steps in a more distant prepared modulation. The previous examples demonstrated prepared modulations to closely related keys in the same mode. Prepared modulations to more distantly related keys generally involve a progressive approach to the target key rather than a direct approach. Given the greater differentiation of major and minor modes within a modal dyad, the shortcut of moving back and forth between parallel major and minor keys is not as useful, although it still serves the function of establishing the tonic note.

Modulations of this kind move through intermediate keys if the modulation is conducted very leisurely but more typically they simply make use of chords from the intermediary keys to act as a bridge to the target key. Using the more familiar Ionian and Aeolian modes, we can see how this approach would function in a modulation from **C** to **B** Ionian (Ex. 43).

Ex.43: Ionian-Aeolian Within-dyad Modulation from C Ionian through Aeolian to B Ionian

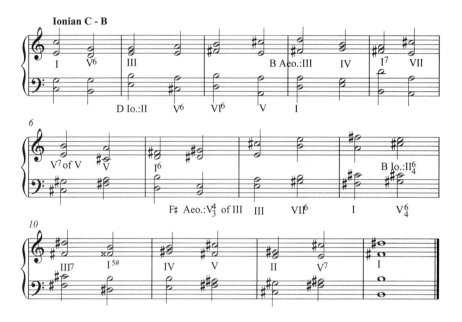

The extended modulation from **C** to **B** goes through **D**, then **B** Aeolian and **F♯** Aeolian. The parallel minor keys offer a real shortcut in the major-minor system that is less readily available in the modal system. However, the use of **B** and **F♯** anticipates and reinforces the tonic and dominant of **B** Ionian. The stepwise modal progressions restore the sense of distinctness and relative distance between keys that was lost in the development of the tonal system. Taking another example, in the Lydian-Dorian dyad, **D** Dorian is the relative minor of **F** Lydian. A modulation from **F** Lydian to **A** Dorian can proceed in much the same straightforward fashion between modal relative keys as occurs in the major-minor system modulating between relative keys (Ex. 44).

Ex.44: Lydian-Dorian Within-dyad Modulation from F Lydian to A Dorian

In the Lydian example we see an extended modulation moving from **F** Lydian through **D** Dorian to **A** Dorian. The nature of the progressions necessarily differs from the Ionian example given above. Example 45 displays a progression from **G** Mixolydian to **A** Phrygian. In the example of the Mixolydian-Phrygian modulation, the use of the minor subdominant modulatory technique (version 2) is still available, even with the greater separation of major and minor modes. Note that the **G** Myxolydian subdominant would be completely subdued in this case, even extending the modulation to the relative key of **A** Phrygian, namely, **C** Mixolydian (the original subdominant key).

As noted in the discussion of the Mixolydian mode in Chapter 2, the minor subdominant progression is particularly useful in the Mixolydian-Phrygian scalar dyad since it provides an alternative to the I - IV progression, which in Mixolydian is rather too easy and a threat to the mode (when modulation is not sought). The minor subdominant progression is not dependent on the harmonic modifications of the minor scale in the tonal system, which allows its use in the modal system. Clearly, the prepared modulation process differs for each mode and has to take into consideration not only that mode but its dyadic partner as well.

Ex.45: Mixolydian-Phrygian Within-dyad Modulation from G Mixolydian to A Phrygian

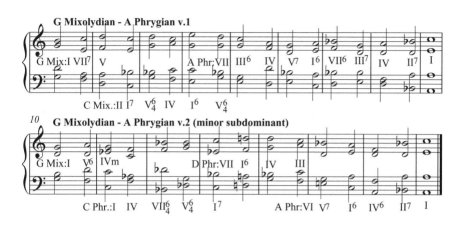

In summary, modulation between major and minor modes within a scalar dyad can make use of the relative key as well as the minor subdominant effect (except in the Lydian-Dorian scalar dyad) in much the same way as occurred in the tonal system. Movement to parallel keys requires more effort since the keys have less correspondence in the modal dyad.

Between-dyad modulations.

The prepared modulation between dyads has no correspondence with the tonal system which obviously had only one major and minor scale. The problem lies in the establishment not only of a new key but also of a new mode. The modes have varying degrees of relationship to each other which means that some modulations would take longer or would require more emphatic procedures to differentiate them from the previously established mode. For example, Ionian and Mixolydian differ by key only in scale degree seven (leaving aside the harmonic and melodic relationships that define the internal organization of the established mode.) Chromatic progressions or alterations have to be carefully used otherwise the new mode can fail to be established or modes can be rendered ambiguous. This may be the effect sought, but it should be done consciously rather than inadvertently.

The problem is analogous to, but more involved than, the modulation to the relative key in the modal dyad. One approach is to modulate to the corresponding major or minor mode of the other dyad. For example, if the starting key is **A** Aeolian and the destination is **A** Mixolydian, then a modulation can proceed to **E** Phrygian which is a modal minor relative and then to the Mixolydian mode (Ex. 46).

In the example, the modulation to **E** Phrygian is emphasized by repeated tonic progressions. A parenthetic harmony [IV of IV] shows the direction of harmonic movement that is soon confirmed by a modulation to the subdominant **A** major. The following progressions solidify the A Mixolydian key.

Ex.46: Between-dyad Modulation from A Aeolian to A Mixolydian

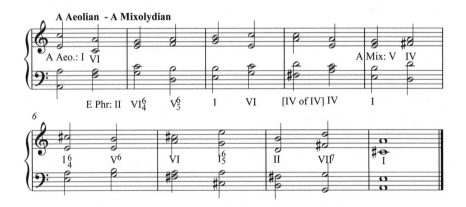

It is probably best not to do more than one modulation to a relative key because the confusability is already high between them and the listener would have trouble perceiving what mode was in effect. Thus, a movement from **A** Aeolian to **E** Phrygian should not generally be followed by a modulation to **G** Mixolydian. Of course, one could also modulate directly from **A** Aeolian to **G** Mixolydian which is a modal major relative. Another approach is to modulate within the existing mode to a relative of the target key and then modulate into the key. For example, a modulation from **A** Aeolian to **F** Mixolydian could move to **G** Aeolian and then make a relative key modulation into **F** Mixolydian.

Parallel keys have different proximity depending on the two modes involved. Using **C** Ionian as a reference, **C** Mixolydian and **C** Lydian have a one note difference, flat and sharp respectively, **C** Dorian has a two-note difference, **C** Aeolian a three note difference, **C** Phrygian has a four-note difference and **C** Locrian a five note difference. The sequence shown in Table 14 indicates the degree of closeness of the modal parallel keys. Each row represents a one note difference between its neighbors. Thus, the parallel keys of neighboring pairs of modes have only one accidental more or less, e.g. Lydian-Ionian, Aeolian-Dorian, Phrygian-Aeolian. A separation of two rows means a two-note difference, a separation of three rows means a three-note difference and so on.

Table 14: Parallel Key Proximity Between Modal Pairs

Lydian
Ionian
Mixolydian
Dorian
Aeolian
Phrygian
Locrian

Thus, parallel keys have a differing utility as a modulation shortcut depending on the pair of modes. If we wanted to modulate from C Ionian to F Mixolydian (2 flats) we could easily use the parallel C Mixolydian (one flat) as the bridge between the two. It is useful to point out that the members of a scalar dyad are always three rows (notes) away from their complement. Thus, the three-note difference between the Ionian and Aeolian parallel keys exists as well within the Mixolydian-Phrygian and Lydian-Dorian dyads.

The closer relations between parallel keys generally facilitate between-dyad modulation. Dorian mode (Lydian-Dorian) has only a one note difference in parallel keys between Aeolian (Ionian-Aeolian) and Mixolydian (Mixolydian-Phrygian). Similarly, Mixolydian has a one note difference between parallel keys in Ionian and Dorian. Ionian and Aeolian is the only dyad in which both members have a one note difference between parallel keys in the other two dyads.

Between-dyad modulations raise more issues of musical form because they represent a greater change in the modal system and because they run a greater risk of modal incoherency if carried out extensively and systematically in a fairly short period. However, between-dyad modulations can be useful in more extended compositions because they introduce not only harmonic variety, but also melodic variety. If there is a musical point to the modulation, for example, a Phrygian melody used as a strong contrast to a predominantly Dorian or Ionian mode composition, and the modulation is incorporated into a larger modulatory scheme, then the results are likely to be musically effective.

The use of unprepared modulations also raises the issue of musical form. Certainly, there is no reason to avoid unprepared modulations given the freedom of melodic and harmonic usage evident in most 20th century compositions, even with relatively conservative composers. However, the increased abruptness requires either greater integration of such effects into the musical style or a musical context which supports its use at that particular point in the work. The distance of the unprepared modulation from the prevailing key and mode will determine how 'surprising' the modulation sounds. Conversely, the unprepared modulation should have some distinctiveness or it loses its point. With the number of similar keys in the modal system, some care has to be taken to avoid creating an ambiguity or unintended effect. Since the unprepared modulation has less confirmation almost by definition, the odds of its misinterpretation are correspondingly enhanced. The modulation can be confirmed after the fact or through repetition through the course of the composition.

Parenthetic Pivots

The increased difficulty in making quick but prepared modulations in the modern modal system, if one adheres to the basic principles, has been mentioned previously. The composer or songwriter is of course free to introduce unprepared modulations or use unprepared chromaticism to effect modulations. The tonal composers used chromatic harmonies such as the diminished seventh, augmented sixth or Neapolitan in just that way. Rather quickly however, the rapid adoption of these harmonic effects led to more intensification of them to retain their affective influence. Since tonal harmony has a smaller range of possibilities than melody, the discovery of them was more or less complete by the beginning of the 20th century. Atonality in its various forms was one way of ending this harmonic chase by a greater equalization of complex harmonies. This proposed modal system offers a different approach based on more subtle and varied scalar relationships than tonality.

Be that as it may, it is worth inquiring as to other procedures for introducing chromaticism or producing modulations that would permit the principled access to more distant keys. One possibility is through an extension of the parenthetic harmonies which introduce harmonies outside the scale without changing the mode. The possibility of chaining parenthetic harmonies was mentioned in passing in chapter 5. For example, a standard parenthetic harmony would be {II of IV} - IV, but we could chain another parenthetic harmony as in {IV of II of IV} - {II of IV} - IV. In the key of C Ionian this would translate into c minor - g minor - F triads.

Obviously, not all parenthetic harmonies or chains introduce chromatic notes in triads and each mode has a different arrangement of scale steps. Interestingly, the Mixolydian-Phrygian and Lydian-Dorian dyads have different key ranges produced through this process of chaining parenthetic harmonies than the Ionian-Aeolian dyad. This is because Ionian-Aeolian parenthetic harmonies are plus or minus one chromatic note while the other two dyads have one or two chromatic notes in the same direction, e.g. parenthetic harmonies for keys based on V and VII in Mixolydian have two less sharps or two more flats than the parent key while Lydian has two more sharps or two less flats for harmonies of keys based on II and IV. A parenthetic sequence in G Mixolydian such as {IV of II of V} - {II of V} - V would translate to **f** minor - **c** minor - **d** minor triads. (Using more complex chords than triads would increase the likelihood of chromatic notes in a given chord, of course.)

The use of this technique has to be considered in light of the compositional practice used in a particular work. In the Mixolydian-Phrygian Study Composition (Chapter 7), elaborate chromaticism would not fit the straightforward, uncomplicated mood of the piece. The other two Study Compositions do make use of this practice, however, to varying extent. This should be viewed as a stylistic resource rather than an essential element of the modal system.

In terms of modulation, parenthetic chaining can be used in a deceptive way. Instead of continuing through the chain as in the {x of x of x} to {x of x} to x, the progression can stay in the key of the initial or middle segment. For this to work, the compositional style must employ parenthetic chains so that the listener has an expectation that these chords obey some systematic practice rather than constituting an unprepared modulation. Since the use of this procedure is so stylistically dependent, examples would have to be examined in the context of musical compositions where the reader can more validly assess their effect.

In summary, the increased number and distinctiveness of the individual modes makes prepared modulation in the modal system more elaborate than in the later tonal system. The added keys increase the degrees of potential overlap, particularly among relatives of the key, and thus the ambiguity in arranging a given modulation. This means that modulations require more confirmation in terms of additional chordal progressions or stronger (or repeated) cadences. In addition, the greater distinction between parallel major and minor keys within a dyad reduces the easy shortcuts that the tonal system made use of to effect modulations to distant keys. (However, between-dyad modulation can take advantage of closer parallel key relationships.) This also increases the length of prepared modulations. Between-dyad modulations and unprepared modulations can have a negative effect on

STYLISTIC AND COGNITIVE CONSIDERATIONS

the coherence of the modal composition so their usage has to be carefully considered and preferably integrated into the overall plan of the composition. The advantage of this modal distinctiveness is considerable, though, since more variety is gained and also an improved sense of harmonic and melodic movement.

Melodic Organization

As with the tonal system, the harmonic aspects of the modal system are the most straightforward to discuss compared with melody and rhythm. Melodically, the modal system permits greater variability and subtlety compared with the tonal system. Some evidence for this can be found in the pre-tonal melodies of the medieval period as well as folk melodies or Indian monophonic ragas in which the melodies can proceed without the constrictions of tonal cadences and voice leading requirements.

Considering the typical harmonic progressions of the tonal era can further support the point. Chromaticism for the most part was generated by secondary dominant chords and other forms of dominant harmony such as the augmented sixth or Neapolitan sixth. The constant appearance of such progressions within a composition had to be varied adroitly by variations in melodic figurations, orchestration, and to a lesser extent rhythms.

The increased complexity of melody compared with harmony is a function of the number of elements that can vary. A chord to be identifiable has to have a relatively fixed set of tones, not have prominent non-related tones and be presented simultaneously or close together in time as in an arpeggiation. It is no accident that tonal music had a fairly restricted approach to rhythm and meter and was similarly restrained in the use of percussive instruments. Rhythmic freedom increases the probability that non-chord elements will intrude in all but the most homophonic music and disrupts the hierarchical status (emphasis) of different tonal chords. Percussive instruments generate significant amounts of noise, particularly in highly audible transients, which also interfere with harmonic perception and balance. The principal tonal percussion instruments were tuned tympani and the introduction of more varied percussion occurred when the tonal system began to break down (although chromatic atonal harmonies can be negatively affected as well by percussive noise and chaotic transients, such as produced by bells and gongs).

Melody by definition is temporally extended, has no fixed set or arrangement of tones (apart from the overall scale set), no fixed duration of tones and no set length. Admittedly, the tonal system constrained melody somewhat to avoid a conflict with characteristic harmonic progressions but it still had far more freedom to vary. The modal system has even more melodic flexibility than the tonal system, if not as much as monophonic musical traditions.

It is useful to contrast the form of tonal melodies with modal melodies since readers are presumably most familiar with the former. To a lesser extent, some comparison of medieval modal melodies with the modern modal system can be made since most modal usage even in the 19th and 20th centuries has been conducted with that as a major influence. Although the increasing availability of (monophonic) music from other cultures reveals how complex and subtle a melodic tradition can become when it's unencumbered by harmony, the enculturation of tonal melodies is still overwhelming. Undoubtedly, tonal melodies have made more progress in other cultures than those cultures' non-tonal system music has made in the West (see Cogan and Escot).

Within that framework, the modal melodic contour will be briefly examined in relation to the governing mode, modal melodic chromaticism, modal bass melody, and melodic cadences. Although the mode doesn't overly constrain the melodic contour, there are more characteristic melodic constructions when support or definition of the mode are sought. Due to the distinctiveness of the modes, the melodic cadences should also be distinctive to confirm the mode. As for melodic chromaticism in the modern modal system, this would occur naturally with parenthetic harmonies and in modulatory passages. Bass melody has a significant role in modal music since it compensates for the milder progressions in providing direction to the music. Interestingly, the more the tonal system predominated, the less that bass melody played a role. The orchestra really has no instruments that can easily play a steady bass melody except possibly the string basses which, however, are weak voiced. Bass notes became almost exclusively based on harmonic considerations. Conversely strong cadences in the modal system require more melodic (and rhythmic) support than in the tonal system for the reasons described.

134

Melodic Contours in the Modal System

One way of distinguishing between modal and tonal melodies is to consider the following analogy. One hierarchy based on royalty approximates the triangular or pyramidal shape with a pointed apex, atop which stands one individual and a steeply sloping angle from that apex. Another hierarchy based on the extended family has a patriarch (or matriarch) at the top but the slope is more gradual between levels of the extended family. The tonal system, in order to maintain the strict organization and direction of extended harmonic forms, imposed constraints on the content and structure of melody. This correspondence forms the so-called deep structure of tonal music that Schenker and other tonal theorists have defined. Tonal melodies tend to confirm harmonic properties of the major-minor scale by careful placement of the tonally significant tones at prominent locations. These placements include melodic peaks, strong beats, extended notes and in the soprano (highest melodic voice) at cadences. They also avoid rhythmic irregularities which would obscure the harmonic progressions and sonorities of the key.

Modal melodies in the medieval or pre-tonal era certainly obeyed strict rules both as single lines and also in contrapuntal voice leading, although the rules became rather more rigid at the height of the modal period than they had been earlier with organum. In particular, melodies had to stay within the range of an octave or so, augmented, diminished or chromatic melodic intervals were sparingly used and dissonances were resolved in a stereotyped manner. (In the 20th century, compositions based on neo-modal styles or containing such passages departed from some of these rules (melodic range and dissonance treatment) but adhered to other (tonal) rules that were not necessarily a feature of medieval modal music. In particular, contrapuntal rhythmic features of neo-modal compositions (e.g. Respighi, Vaughan Williams) were often quite bland and more regular than medieval practice.)

Nevertheless, modal melodies, even when the restrictions noted above are observed, typically sound freer, more wayward and can be quite elongated without recourse to chromaticism. The basis for this effect must lie in the relaxation of the connection between the melodic construction and the harmonic structure, particularly in the ubiquitous tonal cadential formulas. This permits the introduction of more varied rhythmic nuances since a concordance of the different voices is not a constant necessity. In this context, concordance does not refer to the relative dissonance of the chord or to the vertical arrangement of passing tones, but to the relation of the melody tones with the bass (harmonic tones) and the characteristic tonal sonorities requiring temporal simultaneity.

Several examples can lend more concreteness to the characteristic distinctions. In example 47a, we see a typical tonal melody with harmonic accompaniment in a work by Haydn (*Symphony 93*, IV); in 47b, a later tonal melody with increased chromaticism by Mahler (*Symphony 9*, IV); in example 48a, a modal melody from a chanson by Johannes Ockeghem (*Ma Maitresse*); in 48b, modal passages from Vaughan Williams' *Tallis Fantasia* and in 48c, a passage from the first movement of Sibelius' *Symphony 6*.

Ex. 47a: Haydn from *Symphony 93* (IV)

Ex.47b: Mahler from *Symphony 9* (IV)

In the two examples of tonal melodies, despite the difference in style, the characteristic relation between melodic tones and the underlying harmonic structure (cadences) remains quite similar. Tonal melodies often have a Statement and Response form built more or less on the half and full cadence. Generally, more complex or longer tonal melodies have a significant chromatic element. In the Haydn example, the chromatic diminished chord is introduced at the start of the Response or b phrase (5th measure in the example) that quickly proceeds to a return of the tonic a phrase, maintaining the clear overall structure of the piece. The melody, while possessing the characteristic slight quirkiness Haydn was fond of using, still fits into a regular and typical pattern.

The Mahler example has a more expansive treatment of its melody with chromatic inflections which occur more irregularly and often than with Haydn. Nevertheless, cadential progressions have a fundamental similarity between the two pieces. The Mahler melody is held together by the frequent melodic and rhythmic repetitions (e.g. the 16th note turn figure occurring on the 2nd or 4th beat) which help organize the frequent chromatic shifts. As is typical of tonal works, both the Haydn and Mahler works have a strong adherence to metric regularity and relatively sparse non-melodic bass parts. The Mahler passage has only one measure (marked by the asterisk) with even the mildest internal syncopation. Nor is this taken out of context. A perusal of the entire score shows similar traits despite the marked rhythmic effects in the 2nd and 3rd movements. Often, Haydn displays more superficial syncopation than later tonal composers, although it is useful to remember that syncopation is more perceptible when a strong regular rhythm is predominant overall.

The modal melodies also share similarities despite the expanse of time between their composition. Looking at the example by Ockeghem (Ex.48a), the diatonic character of the chanson is counterbalanced by the rhythmic and melodic variety and asymmetry. In the displayed measures, the only rhythmic repetition in a part occurs in the tenor in measures 1 and 2. This low rate of repetition is typical of the entire chanson. Although the nominal meter is 3/4, the actual rhythm constantly fluctuates between that and 6/8, oftentimes simultaneously (e.g. measure 3.)

Ex. 48a : Ockeghem *Ma maitresse*

The following two examples (Exx. 48b and c) illustrate the use of modal ideas in the context of a symphony and a more explicitly antiquarian fantasia. These 20th century examples illustrate some original usage but also considerable tentativeness in handling modal melody and harmony. Additionally, tonal thinking is never far away in either work.

In the *Fantasia*, the principal theme is taken from a Phrygian melody by Thomas Tallis, the 16th century English composer. Although the nominal key is **g** minor, the use of **A**♭ suggests the Phrygian mode. The key of **G** in Phrygian has three flats because the scale degree two must be a semitone above the tonic. Since the piece has considerable tonal passages, chromatic notes are moderately frequent but less so in the modal passages. A few tonally based modulations are also found. It should be noted that the example has a somewhat more contrapuntal texture than the work as a whole. However, the non-melodic bass is quite characteristic.

Ex. 48b-c: Modal passages from Vaughan Williams' *Tallis Fantasia* and Sibelius' *Symphony 6*

The Sibelius example displays a more fully contrapuntal modal texture (**D** Dorian) with a more melodically integrated bass part, but this passage is also not particularly characteristic of much of the symphony. The predominant texture is melody (or melodic fragments) and accompaniment. Sibelius does employ actual modal modulation in an original, albeit modest way (see Pike) with modulations between **D**, **G**, and **A** Dorian in several of the movements. Not surprisingly, the modal ideas are made to fit within the general characteristics of Sibelius' mature symphonic style with respect to chromaticism, rhythm and orchestration. In this respect, a similarity exists between this piece and Beethoven's 3rd movement of the **a** minor string quartet which makes use of a quasi-Lydian mode melody, also within the context of his late style.

Neither example shown above exploits the full range of possibilities in the modern modal system presented here nor even fully reflects past modal practice. Although the Sibelius symphony was one of the few attempts to structurally incorporate modal procedures into the symphonic form, the result was still somewhat tentative. The Dorian mode alternates with the major and minor scale and the Dorian modulations occur only in a few places in the movements. While instructive of the different quality that modal melody has compared with tonal melody, the discussion needs to turn to the other implications of the modern modal system to more fully analyze the character of melodic construction within it. Thus, we will examine modal melodies in light of melodic chromaticism, parenthetic harmonies, increased use of bass melody and the variety of cadences available.

Melodic Chromaticism

Although the modal compositions of the medieval period (and even many neo-modal works) generally avoided chromatic melodies, the modern modal system imposes no such stylistic restriction. Chromaticism can arise through modulation, parenthetic harmonies, melodic voice leading or freely. Another small possibility would be the use of a chromatic dissonant cadence as discussed above. A comparison of the use of modal melodic chromaticism with conventional tonal melodic chromaticism is a useful exercise. To consider these examples

141

in the same order as mentioned above, the difference in modulatory passages varies by mode. Obviously in the Ionian mode, modulatory chromaticism in melodies, while related to the major scale, is stripped of minor scale chromaticism. The other modes have varying characteristic progressions, but are not essentially different in functional terms from tonal counterparts. The 'tonal' triads of the mode rank higher on the hierarchy than the non-tonal notes if the character of the mode is to be maintained. The melody is likely to confirm that hierarchy of scale degrees as much as does the bass or inner voices. Modal melody does have more freedom with respect to their harmonic and metrical placement. There remains a slight but general difference in modal modulation due to the different strengths of the cadences available within the modes. Since the dominant progression in the major-minor system is so strong, modulations can be accomplished in double-time so to speak, although composers often devised more circuitous modulations for the sake of variety.

On the other hand, the melodic chromaticism inherent in parenthetic harmonies, although springing from the same source as modulation, really assumes a divergent character in the modern modal system. In the tonal system, parenthetic harmonies were virtually reducible to secondary dominants, so rare was the occurrence of non-dominant harmonies. In the modal system, the presence of non-dominant progressions is greatly expanded and therefore the chromaticism stemming from parenthetic harmonies and progressions will similarly reflect this tendency.

Melodic voice leading can introduce chromatic notes, particularly when an artificial leading-tone is sought. This was exactly the process that occurred in the medieval modal system with modes that did not have the leading tone to the tonic, inherently present in the Ionian (and Lydian) mode. Of course, this was also the process that led to the abandonment of the modal system in favor of the major-minor scale. In the modal system, the variety of melodic relationships from mode to mode does make it somewhat less imperative to use extensively this particular means of melodic variation. In addition, constant melodic chromaticism not connected to the factors already discussed in this section makes the mode more ambiguous. If this is an intentional effect, the aesthetic results may please, but without careful construction, unintended relations can start to intrude and render the form modally shapeless.

142

The extensive use of melodic chromaticisms unconnected with harmonic ends can most safely occur either in situations typical of their occurrence in the medieval modal system or when the result is the (virtual) construction of a mode outside the modal system discussed here. The first instance is simple enough since medieval chromaticism, until late in the 16th century, was generally limited to the final cadence, simple melodic turns, avoidance of the tritone and an occasional downward leading tone to the fifth of the mode (Ex. 49: Dufay's *Adieu*; Dowland's *Lachrimae*; Dufay's *Vergine*). The chromaticism of Gesualdo and certain other contemporaries, while rooted in principles of medieval voice leading practice, really is associated with the breakdown of the modal system and the concomitant rise of secondary dominant harmonies and other features of the evolving major and minor scales.

Ex.49: Modal melodic chromaticisms: Dufay (*Adieu*), Dowland (*Lachrimae*), Dufay (*Vergine*)

The second instance involves non-standard patterns of chromatically altered notes. The medieval modes were all constructed using only the notes of what is now C major. Logically, however, given the 12 notes of the chromatic scale, there are many more unique permutations possible of a seven note scale with the restriction that no gap greater than an augmented second occurs between adjacent scale points (Ex. 50).

Ex.50: Other Seven Note Scales

The examples violate the tonal and modal order of sharp and flat notes, but are not bizarre sounding melodically for that. However, harmonically these non-standard modes do have augmented, multiple diminished or non-triadic interval chords (to avoid these, the tonal and modal scales start their sequence of flats on **B** and sharps on **F**). Thus, they pose no ambiguity with the modes included in the present discussion. Voice leading melodic chromaticism which produces these non-standard scales are no serious threat to the prevailing mode nor do they introduce unintended references to other standard modes. However, their extended use in a harmonically based system is made problematic by their lumpy chordal structures. These types of modes are probably better suited for melody accompaniment texture or mostly monophonic music where harmonies are limited or drone-like.

More adventurous melodic chromaticism can be employed, however, if the style permits and its use is carefully judged. For example, bi-modality is just as plausible as bi-tonality. Assuming the musical texture makes the division clear, one strand can be in, say, **D** Dorian while another is in **F** Dorian. Obviously, these are chromatic in relation to the other. Chromatic passing notes, short chromatic sequences, arpeggios and arabesques don't seriously disturb the modal framework either. Some melodic chromaticisms would be much more dependent on careful insertion into the plan of the work. For example, a melody that began in **F** Lydian and then suddenly veered into **C** Aeolian would have to be given a plausible context for the effect not to appear aimless. Some possibilities would be a contrasting episode with a return to **F** Lydian, a modulation to **A♭** Lydian or a recurring alternation between the two modes in a quasi-dominant relation. Some of these chromatic features can be seen in the Study Compositions.

Bass Melody

A prime stylistic distinction between medieval modal music and the tonal music which followed it was the degree to which the bass (lowest voice) had a melodic form. While bass melody is not an essential characteristic of modal music, it is a common element and is very congruent with the modal system by providing momentum to the phrase despite the reduction of strong harmonic cadences. Because of its harmonic structure, tonal music has difficulty in integrating a truly melodic bass part with the other voices. Even a contrapuntally inclined composer such as J.S. Bach primarily used figured bass, except in his keyboard compositions with only two parts to control or in fugues and other contrapuntal exercises.

In the medieval modal period, the lowest voice had a roughly equal part in the texture of the whole. Of course, the parts were almost always vocal parts so that the texture was seamless. Occasionally, parts were written with instrumental performance in mind. Often these parts were either extremely basic, as in a repeating cantus firmus or ostinato or were very similar to vocal parts. Gradually, instrumental voices took on a more typical outline with rapid figurations and ornamentation. However, it wasn't until the start of the tonal period around the time of Monteverdi that bass parts routinely assumed their current form as harmonic support rather than a co-equal melodic part.

As unaccompanied vocal music began to disappear and instruments provided the bass part, it was undoubtedly noticed that an active bass part tended to confuse the tonal harmony and also could mask notes in the upper voices. The masking effect is particularly audible with bass instruments since their overtones are often pronounced (sometimes stronger than the fundamental) and there are naturally more notes above them to mask. Orchestral writing is often characterized by bass parts with frequent pauses and notes principally forming part of the chord, as opposed to passing notes or other melodic notes. Bass parts similar to those found in medieval modal music are rarely seen except occasionally in chamber music works where the balance can be more precisely estimated. (Due to the inherent acoustic complexity of masking, there is no exact science in calculating its impact at any given moment of music.) It should be emphasized that a certain amount of acoustic interaction between parts is necessary to create a normal ensemble effect. The negative effect of too great an isolation of voices can be found on many modern recordings in which multi-miking and isolation booths are used. Such recordings have a sterile, artificial sound as if instruments are somehow soloing together.

The lack of a suitable bass instrument for the orchestra posed an additional problem. Wind instruments can't be played as continually as string instruments and the double bass viol is somewhat ponderous with a very low and not particularly forceful sound. Pianos have an overtone-rich lower register while organs because of their size are not in every hall. Their low notes can be made blander through suitable stopping, but they create an overlay of sound rather than a truly integrated or versatile bass part. It should also be noted that modal bass parts were not pitched very low, typically not going below F2, an octave and fifth below middle C and often remaining between C3 and C4.

These comments indicate that certain practical issues complicate the return to the practice of bass melody in the modal system. Contemporary informal music does employ more continuous bass parts in a predominantly tonal context through several methods. First, instruments such as the bass guitar and electric portable organ/synthesizer, which are capable of extended playing, serve as primary bass instruments. Second, electric instruments can have the timbre and overtone structure of sounds controlled through electronic devices. Rolling off prominent overtones significantly reduces the masking effects of such bass parts. Third, in recording or even on stage the sound is often controlled through a mixing panel in which the various instruments can be artificially balanced to create the sound at that site.

Therefore, what guidance can be given to the use of bass melody in the composition of non-a capella works? First, bass melody presents no special problems if the range of the bass part lies above C3 and if the instrument is not overly loud. However, modern music often has a bass part with lower range than C3, particularly in orchestral or amplified music. Second, if amplified instruments or

146

electronically generated parts with rolled-off overtones are used, then many forms of bass melody are practical, assuming of course that the upper voices are also amplified or otherwise collectively in dynamic balance with the amplified instrument. By practical, I mean that the ensemble effect of the orchestration of such works would have a relatively predictable, calculable sound and balance and would not necessarily require external mixing. Third, bass instruments can be doubled to permit one player to rest while the other is playing. This is the approach used in the Study Compositions scored for clarinet choir (in chapters 7-9), in which two bass clarinets alternate playing the relatively continuous bass melodies. Fourth, compositional techniques can simulate to some extent modal bass melody and minimize the conventional tonal organization of the bass part.

The first three points are self-explanatory but the fourth merits some further explanation. In tonal music, the bass mostly plays notes forming part of the prevailing chord. In the early tonal period, chords were generally limited to triads and seventh chords in root position or first inversion. These harmonic based notes were interspersed with scale work or other figuration which kept most non-chordal bass notes on weak beats or otherwise unobtrusive. Later tonal works included more complex chords in all possible inversions, but the character of the bass part didn't fundamentally change.

Modal bass parts in medieval music, as noted, were more integrated into the melodic texture as well as participating in imitative passages with upper voices. That implies a more frequent appearance of bass notes forming part of the prevailing scale without necessarily being part of the typical triadic or seventh chord root. As Schoenberg noted, even the ninth chord begins to stretch the boundaries of tonal chords and composers as a consequence treated it in relatively more stereotyped fashion. Tonal bass typically not only adheres to the meter but also follows the same homophonic rhythmic pattern as upper voices in contrast with the frequent use of cross-rhythms and rhythmic irregularities in modal music. The medieval modal bass part provided more of a melodic than a harmonic impetus even in final or other cadences, often through its participation in canons and other imitative melodic constructions (Ex. 51).

147

Ex.51 : Josquin's *Missa Ave Maris* I

If continuous bass melody is not possible due to instrumentation or not wanted due to compositional requirements, the substantive difference between tonal and modal bass can still be maintained through the use of non-triadic tones, melodic fragments and rhythmic independence of bass notes with upper voices (Ex. 52).

In the examples, we see first a modal bass, then a more conventionally tonal bass. The difference is reasonably audible in the more flowing modal version versus the tighter more short-breathed tonal version. Ostinatos are another device quite compatible with modal forms, rather more so than with tonal forms. Although ostinatos in earlier music were often a purely repetitive note pattern, 20th century music (e.g. Stravinsky) can contain somewhat varying ostinato patterns which retain enough consistency to be audible as an ostinato. The ostinato often contained notes of even or nearly even duration (sometimes called grounds) but this is not required.

Ex.52: Modal bass examples

Ex. 52a

Ex. 52b

The cantus firmus phrase in the tenor of a polyphonic mass formed an ostinato like melodic pattern (e.g. Ockeghem's *Missa Caput*). In terms of the modern modal system, ostinato patterns should be considered with as much creativity and variety as any other musical phrase. They can impart a needed forward direction to the bass and their diatonic non-chord tones (with respect to the upper parts) do not disturb the mode. Of course, modality is not affected by use of a traditional tonal style bass either, as long as its harmony is congruent with the mode and key.

Melodic Cadences

The variety of cadences is one of the strongest differentiating factors between the modal and tonal systems. The typical or possible modal cadences were discussed in the section on modal harmony, but the melodic cadences that can be constructed on these harmonic progressions can vary to some extent.

Modal cadences have two characteristic features in addition to their greater variety. The first is a tendency towards chromatic leading tones in final cadences or less frequently in other section ending cadences. The second is increased melodic movement in most if not all voices in the measure(s) directly preceding the final cadence (Ex. 53).

To repeat, the overuse of chromatic leading tones can undermine the distinctiveness of the mode's melodic and harmonic attributes unless used sparingly. However, this does not apply to progressions with the augmented sixth, parenthetic chords or similar chords. As for increased melodic motion, this is almost always effective in creating a cadential feeling, but it assumes that the preceding musical phrases permit such movement to form a distinct enough contrast.

In medieval music, the fairly slow pace of most of the music made it relatively easy to speed up at the close as shown in Ex. 53. Sometimes the contrast was made against a relatively short preceding slow passage, whereas the bulk of the piece was moderately fast, as in *Credo* mass sections, but this has a somewhat less conclusive sound.

One melodic principle that can be borrowed from the tonal system is the linear arrangement of the ascending and descending lines as defined by Schenker. Although the modes do not have the harmonic properties of the major-minor system, they still have a hierarchical system of scale notes. Therefore, melodic structures conforming to the modal melodic features will provide points of repose at the convergence of these tendencies, for example, an ascending bass line to the tonic coupled with a descending top melody line to the tonic. The key point is that multiple cadential progressions suited to the characteristics of each of the modes are available.

Ex.53a-b: Dowland's *Lachrimae Antiquae Novae*; Ockeghem's *Missa Mi-mi*

Rhythmic Considerations in the Modal System

As noted, the modal system does not have the same degree of harmonic restrictions on the rhythmic variance between the parts. The characteristic chordal progressions and cadences of tonal music are diminished by consistent rhythmic independence and shifting accents and meter. The tonal harmonic progressions impose their own pattern of (harmonic) accents and strong and weak beats which interfere with contrary (melodic) rhythmic accents.

The constraints of the modal system exist more on the basis of scales than of particular progressions or harmonies. Even in the medieval period, progressions had less of the directional character of the tonal system. For example, while tonal cadential progressions such as V - I, II - V and IV - V - I are found in modal compositions, these progressions also are found in reverse order in the same modal compositions (I - V, I - V - IV, V - II). Thus, the characteristic sense of direction that the progressions provide in the tonal system can be reduced or negated. While it is a compositional choice as to which progressions are used or not used, the general reduction of harmonic closure is a fact.

With harmonic direction reduced at least somewhat, it is up to melody and rhythm to make up the difference of musical impetus. But this is no bad thing. Melody and rhythm are well equipped to do just that and in the proposed modal system, enough procedures are available to provide greater harmonic structure when that is desired as well. In addition, the modal system's reduction in harmonic control and reliance on the sonorities of particular chords makes possible a greater use of percussion instrumentation. The percussion can provide rhythmic support that no longer is fighting against the qualities associated with particular tonal progressions. This is particularly true when inversions are used freely. The overtone pattern of inversions blends better than many root position chords with the slightly chaotic overtones of percussion and amplified instruments.

While modal rhythmic freedom greatly exceeds what could comfortably be accommodated in the tonal system, it cannot equal the extreme rhythmic freedom found in monophonic music. Of course, monophonic music can be and often is modal in nature, but it achieves a qualitatively different effect than polyphonic (harmonic) modal music. The clearest side by side comparison can be made in the music of Guillaume de Machaut who wrote both monophonic and polyphonic compositions. However, many recordings of monophonic world music are available as well. The relative rhythmic and melodic orderliness of polyphonic music is quite audible compared to inherently monophonic music.

Notation of Rhythmic Phrasing

Several issues relating to the role of rhythm in the modal system will receive further examination in this section. The freer the rhythmic impulse, the more interpretational questions that arise from the notation of the musical phrase. Thus, notational issues become important to the correct communication of phrase structure and rhythmic organization. This cannot be overemphasized as the modal style depends more on melody that is sensitive to a more flexible harmonic context. A second consequence then becomes the relationship of the barline and meter to the rhythmic organization of the modal phrases. The third issue discussed here is the role of percussion in the establishment of rhythmic patterns in modal music.

In the 19th century, composers became more conscious of the effects of different kinds of instrumental techniques on timbre and rhythmic phrasing. For example, with string instruments, major differences exist between <u>arco</u> and <u>pizzicato</u> sounds. This effect is so striking that even Baroque composers were careful to notate it specifically. But there are many other techniques and notational symbols that clearly affect the rhythmic interpretation of the musical part such as slurs, playing near the bridge, staccato and even subtleties like up and down bowing. Despite the increased use of such techniques, many interpretational questions still are unspecified and rely on knowledge of the musical style to resolve. Fortunately for the performer, tonal music is not rhythmically adventurous for the most part and for much of its history observed the requirements of the meter in effect fairly strictly. (Additionally, the tonal organization itself provided important cues about the correct organization and performance of phrases.)

Earlier music had less explicit notation and the rhythmic interpretation relied more heavily on performers' understanding of the style governing the piece. Different rhythmic styles existed for church music, secular vocal music, instrumental music and even within instrumental music different dances had characteristic styles. For example, in Baroque dance music, the *sarabande* had an unnotated stress on the second beat of the triple meter bar rather than on the first beat. Sacred vocal music was governed by a variety of stylistic and rhythmic conventions related to the old rhythmic modes of duple and triple meters as well as the conventions of chant. (These conventions are only partially known since without a recording it can be difficult to establish actual rhythmic practice of an extinct musical tradition. The same problems would exist in interpreting the performance conventions of jazz or rock music, if recordings didn't exist and the style had lapsed for centuries.)

With modal music, since the rhythmic conventions of tonal music are relaxed, the question of the interpretation of rhythmic phrasing rises to the fore again. Actually, modern atonal music can be ambiguous for much the same reasons. Perhaps partly for that reason atonal composers often inscribe a forest of notational symbols to precisely specify the sound event. Composers primarily familiar with tonal music will have to exercise more attention to the rhythmic organization of the phrase and its notation if they are to avoid performance difficulties with modal music.

The principal factor to establish is the location of primary and secondary stresses since most other attributes can be explicitly notated. The reason that the ordinary stresses should be cautiously specified is the tendency of performers, not to mention conductors, to exaggerate such performance directions. The excessive slowing down and speeding up at the sight of <u>ritardando</u> and <u>accelerando</u> are well known to composers and critics. To some extent, slurring provides an indication of stress points (Ex. 54a-b).

In the example, performers would place light stresses on the first note of the slur group and use the slur to define the phrase. The second example has more asymmetrical slurrings and arbitrary-sounding phrases than the first and sounds slightly awkward as a result.

Ex. 54a-b: Notation of Melody: Slurs

Although slurs are highly useful in showing departures of stresses from the indicated meter, they also specify a particular form of note attack that may not be wanted. Two other possible notational devices can be applied in that case. The first method involves the use of brackets to identify a phrase segment (Ex. 55a) and the second method is the use of beaming across the beat implied by the meter (Ex. 55b).

Ex.55a-b: Notation of Melody: Brackets and Beaming

In Example 55b, the beaming in measure 9 implies a different pattern than the conventional beams of the same measure in 55a. Beaming can also cross the barline as in measure 3, although its aesthetic quality is not good.

The use of brackets to denote a phrase to be played as a unit has appeared less frequently in the literature, although it is occasionally seen in early music scores since the music was composed prior to a real institution of the barline as an enforcer of meter. The brackets function in much the same way as the slur, except they are transparent as far as method of attack or effect on other notations concurrently in effect. In the example 55b, the brackets indicate a displacement of the stresses that the performer would naturally place given the meter. It should be noted that brackets work in conjunction with beaming to indicate the pattern of rhythmic stress within that phrase.

Barline and Meter in the Modal System

The function of the barline in music has often been misunderstood as a direction to stress the first beat after the barline. Originally, the barline was simply an aid to readability of the score. Performers were assumed to be familiar with the material and know how to sing it. Oftentimes, the composer was physically located at the court or church where his music was performed. The rise of the tonal system, by regularizing rhythm, made the concept of the measure and barline more useful. However, the barline has only a modest relationship to stress even in tonal music.

Oddly enough, modern composers have sometimes made the barline a better indicator of stress due to their willingness to alter the meter frequently. In tonal music, changes in meter were relatively rare even at the beginning of the 20th century. Though soon thereafter, many different time signatures became more widely used or even commonplace, filtering down into jazz and other informal music. Actually, this recent practice makes a great deal of sense in terms of better conveying compositional intent. The drawback of the older system appeared when phrases and stresses were more irregularly placed in the measure and thus depended on the stylistic knowledge of the performer for interpretation. In the current environment, however, the stylistic range exceeds past practice by several orders of magnitude and even individual composers can write two different works in distinct styles.

Even if we adjust the barline and time signature to fit the phrasing, there still remains the question of the precise way that stresses are organized within the nominal meter. The same time signature can have its beats subdivided in numerous ways. The standard 4/4 measure is assumed to have four evenly spaced beats on the minims with a primary stress on the first and third and a secondary stress on the second and fourth. Yet blues and rock music customarily reverse the stress pattern forming a backbeat. More complexly, the beats can be divided irregularly as with a 8/8 measure divided 2 + 4 + 2 or 2 +3+3. Odd time signatures such as 5/8 or 7/8 have an inherent asymmetry that can be reversed either explicitly or implicitly (e.g. 2+3, 3+2). In general, irregular subdivisions of meter should be explicitly notated if there is some consistency in that subdivision over an extended series of measures. Otherwise, it is best to use the notational devices mentioned above to indicate the phrase structure.

Percussion and Rhythmic Organization

Tonal music made sparing use of percussion as a rhythmic force not only for stylistic reasons, but also because of its disruptive effect on chordal sonorities and the progression of tonal harmonic rhythm. The rise of atonal music freed percussion to assume a larger role in modern formal music. As for informal music, stylistic reasons were favorable, but the inherent loudness of the instrumentation of jazz, big band and pop music made the effects of percussive noise mostly irrelevant to harmonic sonorities.

Because of the flexibility of modal rhythmic and harmonic progressions, rhythmic accentuation through the use of percussion can add to the sense of propulsion in the other voices, particularly in highly contrapuntal settings. Clearly, all percussion is not the same nor does it have the same interaction with pitched voices. The safest percussion from a harmonic, and to some exten, a melodic standpoint are the various unpitched drums without excessive upper partials. Tom-toms, congas, and bongos blend easily with pitched voices.

Percussion which has a greater interaction with other voices due to greater transient noise or strong upper partials obviously has to be used more carefully as a rhythmic adjunct, particularly in unamplified settings. Cymbals and bells have particularly strong interactions, albeit in different registers. Bells have a fairly chaotic overtone pattern, unlike most acoustic instruments, but also have some partials which are extremely prominent. Overall, they tend to muddy the sound from acoustic instruments. The problem is less severe with amplified instruments since they are louder and usually have a somewhat chaotic overtone pattern as well. Cymbals have particularly prominent upper partials and are difficult to use as a rhythmic adjunct

158

without external mixing unless they are played with softer sticks or brushes or are playing with other loud instruments. Nevertheless, greater latitude exists in modal music for percussive transients.

The rhythmic accents that the percussion would project would typically fall into three main categories: a) congruent with the meter but not the bass, b) congruent with the bass not the meter, c) congruent with the bass and meter. The third case is more often found in pop and other informal music. With tonal music, the percussive accents are emphatic more than musically essential, since the tonal progressions demarcate the often straightforward phrases. Within a modal framework however, the percussive accents would provide an element of propulsion that is less forcefully provided by the modal harmony. It could well be that the melody and rhythm of the voices were energetic enough without added percussive rhythm, but the modes do differ in their essential character in this respect.

The first case implies a melodic bass part since modal melody does not have to bind itself as rigidly to the straitjacket of the meter. The texture would generally be contrapuntal and the percussion would perform a function that would not be evident in the other parts, at least on a consistent basis. In this situation, the percussion part would provide more accentuation than the free flowing melody or at least provide an element of contrast. The second case is probably the least likely to occur and would seem to imply a syncopation or ostinato pattern in the bass that the percussion further emphasizes. This kind of role would be difficult to sustain for more than a short passage or a brief song.

General Issues from a Psychological Perspective

In this section, we will step back from the specifics of the modal system to consider some more general musical and psychological issues relevant to its compositional use. No simple-minded or slavish linking of psychological processes with musical style is being advocated. Through learning and experience, listeners can acquire a taste or preference for vastly different musical works and through boredom (habituation) can grow tired of any given work or entire style. However, it is useful to bear in mind (within our present knowledge) how the typical listener will perceive, categorize and remember musical forms and syntax.

Without memory, it is safe to say, music would be an undiscovered art. Temporal sequence forms the essence of musical expression as it does not for painting or sculpture. How memory specifically affects musical perception and comprehension would easily full a large book and still fail to break the surface. The present discussion must be limited to a few central points, mainly revolving around the concepts of short and long-term memory and primacy and recency effects.

Short Term (Working) Memory Processes

The well-known distinction between short-term (working) and long-term memory almost certainly has a basis in different brain mechanisms and the two kinds of memory have different properties. Short-term memory generally is considered to be limited to thoughts and perceptions that are in immediate consciousness or no more than a few seconds out of consciousness. Short-term memories are subject to total loss unless they are quickly converted to the more permanent long-term memory. Conversely, memory is nearly perfect for items in short-term memory. In this section, we will predominantly focus on short-term memory and musical processing since long-term memory has a much more widespread and complex relation to other forms of music processing such as judgment and categorizing.

As common experience will confirm, short-term memory has significant constraints on the number and complexity of thoughts and perceptions that can reside in it at any given time. The well known rule of seven plus or minus two states that short term memory can comfortably contain between 5 and 9 items and research confirms its wide applicability. However, people can work around these limitations by either 'chunking' or recoding of information. For example, telephone numbers are seven numbers split into chunks of 3 and 4 numbers. The area code is another 3 number chunk. Trying to remember a random string of ten numbers is more difficult than remembering those 10 numbers split into three chunks, particularly when one of the strings (the area code) has an implicit verbal label (a city or a region of a state). Many other examples could be provided that confirm these limitations and the noted strategies that help to mitigate them.

The effects of short-term memory processes express themselves in a number of ways in music. Perhaps the most striking is the almost universal limitation of musical scales around the world to less than nine distinct notes within the octave. The diatonic scale has seven notes, the pentatonic five. The one major exception is the chromatic scale, which, on the evidence of the listening public, is perceived as more difficult to comprehend when used as the basis of a composition; more precisely, when the 12 notes are used as freely as notes within a diatonic scale are used. Obviously, over the course of a composition, tonal composers present different subsets of the 12 notes and often all 12 notes are present somewhere. But in any given section, some of the 12 notes have a subsidiary (infrequent) occurrence. Memory for these subsidiary notes is usually poorer than for main notes.

Similarly complex scales, such as the 22 note Indian scale, are also not used within a single composition by composers and musicians. Conceptually, some of the 22 notes serve more as embellishments of a neighboring primary note. In practice, compositions employ a restricted set of the 22 potential notes, much in the same manner that diatonic scales make use of a particular subset of the chromatic scale (see Wade).

Concurrent musical lines, as exist in polyphonic compositions, produce an even greater strain on short-term memory due to the increased density of information presented in each period of time. The norm of 4 parts is rarely exceeded and frequently reduced to three or two parts in extended passages. True polyphonic music, characterized by melodically and (especially) rhythmically separate parts, evolved in Western European formal traditions and is rarely found in more than incidental fashion elsewhere, even in the otherwise sophisticated Indian or Oriental art music. (However, some African music does have true polyrhythmic accompaniment to a monophonic chant melody.) Actually, true polyphonic music has always been resisted in informal styles and in a fair proportion of Western formal music. Melody and accompaniment or homophonic music is predominant in the music between Mozart and Brahms and 20th century informal music is almost exclusively in this style.

Another memory process related to short-term memory is the *recency effect*. If a person is given a string of items (notes) to remember,

161

they are more likely to remember the items at the end (most recently presented) than items in the beginning and especially in the middle. Items in the beginning are remembered better than middle items, known as the *primacy effect*. The primacy effect is somewhat more complicated than the recency effect since it is the result of both short and long term memory processes. The beginning items are no longer in short-term memory, so the probability of their recall is accordingly reduced. However, since they were the first to be presented, short-term memory had no (similar) previous items competing with them. Thus, these initial items could be processed more fully and transferred more effectively into long-term memory

Composers have always coped with the practical implications of the recency and primacy effects in extended compositions. Since the recency effect is the strongest, particular attention has to be paid to the sequence of local progressions. Discontinuities between adjacent passages are highly likely to be perceived, while such differences between less proximate sections may pass unaware or be noticeable only upon repeated listenings to the entire work. Composers have often varied the degree of continuity and discontinuity to create particular effects or moods. For example, Beethoven's *Piano Sonata 32* has striking adjacent discontinuities in the first movement in terms of the melodic, rhythmic and musical dynamics elements. Within the second movement, however, a significant change in motion is achieved gradually so that the discontinuity between the beginning and later passages is not as evident.

Divisions or sections are another way that composers can clarify musical thought for the listener. Generally, the division or section is initiated by an overt pause or at least a reduction of harmonic and melodic activity between the preceding section and subsequent section. The division has the effect of renewing the primacy effect, although probably not to the same degree as the actual beginning of the work. Of course, recurrences or similar passages and themes can be placed across different sections which tends to connect such otherwise separated sections in a more specific way than in a less sectionalized work, since the sections permit better temporal marking.

When composers want a more distant section or passage to be remembered by the listener at a later point in the piece, they generally use either the passages at the start (primacy) or passages made highly distinctive through other means. For example, composers can highlight a passage either melodically, rhythmically, through orchestration or through harmony and the reader can easily find examples of each in most periods of music. A more facile means of highlighting is provided by repetition, which generally marks the third rate formal or typical informal composition. The net effect of such highlighting is to displace other information from short-term memory, thus ensuring maximum processing of the distinctive material. Of course, distinctiveness is a relative concept and what might seem distinctive to the composer or music analyst might seem not distinctive to a listener. Generally, melody is the most effective and harmony the least effective means to highlight a particular passage (not considering repetition), with rhythm and orchestration (with dynamics) falling in the middle.

The use of primacy effects goes back to the medieval and Renaissance period and can be found in clear form in the cantus firmus mass cycles in which the tenor part was based on a quotation from a well-known chant or secular melody. The chant melody was generally used prominently at the start of each mass movement to provide some bridging of the quite separated performances of the movements in church services. Many examples can be found in later music. One obvious example is the use of the overture in operas and operettas to introduce the main themes found later in the work.

The use of thematic integration, much favored in late Romantic and 20th century works, has a somewhat complex effect on primacy and recency processes. Thematic integration, by using the same or similar melodic, harmonic and rhythmic motives throughout a section or work, clearly affects recency since such motives are more often in short term memory, enhancing memory for the repeated event. If the motives are inherently distinctive (e.g. octave leaps, syncopated rhythms) or made that way by compositional highlighting, then de facto primacy effects can also occur. This comes about because the distinctive material tends to push out less salient information and tends to function as a quasi-beginning or at least as a defined passage. The transfer of a particular set of information from short to long term memory and subsequent ability to recall or recognize it again is enhanced when that information set is subjected to less competing (interfering) information. In related fashion, the reduction of competing information also gives the listener more time to process various aspects of the information which also enhances later retrieval.

At a more general level, thematic (motivic) integration necessarily reduces the amount of musical material with distinctive features at variance with the established thematic material; in a word, its variability. This tends to create a polished sound to musical passages and works as divergent as a melody by Bernart de Ventadorn, Debussy's *Syrinx* or some of Webern's later chamber music. This is not to say that such motivic integration is always audible in a direct sense. In many cases, the listener may not be able to identify the precise motives which form the basis of such works. They simply perceive that there are fewer marked contrasts on the particular dimension or feature (e.g. melodic motive, rhythm, harmony, instrumentation) integrated in the work.

The theoretical emphasis on motivic integration has overshadowed the other dimensions which foster a sense of integration. Other things equal, a string quartet or clarinet choir gives a more coherent impression simply because of the homogeneity of the sound (timbre) compared with an orchestra or varied instrumental combination. Similarly, compositions with a restricted set of rhythms (note durations) seem more integrated than those with varied rhythmic effects. Conversely, a melody where each note is played by a different instrument would sound less coherent and integrated than if it was played on one instrument or a stable group of instruments.

Listeners perceive such musical integration most strongly when the set restrictions are relatively obvious. Formal relations in complex music, whether tonal, modal, or atonal, can easily exceed the capacity of experienced, let alone average audiences to analyze the score. Atonal works, either based on the chromatic scale or using pitched and unpitched sounds, require even more care in their construction since they tend to favor symmetrical relationships which are inherently more difficult to remember than hierarchical relationships. A simple example is the greater confusion people have determining right and left compared with up and down. Up and down have gravity as a reliable reference (at least on the Earth) whereas right and left are dependent on changeable orientation. (Bodies tend to reflect this as well in that the vast majority of animals are symmetrical on right and left sides but less so top to bottom.) Hierarchical relations also favor chunking of presented information since less memorable elements can be related to more memorable elements (e.g. a cadence).

164

Since music based on symmetrical relations tends to have less internal structure, compared to a hierarchical scale, pieces in this style often have more external structure to compensate. Atonal music which makes use of even limited hierarchical relations such as the 12-tone music of Alban Berg or Stravinsky tends to sound more conventional. Conversely, tonal or modal music that employs symmetrical constructions tends to sound less tonally definite and more atonal, as with music favoring the whole tone scale (major thirds), diminished seventh chords (three minor thirds) or the tritone (two minor thirds).

The number of scale elements has also played a role with historical styles of atonal music in the 20th century, since in most cases, the 12 note chromatic scale was used. Serial music generally involves using the 12 chromatic notes in a specified order before repeating any. As noted, the 12 note sequence exceeds the number of different elements comfortably held in short term memory, particularly if the listener can't easily group (chunk) the notes. By the same token, a pentatonic atonal piece should be more easily remembered and analyzed by the listener, since only 5 elements have to be followed before repetition, while a 24 note sequence would be far more difficult.

Complexity in the relations of the different musical events affects the comprehensibility of all musical styles. Different serial techniques, for example, influence the exact way in which the sequence is played out in each instrument and in the harmony. To the extent that they introduce more elements that need to be remembered and minimize primacy and recency effects they will be perceived as more difficult examples of the style. If the original melody, 12-tone or otherwise, is not remembered then there isn't much chance that variations of it will be perceived as related to that melody (theme). While the particular 12 note sequence specifies the order of the notes (e.g. A♭, **B**, **E**), it does not indicate the note duration. (Total serialism, however, may also apply a serial sequence to dynamics, note values etc.) The ability of listeners to recognize such complex alterations as the music is being played is doubtful. Even the variations in tonal works such as the Bach *Goldberg Variations* are too complexly related to the original theme for most listeners to be able to perceive the exact nature of their relationship without studying the score.

Variations that are related melodically as well as harmonically should be easier to perceive (e.g. the variations in Beethoven's *Piano Sonata 30*). This is because a distinctive melody is generally encoded as

165

a unitary element in the same way that, through chunking, a sentence is easier to remember than the equivalent string of letters. This would presumably be true for atonal works as well if the theme was melodically distinctive. A melody specifies a sequence of notes with associated durations intentionally constructed by the composer to be identifiable and memorable in the context of the work, in contrast to a less easily defined sequence of notes. In addition, the melody or theme is usually repeatedly presented in straightforward transpositions and simple variants.

A related concept, the *'spacing effect'*, also plays an important role in the listener's perception of musical organization and coherence. The spacing effect refers to the increased memory retention of information that is presented once and then presented again after an interval of time compared with retention of information that has had immediate repetition. For example, a list of 20 words presented sequentially has one word presented in position 3 and then again in position 15 while another word is presented in position 6 and then 7. The interval is typically long enough that the first presentation of the information is no longer in short-term memory but not so long that the person can't even remember having seen or heard it before. Although the psychological basis of the spacing effect is quite complex and too involved to go into here, it is a very wide-spread and stable memory phenomenon. As might be expected, the closer the repeated event is to the previous presentation the greater the likelihood of recognizing a repetition has occurred.

Composers intuitively make use of this effect by using spaced repetitions as with refrains and rondeaus or more complexly in for example, sonata form or Wagnerian leitmotivs. Song refrains are perhaps the simplest example, but the somewhat equivalent rondeau form is very wide-spread even in formal music. Generally, formal music is more likely to vary the repetition of material, but it should be remembered that as late as Beethoven and Schubert exact repetitions of material were still quite common. Rondeaus are usually perceived by even the most inattentive listener since there are usually multiple repeats. However, a single repetition of an extended section of material may or may not be obvious. The listener may clearly perceive that some repetition is occurring without being able to specify the actual extent of it in the absence of complete concentration and multiple hearings. This probably could be demonstrated with a significant

166

portion of the classical literature depending on the distinctiveness of the start and end of the repeated material.

Sonata form can be viewed as a method of managing spaced repetition of musical material. The first subject (melodic material) is followed by the second subject before the return in varied form of the same material in the development section. A more exact repetition of the opening material occurs in the recapitulation. Atonal music, mainly for stylistic reasons, rarely makes use of clear (varied) repetition of distinctive musical material but when it does, its effect is similar as in tonal works (e.g. Berio's *Coro*.)

There is also the related effect of using subsets of the total material at any given time as opposed to the total set. A simple analogy might be a diatonic or chromatic scale played one note at a time or as a chord with all the notes sounding at the same time. Even if the spacing or arrangement of notes were to change in the chord, the same basic elements are still present. In polyphonic or harmonically-based music, movement is felt by chordal progressions involving different scale degrees (see Schoenberg). Too similar chords create a loss of felt motion or static quality. Music that is very simple or very complex can arrive at a similar point if their pitch elements don't vary much from one segment to the next.

Despite the lack of clear rondeau or repetition, works using the 12-tone series or other atonal works constructed on similar plans (e.g. Messiaen) nevertheless do often have a perceived consistency or coherence. The basis for this probably occurs indirectly. Instead of perceiving a particular series or motive in all its permutations and harmonic constructions, listeners are sensitive to the repeated occurrence of particular adjacent melodic intervals and harmonies and the exclusion of many other intervals and harmonies.

As long as the listener's expectations are not upset by something too definitely different from the established norms of the work (e.g. a regular scalar passage or dominant cadence in a 12 tone work), they should perceive local consistency and perhaps even overall consistency. The perception of consistency would depend on more than the piece's adherence to a complex and varied set of material too extended to reside in short-term memory and lacking in the aids to memory provided by a hierarchically organized scale.

Repeated listening to a composition can overcome to some extent the difficulties that the listener has in relating non-juxtaposed passages to each other. However, it is probable that composers and analysts rather overestimate the influence of such processes compared to the very strong effect produced by recency and primacy effects (see Cook). In the context of a musical work therefore, the sense of continuity or coherence should be based most strongly on local progressions and their relation to the initial passages. In other words, if one passage moves smoothly into another passage, continuity is likely to be felt even if the differences between beginning and ending passages are quite noticeable.

Sufficiently extended tonal compositions show no particular loss of coherence by ending in different keys than were used at the outset. As noted previously, composers such as Mahler and Nielsen ended compositions in remote keys from the initial key without thereby disrupting the unity of the composition. Additionally, the tonal pattern of symphonies became so complex that remote keys were used throughout the work, even in large sections of the final movement. The return to the tonic key at the end could occur through some tonal sleight of hand such as the augmented sixth chord.

It is highly questionable that a sudden return to the tonic under these circumstances could convincingly restore a sense of unity that would be lacking if the work ended in a strong cadence in another key. If recency effects have greater strength, then the coherence of extended tonal compositions stems from the nature and consistency of local (sequential) progressions and melodic memorability far more than from a complex and abstract tonal schema.

Music score readers remember music with the support of verbal or symbolic labels supplementing the memory of the sounds themselves that aid in the memory and processing of certain aspects of musical form. Such labels effectively reduce the amount of information that needs to be remembered or processed and aid memorability. The process is similar with pictorial information. The label *Mona Lisa* is a sufficient cue that brings to mind a complex pattern of graphical and coloring relationships that exist in the actual painting by Leonardo. However, the cue or label is not a simulation or fuzzier image of the sound or image; it is a totally different and simpler way of characterizing aspects of the work.

Providing verbal labels for musical passages certainly reduces the complexity of information needed to remember something but it also creates a distortion of the original event. The verbal label selects certain features of the musical passage for emphasis and minimizes others. In many cases, the aspects selected are those more susceptible to verbal description than those that are not. In some cases the label describes the structural aspect of the passage rather anything to do with the sounds themselves, as is the case with labeling a sonata recapitulation or a fugue or a rondeau. The structural relationship exists independently of the particular notes used to implement that musical form (see Sloboda).

A listener who does not use such abstract labels might remember a recapitulation section of a sonata instrument by remembering a particular melodic phrase or the use of particular instruments (e.g. trumpets, cellos) that forms its musical substance. The disadvantage is that commonalities between such works are not easily perceived by focusing on the precise musical realization of the sonata form. However, the advantage is that the individuality of works is perhaps more directly experienced.

It is hardly an accident that musical criticism concentrates so heavily on harmonic and motivic analyses and major structural regularities and so little on melody, rhythm and sonority, let alone the conjunction of all these elements in any given musical work. Even complex harmony is easy to describe verbally, while rhythm or sonority are quite difficult to describe in a meaningful or analytical way. Yet it is doubtful that the listener puts the emphasis on harmonic relationships when a work is played or in trying to remember it except in the most general way (e.g. romantic, atonal, modal harmonies). It is clear though that making use of such labels and descriptions does reduce the amount of information that would need to be processed through short-term memory.

Thus, short-term memory limits, while a universal constraint, can be alleviated through various strategies of processing information such as chunking or labeling. Such strategies, however, are not always useful in accurately remembering the original musical sounds and generally involve the recoding of the original musical event into a combination of verbal descriptions and simplified representation of the sounds. Recency effects are associated with higher levels of recall; in a musical context, the character of local progressions and sequences are easily perceived by the listener. Dissonance between two adjacent chords is immediately apparent to the typical listener, whereas non-sequential dissonance such as might occur between a chord in one measure and another chord occurring two measures later is rather difficult or impossible to perceive under normal listening conditions. Non-adjacent relations are mostly learned from analysis of a musical work rather than listening except where repetition or obvious highlighting are used. Stylistic attributes can have significant effect on the memorability of a piece if they are facilitative or contrary to memory processes. The effect of particular musical forms typically has similar effects even across genres such as tonal or atonal music.

Recognition vs. Recall of Musical Passages

Recognition and recall are the two main procedures which are used to test memory. Recognition is considerably easier since the to-be-remembered event is presented again and the person simply needs to decide if they have seen or heard it or if it is something new. Recall is a more active process since the person must remember previous information with some cue other than the item itself. For example, a recognition test could present the melody to the *Star Spangled Banner* and the person would have to say if they have heard it before. In a recall test, the person would have to sing or play it from memory based only on the verbal cue. In terms of listening to a musical work, the return of the main theme or refrain would involve recognition by the listener that the melody or passage is a repetition of something presented earlier. Generally, listeners can identify identical repetitions of simple or distinctive musical material. However, recognition can become more difficult if the repetition of a musical event or passage is modified or varied in some way. Almost invariably, a musical repetition involves a change in the context of that passage even if the passage itself is unchanged.

In simpler music, a refrain or other repetition is usually presented in identical or nearly identical fashion on each recurrence. What variety exists in the work is kept to the intervening sections or passages. The composer or songwriter makes an effort to ensure the recognition of the repetitions often through a change in some important aspect between the refrain and the intervening passages (e.g. a distinctive melody, change of instrumentation, rhythmic shift).

In formal music, musical material that is presented more than once is typically modified, sometimes considerably from occurrence to occurrence. The likelihood of recognition by the listener decreases as a function of the amount of change and degree of distinctiveness in such circumstances. If the repeated (and unchanged) passage is more extended, complex or less distinctive, recognition will become less likely in the absence of many re-hearings or analysis of the score. As one would expect, increasing the time interval between successive presentations also negatively affects the likelihood of recognition.

The above examples involved recognition of a repeated musical passage or material. Musical recall possesses a higher order of difficulty that most listeners cannot be expected to accomplish. For example, in a set of variations, the listener has to recall the initial theme in order to assess the nature of the difference between the theme and a given variation. The greater the interval between theme and variation, the more difficult the task. Composers usually make the task easier by making gradual changes in the theme and by putting similar variations together. Another example, would be recalling the context of a previous presentation. Wagner's later operas contain sets of motives tied to particular characters and ideas. One motive can be juxtaposed with another motive to musically illustrate some action in the drama. A later presentation of the motive might occur in a different context. The listener might recognize the repeated motive (if not too modified) without recalling the prior context or particular juxtaposition with other motives. Recall would be much less likely than recognition in this and similar circumstances.

Judgment/Categorization

Although the primacy effect is weaker than the recency effect in short term memory, it is also true that in the context of musical works, the initial passages have a strong impact on the listener's categorization of the work into particular styles. Categorization is not dependent on short-term memory constraints since it stems from the long-term memories of past musical experiences. A musical style represents a collection of standard progressions, instrumentation, rhythms and so on that the listener has come to group together in a category based on some distinct set of features. Western music is typically divided into romantic, neoclassical, baroque, jazz and other well-known musical categories.

171

The listener, when they hear a new work, attempts to place it in a known category as they would for non-musical events. Thus, the initial measures of a work have a disproportionate influence since the listener expects them to define what will follow. For example, if a piece starts out in a Baroque style and then suddenly switches to a Romantic style, the listener regards this as bizarre and disconcerting even though the actual differences in purely musical characteristics between the sections may be no greater than the typical discontinuities within an extended stylistically consistent work such as a symphony.

The adverse reaction is due to the abrupt disconfirmation of the listener's firm expectation that the category of a work can be ascertained in its opening section. The same reaction would occur if the sound of a siren were interjected briefly in pianissimo in the middle of a 12-tone work. The siren noise heard at low volume is not necessarily more dissonant than the preceding music but the 12-tone style does not customarily contain such noise since it disturbs the harmonic consistency of the series.

It is important to note that atonal music is a much more open-ended category since it can be almost anything not tonal or not modal. And yet a listener will still try to use the initial section to categorize what will follow. Atonal works that maintain the general style of their initial section as well as specific motivic forms thoughout are likely to be perceived as more 'normal' than those that do not.

The tendency to categorize musical works of course makes the appreciation of new styles more difficult. A work which represents a stylistic innovation typically incorporates many elements from traditional or current styles, while adding new elements or exaggerating existing characteristics. (The more extreme innovations or experimentations of the 20th century have generally moved beyond connoisseurs only when tamed by use in a dramatic context or by incorporation into a simpler, more conventional setting.) The listener has certain expectations set up but receives less reliable confirmation compared to a work in a familiar style.

People are excellent at judging relative frequencies of different events or outcomes. This implies that they recognize a repeated event as a repetition rather than something new as we noted above. The various stylistic features that composers use, whether common to a more universally accepted genre or personal idiosyncrasies and tendencies, all exert their pervasive effect on the relative frequency or probability that some events are followed by other particular events. In other words, a musical style promotes certain event frequencies and correlations with other events and minimizes others. To take an obvious example, the tonal music style ensures a higher probability of dominant progressions than found in modal or atonal music. This is why composers feel the need for a system that they can work within rather than simply writing down what seems right (see Schoenberg).

So-called difficult music (not simply dissonant) probably stems from the same cause of relative unpredictability. In terms of music scales, styles that have a defined subset of the total possible notes are generally judged simpler than those that use the total set of elements, e.g. diatonic vs. chromatic scales. However, the true factor is the degree of restriction and correlation of note sequences inherent in the style. For example, the works of the early organum composers sound stranger and more complex than many later medieval works because of the relatively high degree of freedom of movement between possible scale (hexachord) notes and the less predictable vertical sonorities. The range of each voice is quite restricted and diatonic all the same. A vague parallel exists between the above comparison and that of Ockeghem in the 15th century or by the 20th century neo-classicists. In both cases, these works sound more complex (because of greater variability) than the relevant parallels (Ockeghem's contemporaries or the classical composers, e.g. Haydn, Mozart), although maintaining a diatonic melodic and harmonic style.

It is through repeated listening that audiences begin to develop a grasp of an innovative work's structure. But this is simply a case of external repetition, so to speak, compared with the internal repetition (however disguised) that a composer inserts into the composition itself. The conductor Toscanini would sometimes repeat a work in concert (e.g. Sibelius' *Symphony 4*) that the audience failed to react to as Toscanini felt they should. However, such external repetition cannot substitute for audible internal organization, at least as far as a listening audience is concerned, although the repetition may permit internal organization to be grasped.

On the other hand, people find total predictability boring. For example, the psychological research indicates that with most (non-paying) tasks people generally prefer an approximately even chance of success versus failure because of the relative challenge. This finding is hard to transfer directly to music listening partly because the process of listening is more passive than active for most people. Nevertheless, even the most casual or uninformed listener prefers some modest deviations from total predictability in the musical flow. This preference does not necessarily depend on harmonic novelty; melody, rhythm or instrumentation can also afford relief from too great predictability. In this, music shows itself not far from drama or even literature, which also depend on some conflict and eventual resolution for their affective power, as opposed to painting and sculpture, which rely on balance and analogy (see Meyer). The reason of course lies in the temporal extension of the former (even a short story can't be read in one glance) and the purely spatial extension of the latter art forms.

6

Modal Study Song (Ionian-Aeolian)

A Study Song Composition is provided to illustrate the procedures and stylistic issues related to composing modally as described in previous chapters. To make the discussion as straightforward as possible for readers still much more comfortable with the standard tonal system, the Ionian-Aeolian modal dyad was chosen. The Study Song is meant as a simple example but the following chapters will present longer study compositions in all three modal dyads to explore more aspects of modal composition. The Study Song composition is displayed in the next section. The work is scored for clarinet and piano. To make the analysis easier, the Study Song follows a conventional form with a short Intro, Verse 1 and 2, Chorus, Verse 3, Break with Bridge, Chorus and Outro.

To assist the reader in their own composing and songwriting, a practical orientation guides the detailed measure by measure analysis of significant aspects of the work. The analysis focuses on the particular ways that musical features discussed in this book are used in the piece as well as some of the compositional decisions that should be considered in writing modal music. It is not intended to provide a rigorous musicological description.

Readers are encouraged to re-compose measures or even whole passages of the composition to see the extent and musical value of the difference on the part and the whole. In addition, writing a similar Study Song in the other two dyads will be a highly useful exercise. Although an effort was made to give it at least some aesthetic value, the composition was purposely kept fairly straightforward so as not to complicate the discussion; in other words, pedagogical concerns outweighed aesthetic concerns.

As part of the analysis, chords are named according to their position in the operative mode, e.g. III, V^7 etc. This is no different than with tonal system analyses. It should be noted that in these modal pieces, however, the greater rhythmic flexibility and increased melodic character of the various parts, including the bass, make it more difficult to specify the chordal sequence as precisely as in most tonal music. This is because there is more likelihood of chord notes being spread over a few beats in the parts and the greater possibility of notes outside that chord occurring in one of the parts. When a chord assignment is particularly problematic, a justification will be offered in some cases.

The reader should also view this analysis as a starting point rather than a final conclusion. In the case of disagreement between the given reading and their own, readers should consider the context of the different chord notes, such as their position in the phrase or doubling in addition to their hierarchical status in the mode. Briefly presented or incomplete chords are not always specified in the analysis either.

With respect to the overall character and compositional stance taken in this Study Song, a preference was given to finding fresh ways of creating musical flow and texture. Since thousands of scores and musical analyses are available on traditional techniques such as imitative counterpoint, canon, fugue, typical suspension effects, tonal sequences and bass accompaniment, these have not been emphasized. Of course, these techniques are not incompatible with modal composition or even with the scalar dyadic system proposed here. The reader may use these traditional techniques in their own compositions or try some of the effects presented in the Study Compositions.

The Study Song is set in the Ionian mode, but does make use of Aeolian brief modulations and parenthetic harmonies. As noted before the Ionian mode is the basis for the current major scale while Aeolian is the basis for the current minor scale. But the use of harmonic and melodic minor scale variants is not available with the Aeolian mode, which retains its basic minor harmonic status throughout. The key structure is quite simple since it begins and ends in **C** Ionian, with brief diversions to neighboring keys for both **C** Ionian and **A** Aeolian. The Break is mostly in **D** Aeolian (one flat) and **G** and **F** Ionian are most frequently touched on for harmonic variety.

The time signature should also be noted. Since the modal system permits more rhythmic independence, the parts don't necessarily observe true 4/4 meter which is why the time is set at 8/8. Within the measure, the division of the beats is not entirely predictable and may differ between parts in the same measure, although the barline itself is a somewhat more reliable guide to stress. To avoid confusion, references to particular notes will include the (piano) octave too (e.g. **C3**, **A5**). The score is presented at concert pitch (in **C**).

176

Analysis:

Measures 1 - 17

The first measure is an upbeat half measure (4/8) on a **C** Major seventh chord arpeggio. This half measure and measure 1 constitute the Intro. Note the arrangement of notes in the arpeggio which emphasizes the seventh (**B**) to provide a bit of harmonic tension. An arpeggio just on the **C** Major triad would be very static sounding and provide little forward movement. In the first full measure the arpeggio continues in the bass while the treble staff has an introductory melodic phrase. The melodic phrase emphasizes the upper triad of the **C** major seventh from **E** to **B** before falling back to **C** at the start of the Clarinet melody in m.2. Note that the first three notes of the Piano melody are the same first three notes of the Clarinet melody.

Let's take a closer look at m.1. The bass arpeggio is slowed down to eighth notes. This better prepares the rather moderate melodic movement of the Clarinet. The **B** is included but in a less prominent way and it is the widely spaced **C** major triad which ends the measure. In the treble staff, a chromatic note in introduced the **A♭**, which has a melodic and harmonic implication. Harmonically, the **A♭** points to **C** Aeolian with its 3 flats. Melodically, the **A♭** provides a motif of a semitone and whole tone sequence also present in the opening Clarinet phrase, albeit ascending there.

The phrasing is somewhat irregular as well and produces a gentle clash of hemiola with the regular rhythm of the bass. The first triplet is displaced an eighth note by the two sixteenth notes. Also the slurring indicates a phrase grouping of two 3s and two 2s. This phrasing creates a bit more momentum to the **C** ending the motif. Also looking back at the upbeat half measure we see an asymmetric grouping with the slurs. The first goes from **C2** to **G2** and the second slur from **C3** to **C4**.

In m.2 the Clarinet melody begins with the half step whole step motif in a triplet but then unexpectedly pauses before leaping a sixth to **E**. An unexpected rest can be as noticeable as a note but obviously they have to be used for a purpose and not overused. Pauses at the end of phrases are almost unnoticed. Here the pause highlights the leap and shapes the phrase by making the top note a clear balance point and setting up the descent in mm 3 and 4. The Piano in m2 performs a mostly harmonic function starting with **F**, the Subdominant, moving to **G**, the Dominant, before easing back to the **C** Major triad in m.4. So **C** Ionian initially is

177

established by melodic phrasing as well as by harmonic movement. Note also the rising and falling lines of the Piano bass part. While not really a walking bass line found in jazz it does provide motion and impetus often lacking in tonal bass parts that are more purely harmonic in their function.

In mm. 3-6 the main Clarinet melody unfolds. Motives from this melody will be found in succeeding Clarinet and Piano phrases. The Clarinet melody starts out over a **C** Major triad and ends on a **G** Major triad. The harmonies move in various root and inversions through **C**: VI III II I⁶ V. However an unexpected **F♯** in m. 5 gives a mild suggestion of **G** Ionian to the **G** Major triad in m.6. The **G** Major triad is emphasized in m.6 as preparation for a parenthetic modulation to **G** Aeolian in the next verse phrase, the parallel key obviously to **G** Ionian.

The point of these different maneuvers is to clarify by distinction and contrast the different modal keys in the piece but most importantly clearly define **C** Ionian without the usual major-minor system formulae. The IV and V are the major threats to the stability of the Tonic key because they lie on the circle of 5ths. The other potential confusion is with parallel keys in the other modes. On **C** for example there are 7 different modes using it as a key, only two of which are part of the dyad, in this case the **C** Ionian and Aeolian.

The second verse is telescoped soon after the end of verse 1. One of the characteristics of the tonal system is the tight control maintained by the harmonic rhythm. This is what produces in less expert hands the vamping at the end of a phrase. The looser harmonic structure of modal music permits more flexibility phrasing or at least makes it easier to create. The intent here is to maintain a bit of urgency to the basically gentle melodic content of the Clarinet part. The second verse starts with a two note upbeat in m.6 which sounds like the initial triplet phrase in m.2. The actual triplet though occurs in m.7 in inverse (descending) form to m.2. It also introduces a chromatic note **E♭** as the pivot between the m.6 upbeat and the triplet figure. Actually the chromatic alteration is required in **C** Ionian to maintain the half step whole step relation initiated in m.2 when descending from **E** to **C**.

The **E♭** also establishes the start of a move to **G** Aeolian from its parallel key **G** Ionian, confirmed in the Piano part in the same measure. But then the key slips into **D** Aeolian in the next measure downwardly sliding VI, V, IV and then to the Tonic **D** in m.9. The harmony then moves on in .10 back to Ionian **C**. The Clarinet melody in the second verse very loosely follows the outline of the first verse melody, but with many changed details. One of the more interesting details is the

178

diminished octave relation of between the two verses in their initial triplet figure. Also note that the melody descends at the phrase end in verse 1 and ascends in verse 2. Modal music is dependent on a melodic and rhythmic impetus so a bit of dissonance and attention to melodic/rhythmic balance and contrast is part of the style. Also, occasional wider leaps of the melody or in the accompaniment are more important in modal music to give inner life to the movement.

The second verse melody ends in m.11 with the Clarinet melody returning to **C**. Note that the harmony on the downbeat is actually **C**: IV (preceded by **C**:V in the prior measure) with a Tonic **C** arpeggio only on the second beat. This interposed plagal cadence suits the mildly chromatic sinuous nature of the second verse. Unlike the foreshortened segue between the first and second verse, mm. 11 and 12 contain a slightly expanded sequence. This expansion permits a more energized push into the third verse. As was mentioned above, harmonic vamping between verses is found fairly often in tonal songs. Here with more harmonic flexibility it is useful to better integrate such transitions.

The transition has the top staff change from the treble to the bass clef in order to more easily create a rising sequence that will still end below the Clarinet melody in m.13. The syncopated rhythms with both Piano staves mostly within an octave creates a bit of a rumble and change of register from the preceding measures. The Clarinet melody in verse 3 opens with a combination of the verse 1 and 2 openings. The triplet figure is back to what it was in verse 1 but the pause is replaced by the upbeat phrase from verse 2. Thus the leap of a sixth in the first verse is softened to a leap of a fifth. The verse 3 melody stays closer to the form of verse 1 until m.15 where the upward sequence is interrupted by an unexpected move down to **A**4 and then followed by the leap of a sixth to **F♯** that went missing back in m.13. After this bit of excitement the melody returns to the basic outline of verse 1 to the close in m.17.

Measures 18 –27

The Piano part in verse 3 is quite different from that found in verse 1. Just because the melody is similar doesn't mean that the accompaniment must also be the same if there is a reason to change. Here it seems useful to continue the syncopated rhythms of the transition to verse 3 particularly as this verse is followed by the Chorus. A complete return to verse 1 melody and accompaniment creates a somewhat static section and a weak lead-in to the Chorus. The rhythmic syncopation does slow down appreciably so that the Clarinet melody is not overwhelmed by too active accompaniment.

Harmonically, the F♯ does push the key to **G** Ionian at the verse 3 end as with verse 1. The key switches back to **C** again in m.17. Due to the emphasis on the **C** Ionian Dominant and its parallel Aeolian key it seems useful to more definitely fix its relation to **C** Ionian headed into the Chorus. To this end, an augmented chord on **C**:V occurs in m.18 which resolves to **C**:I at the start of the Chorus, or more precisely on the second eighth note of the downbeat. The slight displacement creates more momentum to the Clarinet fanfare in m.19.

The Chorus melody in the Clarinet part is a fairly simple fanfare melody, however the character is altered by its rhythmic irregularity. The fanfare melody is repeated in m.21. Interspersed with the Clarinet melody are the Piano responses to it in m.20 and 22. The first response is in **F** Ionian and the second response is in **G** Ionian. Thus **C** Ionian is bracketed by the Dominant and Subdominant. Since they are just transient brackets around **C** Ionian they present no danger to the key but in fact center it between them.. Note also that the block chords of the Piano part differentiate it from the verses.

Measures 28 – 40

There is a short transition from the Chorus back to the verses. It switches back to **F** Ionian as the Dominant key **G** has been dwelt on enough in the first part. Note the even ascent in the Clarinet in m.25 which slows the movement as preparation for the return of the verses in m.28. Similarly in the Piano bass staff in m.27 there is a scalar descent to **C** in octaves planting the return of the verse firmly in **C** Ionian again. In m. 29 after the two note upbeat the triplet phrase is shifted down a minor third to the **C**5, which permits the phrase to be used without chromatic alteration. This also scales back the tension in the melody.

The remaining two verses have a Clarinet melody that adheres to the opening verse melodies more closely than the immediately preceding verses have. However there is a new Piano part accompaniment. In this situation, the Piano part is more gently rocking with an eighth note motif derived from m. 3. Note that the Piano bass part has less of an ascending and descending motion, moving within a narrower range. This general reduction in tension has the purpose of providing a bit more surprise and excitement to the instrumental break that follows.

The last verse has a bit of mild embellishment to the Clarinet melody which unexpectedly ends on a rising chromatic ascent to the **A**. **A**

180

Aeolian is the last remaining unexplored member of the close keys to **C** Ionian in this case obviously the relative minor. Could the **F♯** and **G♯** be unauthorized indicators of the tonal harmonic minor? The harmonies in m.37 make it clear that rather than the harmonic **a** minor of the tonal system this is a parenthetic harmony in **A** Ionian as is established by the **C♯** and the positioning of the **F♯** and **G♯**. This unexpected segue into the break quickly moves on quickly to the more normative **A** Aeolian the relative of **C** Ionian in m.38 then to **D** Aeolian then to an augmented sixth chord **F♯-A♭-C-E♭** resolving to the Dominant of **C** or **G** in m.42.

The character of the break is more typical of instrumental performance than the melody and accompaniment of the verses and chorus. So the speed and range of notes in the Piano part exceed what has occurred before. The Piano ascends to **G**6 in m.41 but note the scalar pointing of **D**, **E**, and **F** in the preceding measure.

Measures 41 – 54

The bridge passage between the break and the return of the Chorus starts in m.42. Although the augmented sixth chord strongly pointed to the **C** Ionian Dominant, the verses preceding the break were pointing to the key more directly as well, as can be seen in mm. 27 and 28 in the Piano bass part. The break has a strong confirmation of the Dominant followed by the Tonic **C** in m.43. The next measure returns to the Dominant that leads to a surprising return of the opening arpeggios in the Piano bass. Unlike the opening this time there is a rhythmic figuration in the treble which changes the character of the bass part. This prepares the return of the Chorus in m.46.

There are some changes to the Chorus accompaniment and just a minor added grace note in the Clarinet part. It is worth pointing out that the fanfare triplet has the same step pattern as in the verses. The falling 4th is also present in similar fashion in the previous verses. In the Piano bass part is the first appearance of the closing cadential figure fixed clearly on the **C**^{M7} chord. Note also the slightly spiky responses o the fanfare by the Piano in **F** and **G** Ionian. This was an attempt to avoid too harmonically and melodically smooth and answer to the rhythmically skewed fanfare. Thus the leading tone triad was used to progress to the temporary tonic **F** or **G**.

In m.50 the Outro begins with a falling 4th from **C** to **G** and a quiet ending type phrase. In m.51 the repeated cadential figure in the Piano shifts off **C** to the Supertonic **D**. This initiates a short linear sequence **D-E-F-G** which falls to **C** at the end. The Clarinet has the sequence on the downbeat of **C-F-G-C.** Note also that closing phrase of the Clarinet in m.52 is the same as in m.25 except the **B♭** has become a **B♮**. To avoid too much repetition of the cadential figure in the Piano bass part, the penultimate measure contains an arpeggio in the bass and treble

In the final measure the cadential reaches **G** which serves as the bass of a I six-four chord. Note that the treble melody outlines the $\mathbf{C}^{M7}$ chord with the **B** serving as the melodic leading tone here. The feeling of closure is based as much on linear movement as harmonic progression which has avoided typical tonal formulae.

This Song Study Composition though brief is a bit loaded with various effects and procedures for pedagogical reasons obviously. A songwriter might simplify the material in a more commercial way of course. But it is also true that there are other effects and progressions that could be used in concert or as substitutes for the ones present here. The reader is encouraged to write similar songs in the Lydian-Dorian and Mixolydian-Phrygian dyads. In the next 3 Chapters, more extended Study Compositions are provided for all three dyads.

Modal Study Song

Ionian - Aeolian

7

Study Composition in the Mixolydian-Phrygian Scalar Dyad

A Study Composition is provided to illustrate the procedures and stylistic issues related to composing in each dyad. The Mixolydian-Phrygian composition (M-P for short) is displayed in this chapter. The work is scored for six part clarinet choir in order to minimize issues related to orchestration and timbre, and also to provide more flexibility for part writing compared to keyboards. To assist the reader in their own composing and songwriting, a practical orientation guides the detailed measure by measure analysis of significant aspects of the work. The analysis focuses on the particular ways that musical features discussed in this book are used in the piece as well as some of the compositional decisions that should be considered in writing modal music. It is not intended to provide a rigorous musicological description. Readers are encouraged to re-compose measures or even whole passages of the composition to see the extent and musical value of the difference on the part and the whole.

Although an effort was made to give it at least some aesthetic value, the composition was purposely kept fairly straightforward so as not to complicate the discussion; in other words, pedagogical concerns outweighed aesthetic concerns. To this end, 'stylistically generated' chromaticism was severely restricted to avoid analytic complexity. The chromatic notes in the score represent the essential minimum necessary to maintain modal structure, within the present system and the overall form of the piece. In addition, to avoid analytic complexity, noteworthy musical features were spread through the score and essentially presented one at a time. This allows the effect of a particular feature or progression to be heard and assessed more clearly.

187

As part of the analysis, chords are named according to their position in the operative mode, e.g. III, V^7 etc. This is no different than with tonal system analyses. It should be noted that in these modal pieces, however, the greater rhythmic flexibility and increased melodic character of the various parts, including the bass, make it more difficult to specify the chordal sequence as precisely as in most tonal music. This is because there is more likelihood of chord notes being spread over a few beats in the parts and the greater possibility of notes outside that chord occurring in one of the parts. When a chord assignment is particularly problematic, a justification will be offered in some cases.

The reader should also view this analysis as a starting point rather than a final conclusion. In the case of disagreement between the given reading and their own, readers should consider the context of the different chord notes, such as their position in the phrase or doubling in addition to their hierarchical status in the mode. Briefly presented or incomplete chords are not always specified in the analysis either.

With respect to the overall character and compositional stance taken in these pieces, a preference was given to finding fresh ways of creating musical flow and texture. Since thousands of scores and musical analyses are available on traditional techniques such as imitative counterpoint, canon, fugue, typical suspension effects, tonal sequences and bass accompaniment, these have not been emphasized. Of course, these techniques are not incompatible with modal composition or even with the scalar dyadic system proposed here. The reader may use these traditional techniques in their own compositions or try some of the effects presented in the study compositions.

M-P is set in the Mixolydian mode, but does make use of Phrygian parenthetic harmonies. The key structure is quite simple since it begins in **A** Mixolydian, modulates to **G** Mixolydian, then back to **A** through **D** Mixolydian. Although two bass clarinets are used, it is mainly for the purpose of providing a continuous bass line. The two parts could almost be combined into one if an instrument that could be played without pause were used instead. The time signature should also be noted. Since the modal system permits more rhythmic independence, the parts don't necessarily observe true 4/4 time which is why the time is set at 8/8. Within the measure, the division of the beats is not entirely predictable and may differ between parts in the same measure, although the barline itself is a somewhat more reliable guide to stress. To avoid confusion, references to particular notes will include the (piano) octave too (e.g. **C3, A5**). The score is presented at concert pitch (in **C**) but note that the Bass Clarinets sound an octave below the written part.

Section 1 Analysis: Measures 1 - 16

The first measure shows right away that the parts will not strictly follow 4/4 time and that different parts may have conflicting meters. The 2nd B♭ Clarinet (2.B♭) has a 3-2-3 division of m.1 while the Basset-horn (Basset) has a conventional 4/4. The listener then should not be unduly surprised by flexible rhythms and mildly conflicting meters in subsequent passages. Melodically, the 2.B♭ phrase has a somewhat unusual structure, at least if this were a conventional work in the major-minor system. The leap of a minor seventh to **B4** not only occurs on the 4th beat of the measure (in 8/8) but also rises a major ninth above the opening **A3**. This gap-fill phrase is then filled by ascending motion instead of the more typical descending motion. The Basset part in m.1 has a different phrase structure, although it is only at beat 5 that the listener first detects that something is not quite regular between the two parts. Because of the entrance of the 1st Bass Clarinet (1.Bass) on beat 5, the 2.B♭ is spotlighted as having the discrepant rhythm.

The first harmony is **A** followed by **G^{M7}** at the entrance of 1.Bass. Presumably, the listener is expecting a tonal major or minor key to assert itself. Since this is m.1 the listener can't assume that **A** is the major key just because the first chord is **A**. So when the **G♮** enters in the bass, the implication is that this is a piece in **D** major (Ionian) and that **A** is the dominant. Notice that m.1 already contains every note in the scale of **A** Mixolydian. In m.2 the harmony reverts back to **A**, although not in decisive fashion, since the first two beats show no clear chord. The harmonic movement from **A** to **G** to **A** presages the Mixolydian key progression in the work as a whole as we will see.

The melodic phrasing comes back into alignment at the m.2 barline which defines the 8/8 meter. Note the congruence of all the parts at the beginning of the bar. This will prove the rule in the piece with only occasional exceptions. For example, in the first 20 measures, only 5 have tied notes crossing the barline in any of the parts. Thus, despite the metrical variability of the parts, a basic pulse is still present, though governed more by bar (line) than metric organization within the bar.

The first B♭ Clarinet (1.B♭) begins here with its own melodic leap of a major sixth. While similar to the minor seventh leap of the 2.B♭, it is also clearly not identical, indicating that the precise melodic intervals will not necessarily be confirmed across parts or in repetitions. The 1.B♭ melodic leap occurs in a more regular metrical position than the initial 2.B♭ leap. The variation between metric regularity and irregularity provides not only a certain level of variability, but also a comparison standard. Whether music is metrically constantly regular or constantly irregular amounts to much the same thing within a piece; it is only when there are changes between the two that the musical effect of irregularity can be assessed.

Although the barline does exert a consistent effect on the coincidence of notes, it is also true that the phrase structure is not governed by it to the same extent. Phrases are of varying length and, in addition, start and end at different parts of the measure. The reader should examine the initial phrases of the two B♭ Clarinets and the E♭ Clarinet in the initial seven bars and assess their relations and differences. Consider the effect of making them more regular in length or form as well as even more irregular while keeping the harmonic progressions the same. The relationship of the different voices (parts) to meter, barline and phrase length forms an important aspect of modal style. These features have a narrower range in most tonal compositions, so time spent analyzing them and trying out different balances in the reader's own compositions and songs should be valuable.

Returning to the Study Composition, in m.3, if the listener is expecting **D** major to assert itself, the movement from the **A** major chord to the **e** minor chord is disconcerting. While this makes sense within Mixolydian since it is a I - V progression, it would be a V - II progression in the key of **D** major. As noted previously, the tonal system generally did not use retrogressive (backward) moving progressions such as V – II, since it interfered with the dominant motion. The **e** minor (Mixolydian A:V) chord is followed by a Mixolydian IV⁶ which would be the **D** major tonic in the tonal system. Here, however, it is nothing more than a passing chord between two occurrences of Mixolydian V. Incidentally, this mirrors the movement from the Mixolydian Tonic to VII and back in m.1. The return to V here though occurs as a definite $V^6/_4$ since the **B3** in the 1.Bass arrives by leap. Again, the tonal system mostly avoided the six-four chord, except with the tonic cadence.

Modal composition should involve careful treatment in specifying a given mode. As noted, with seven modes, most short progressions can validly suggest two or more modes. Modal ambiguity can sound effective in the proper location but it should be composed rather than inadvertent. The modal composer has to consider using somewhat longer series of progressions to define a mode adequately and therefore can't rely as much on the short harmonic phrases that can be safely used in the tonal system. Given the universal acquaintance with the major (Ionian) scale, the assessment of modal ambiguity should always begin with it. For example, if a Lydian melody were ambiguous with both the Ionian and Mixolydian modes, distinguishing the Lydian mode from the Ionian mode would have a disproportionately large effect in reducing modal ambiguity. The contemporary listener, who currently tends to hear things in terms of the major-minor scales, is less prone to trying to force fit modes to a non-Ionian standard.

Before leaving m.3 there are some melodic features worth mentioning. Remember that melodic definition and shaping are an important aspect of modal composition. The notated barring and slurring shape the melodic phrasing in the 1.B♭ and the 1.Bass parts. In the 1.B♭ part, the slur and separated crotchets keep the eighth notes from dividing the measure irregularly. (If the eighth notes were barred together and slurred, they would create a 3-2-3 division which would parallel the division in m.1.) The 1.Bass slur, however, creates a slight irregularity since it pulls the **F♯** away from the **B4** with which it would normally be grouped in regular 4/4, thereby making the $V^6/_4$ more noticeable. The slur brings the 1.Bass rhythm more in line with the Basset rhythm in the measure.

In m.4 we have the first chromatic departure from **A** Mixolydian with the **C♮**. Since it occurs by skip, it won't be interpreted as a passing chromatic note and it is too soon for a modulation. The odds are then that the listener assumes it is a secondary dominant chord if they still think that the work is in the major-minor system. However, it makes no sense as a secondary dominant in the key of **D** major since it is an **a** minor (seventh) chord. Yet the chord which follows is a **D** major chord. In Mixolydian, this progression is {V⁷ of IV} - IV and is an example of a Mixolydian parenthetic harmony. In the key of **D** major, the progression has no particular meaning. Notice that the interpretation of the piece as possibly being in the key of **D** major (or Ionian) has been negated even though the root progression has gone from the dominant (albeit with flattened scale degree seven) of **D** to the (supposed) tonic! If the parenthetic harmony had not been introduced, the Mixolydian mode would be in danger at that point since there would have been a II - V - I cadence in **D** major instead of a V - {V of IV} - IV progression in **A** Mixolydian. The harmony swings back to V at m.5 on its way through VII to a definite cadence on I. Remember that in Mixolydian, the VII and the IV are in agreement with the tonic whereas V is not.

Turning to the melodic phrasing, m.4 marked the first switch between 1.Bass and 2.Bass. The two bass clarinets allow a continuous melodic bass part despite their individual inability to perform that function. It is worth pointing out that the bass part emphasizes the **A** and **E** in support of **A** Mixolydian in these initial measures, but does so in a melodic context. Also, the E♭ Clarinet makes its introduction here with a melodic leap of a fifth. The leaps now form a definite descending progression from minor seventh to major sixth to fifth. Additionally, the leap occurs at a different metrical point than the first two, confirming the melody's lack of regularity.

In m.8 a new rhythmic idea appears. Actually it appears in two different variants simultaneously, one of which is metrically irregular (compared to 4/4). The harmony in m.6 has moved off from the tonic towards the now neutralized subdominant and then to the diminished Mixolydian III in m.7. This paves the way not only for the m.8 rhythmic variant but also another parenthetic harmony, this time {IV of V}. However, instead of resolving to V it progresses to another parenthetic harmony {VII of V} before proceeding to V. Note that since Mixolydian V is a minor triad, the parenthetic harmony is in the Phrygian key of **E**.

Unlike the major-minor system, parenthetic harmonies in the Mixolydian and Phrygian modes can sometimes involve a double chromatic alteration. This occurs with parenthetic harmonies on Mixolydian V and VII for example. As we saw though, parenthetic harmonies on IV and II involve only one chromatic alteration. For this reason, parenthetic harmonies on V and VII are more noticeable. The selection of {IV of V} and {VII of V} as the parenthetic chords are in

192

keeping with the Mixolydian-Phrygian scalar dyad since triads on both scale degrees are in agreement with the tonic. The progression from III to {IV of V} is smoothed by the delayed appearance of the second chromatic alteration (F♮ in m.9).

After V is reached in m.10, there are two progressions to I through VII before a half-cadence on the dominant in m.13 occurs. This initiates a transitional passage, in which progressions of a major second briefly predominate, that will lead to a modulation to G Mixolydian. Note the descending triplet figure in the E♭ Clarinet since this will reappear at key points later in the piece.

Notationally, two features of phrase marking should be pointed out in these initial measures. In m.5 the Basset part has a combination <u>tenuto</u> and <u>staccato</u> on the G4 note. This marking is intended as a phrase shaper by slightly and only slightly stressing and detaching the note from the previous and following notes. The following note should be played as if it is the upbeat to the beginning of a phrase, or more likely, a subphrase, and by analogy this feature might be regarded as a slight intake of breath by a speaker. The other notational feature, the phrase (subphrase) bracket, appears in m.8 in the 1.B♭, 2.B♭, and the 1.Bass Clarinets. As discussed in Chapter 5, the bracket is used to mark a group of notes to be played as a unit without adding any indication of attack or articulation beyond what is already specified in the score. In this case, the eighth note E4 is played as more of an upbeat to the A4 and the preceding E4 quarter note becomes more attached to the melodic phrase in the previous measure.

Section 2 Analysis: Measures 17 - 40

In modulating from **A** Mixolydian to **G** Mixolydian, there are 2 overlapping triads **A**:V (**G**:VI) and **A**:VII (**G**:I) that could be used in a prepared modulation directly between the two. Using VII is a bit awkward since it is the tonic in **G** Mixolydian although it can be done with a little care. The V of **A** is more easily used since it can be reinterpreted as VI in **G**. However, a direct modulation could be somewhat abrupt sounding since there are two chromatic notes between the two keys. The reader is invited to try out different modulatory schemes to see what effect they have. One thing that should be remembered though is that the two note difference is also heard in Mixolydian (Phrygian) parenthetic harmonies as we saw. Thus, some preparation may have already occurred for that kind of movement, even in a mostly diatonic composition such as the present one.

Be that as it may, while V is used as a pivot, it really takes a quick motion through **D** Mixolydian as seen in the following progression VII - I - V^2 in m.17 and m.18 before settling firmly in **G** in mm.19-21. The movement is aided by a bit of parallelism in the progressions in m.17 compared with m.19. Melodically, yet another variant of the m.8 rhythm is introduced in the E♭ Clarinet melody in m.19, the first time that the rhythm is incorporated into a melodic figure. The slurring and the mild metrical rubbing of the two B♭ parts makes the cadence on I (**G**) more noticeable in m.21.

A more emphatic melody starts out in m.23 with a similar irregular division of the measure as in the beginning. Harmonically, this section has a variety of parenthetic harmonies based on each step except for VI (other than the diminished III and tonic, of course) that the reader should carefully examine. The location of the chromatic element in the parenthetic harmony will vary depending on its relation to its parenthetic tonic (as a triad in the main key). For two of the scale degrees, the parenthetic harmony can have two chromatic notes. In Myxolydian and Phrygian, the parenthetic harmonies have fewer sharps or more flats than the main key. For example, the {II of VII} in **G** Mixolydian is the II in the key of **F** Mixolydian (two flats) or a **g** minor chord (**G/B♭/D**) while {VII of VII} is an E♭ major chord (**E♭/G/B♭**).

The 1.Bass part assumes a more forceful role in mm.23-26, in part because of the emphasis on the low **D,** but also due to the prominent chromatic E♭ as part of the parenthetic chord {VII of V}. The reader should also note the phrase brackets in the 2.Bass part starting in m.30. These are guides to the player on how to shape and demarcate rather long and somewhat ambiguous lines. They should not just be viewed as specifying where a phrase begins and ends but also give an indication of the interior stresses as well when necessary.

The measures between 23 and 38 are essentially a build-up to a weak climax on G5 in m.39 but which also serve as an anticipation of the more forceful crescendo in the following section. Although **G** is the tonic at this point and does serve as an adequate target for a melodic peak, its position in the measure and in the melodic phrase tend to not reinforce its position. The reader should consider the enhancing and retarding factors at work in this passage. Perhaps the most obvious enhancing factor is the chromatic ascent from **D5** to **G5** in the E♭ Clarinet from mm.35-39. Another positive factor is the greater degree of rhythmic synchronization between the 2.B♭ and the Basset. On the other side, the G5 has been reached at the beginning of the section in both the E♭ and 1.B♭ and the A5 reached in the E♭ Clarinet in m.27. The A5 is ambiguous since it represents the top of a brief melodic arch rather than a culmination of any kind. The **A** is also not a principal melodic target in **G** Mixolydian since it is the second scale degree. It does provide a reminder of the initial **A** Mixolydian in a slight way. The reader is encouraged to further analyze this section both in terms of itself and also in relation to the piece as a whole.

Section 3 Analysis: Measures 41 - 64

A variation of the two 16th notes figuration in mm.17-18 appears in the 1.B♭ part in mm.40-42 as the E♭ Clarinet quickly descends from the G5. A more or less unprepared modulation to **D** Mixolydian occurs in m.41, although the effect is quite mild because of the essentially melodic way that it is introduced. There is one V - I cadence in **D** at m.43 but remember that in Mixolydian mode V - I progressions are not particularly strong. Another transitional passage ensues as the two 16th notes expand to four and the m.1 figuration is revealed in varied form. At m.47 a modulation back to **G** occurs using **D**:II as the pivot, with the IV - I cadence in **G** occurring at m.50 and again two measures later (IV – V - I).

At m.53 the 1.B♭ begins another melody, but with some structural significance. An upward leap of a tritone to **F5** on the 2nd (eighth note) beat, used for the first time, is promptly followed by a downward leap at the 4th beat of m.54. In m.55 the melody ascends to G5 on the 3rd beat followed by a downward leap. However, the E♭ Clarinet enters on the 6th beat of the same measure with a premature A5 and a cadence on **G**. The 2.B♭ picks up when the 1.B♭ stops in m.58 and continues on in the same way with the E♭ Clarinet until m.64.

There are two significant aspects to this duet (with three instruments!). The first is the role it plays in reinforcing the Mixolydian mode, but through an essentially melodic cadence rather than a harmonic one. The second is the way the beginning of the passage prefigures and prepares the very end of the piece, although this relationship might require more than one hearing of the work to be audible to the average listener because of the temporal separation between them.

In terms of the first aspect, there have been relatively few instances up to this point where two parts moved in melodic or even rhythmic unison, but all of those involved interior parts. This is the first time that the principal melodic part at a given point has moved in (rhythmic) unison with the second melodic part (counter melody). The premature entry of the E♭ Clarinet adds some tension to the duet, which is resolved when the falling 1.B♭ cadential figure fixes the tonic triad in m.57.

The second aspect is a little more tenuous simply because of the separation between the appearance of the premature **A5** in the E♭ Clarinet and the similar premature re-appearance in the penultimate measure. However, the **A5** is a stressed entrance note and completes an ascending sequence of **F - G - A** but in unexpected fashion. It is also worth pointing out that **A** is the tonic note of the initial (and closing key). We will revisit this when we reach those final measures.

Section 4 Analysis: Measures 64 - 82

Starting in m.65 and going to m.82, we have a varied recurrence of the passage from m.23 to 40. Note that the variation does not follow standard tonal practices. No measure is exactly the same as before and most are quite different, the harmonies are changed, the progressions end up in a different key and yet there is an unmistakable similarity (to my ears). The similarity is primarily due to occasional rhythmic or melodic agreement at key points and a gradually rising melody in the E♭ Clarinet which reaches **D6** at m.82. In a sense this section represents an inversion of the practice of variation in the tonal period (including harmonically-based jazz improvisation) in which stable harmonic progressions underlay changing melody and rhythm. If this variation has a more tangible relation to the original than many tonal system variations, it is testimony to the greater salience of melody and rhythm compared with harmony. Given the more relaxed flow of modal harmony (except in the Ionian mode), variations based more on melody and rhythm provide a more forceful way to organize the musical relations.

A measure by measure comparison would be overly tedious to present here but the reader might find it a useful exercise. I will compare the first 4 measures in each section just to start the reader off. Note that the lead-in to these two sections is completely different. In m.64 there is a parenthetic harmony with a falling melodic line and decrescendo followed by another parenthetic harmony at the start of the variation section in m.65. The m.22 lead-in, on the other hand, is a parenthetic harmony with a rising melodic line and crescendo ending in a trill.

Turning to the corresponding sections themselves, m.65 has rather more similarity with its progenitor m.23 than many in this section. The reader will notice that there is more correspondence in the beginning of phrases, which are more likely to be remembered across a temporal separation as exists here. The m.65 rhythm of the 1.B♭ part is identical to m.23 while the melody is similar but with noticeable changes in melodic skips. The Bass part is completely different not only in melody and rhythm, but also in total effect, being softer and smoother. It also changes the harmony of m.65 to a parenthetic chord compared with the IV^6 in m.23.

It is the Bass part in m.66 that rhythmically resembles the Bass of m.23, entering a bar later this time. Above it the Basset has the same rhythm as in m.24 but a different melodic line. The B♭.1 part is very different and more regular than m.24 but resumes close correspondence in mm.67-68. The reader can observe more detailed differences and correspondences at their leisure.

From here, we'll just describe the current section without reference to the prior. Measure 69 also contains the pivot chord G:IV (D:VII) to a modulation back to D Mixolydian, revealing the first modulation to D Mixolydian in the previous section as a genuine anticipation. However, the first occurrence of the tonic chord is reached in a slightly unorthodox sequence of progressions (II – VII – IV – V – II – I), but does occur cleanly on the first beat of m.71 with the tonic note in the 2.Bass. This kind of sequence would have been more problematic at the beginning of the piece, but not now that Mixolydian is well established.

The music in mm.68-75 now becomes more active with melodically crossing parts. In m.75 a parenthetic sequence on VII

197

introduces a two note chromatic change moving in fourths on the Mixolydian triads in agreement {VII of VII} – {IV of VII} - VII. In contrast, m.78 contains a parenthetic Phrygian harmonic sequence based on the key of V (**A** Phrygian). In this connection, note that the cadence in mm.80-81 has a semi-Phrygian cast even in the II - VII - I progression.

The reader should consider the relation between sections 2 and 4 in terms of the structure of the piece. What would be the effect of making the Section 2 ascent more forceful and structured? What would happen if the parallels between these 2 sections were reduced or changed? What is the effect of the kind of varied resemblance found here compared with traditional tonal techniques of variations based on harmonic progression or sonata exposition versus development?

Section 5 Analysis: Measures 82 - 131

Immediately after the peak, the key modulates through a melodic sequence of parenthetic harmonies {IV of x} into **A** Mixolydian before a delayed cadence on I^7 in m.92. Note that the melodic line in the mm.84 to 89 has a 16th note figuration which shifts position every two bars. More significantly, it represents a completely different texture from the entire preceding portion of the piece, with its staccato notes, repeated measures and short isolated figuration. The reader should consider the effect and placement of this short passage right after the major climax. What would be the effect if it occurred elsewhere in the work?

In the preceding sections, the Mixolydian mode has been made to display a more forceful, focused light, almost quasi-tonal at least in the sense of its forward motion. This final section shows a more relaxed modal aspect of Mixolydian. In mm.94-95, there is an extended parenthetic progression on II ({IV of II} – {VII of II} -II). Remember that in Mixolydian, parenthetic harmonies on II and V follow the Phrygian mode. Of course, since Phrygian is the minor mode of the scalar dyad, steps IV and VII are minor in Phrygian as they are major in Mixolydian.

Measure 97 contains a reminiscence of the E♭ Clarinet melody from m.19, although in more relaxed and rhythmically regular form. Harmonically, the music oscillates between VII, II and I, but with the tonic chord either in inversion or not sustained in a prominent way until m.103. The next four measures feature another varied reminiscence of the rising E♭ Clarinet melody but which atypically fades away as it ascends rather than growing louder. This leads into a prolonged parenthetic excursion on IV and a soft cadence on I. The measures from 97 to 112 provide a bit of rest from the strong melodic direction of the prior section; what Meyer has termed the weakening of shape.

At m.112 the music takes on a bit more forward direction again as the slow syncopation returns in the Bass, with the progressions avoiding IV while moving between II, V, VII and I. At m.117 the two Bass parts begin moving forcefully in unison in preparation for the end. At m.123, the 1.B♭ plays a loud descending rhapsodic phrase that peaks significantly at a C♯6 on the 3rd eighth note beat with a I7 harmony (in inversion), a semitone below the high D in m.82. This confirms the descending melodic line (see Schenker) from its peak until the end of the piece on the tonic A. In tonal pieces the descending melodic line is usually from the fifth to the tonic, but remember that in Mixolydian IV is a 'tonal' degree whereas V is not.

The progressions now favor IV and V as the 16th note figuration from m.1 makes a return on the 2.B♭. The rhythmic structure becomes more complex rather than simplifying while the harmonic progressions become more straightforward. Note the E♭ Clarinet flourish which suddenly leaps a fifth to A5 in the penultimate measure on the 5th beat. This is the corresponding effect to the premature entrance of A5 in m.55 noted previously. The appearance of the A5 in m.130 also sounds premature (I think). Notice that the descending linear sequence from D6 had the C♯6 enter on the 3rd beat (in 8/8) and the B5 enter on the 7th beat in m.127. The A5 however splits the difference by appearing on the 5th beat which even though more regular sounds almost offbeat. As in the duet to the tonic chord beginning in the m.55 sequence, this unexpected entrance more strongly prepares the conclusive final tonic chord (to my ears).

Study Composition 1
Mixolydian-Phrygian

M-P

M-P

M-P

M-P

M-P

M-P

M-P

M-P

M-P

M-P

M-P

M-P

M-P

M-P

M-P

M-P

M-P

M-P

8

Study Composition in the Lydian-Dorian Scalar Dyad

The Lydian-Dorian study composition (L-D for short) is displayed in this chapter. The work is scored for seven-part clarinet choir in order to minimize issues related to orchestration and timbre, but also to provide more flexibility for part writing compared to keyboards. To assist the reader in their own composing and songwriting, a practical orientation guides the detailed measure by measure analysis of significant aspects of the work. To repeat, the analysis focuses on the particular ways that musical features discussed in this book are used in the piece, as well as some of the compositional decisions that should be considered in writing modal music. It is not intended to provide a rigorous musicological description. Readers are encouraged to re-compose measures or even passages of the composition to see the extent and musical value of the difference on the pasage and the entirety of the work.

The Lydian mode is a rather 'exciting' mode not only due to the melodic tension of the hard-to-avoid diminished IV, but also due to the compositional challenges it presents. In diatonic passages, the pull of the Ionian dominant has to be constantly minimized, while chromatically lowering the subdominant is a problem; the Lydian mode can be in danger of direct confusion with the relative and parallel Ionian modes (for example, F Lydian with C Ionian or F Ionian respectively). The proposed modal system has resources available to control these tendencies, including the Dorian mode as the scalar dyad complement, but the composer/songwriter must effectively deploy them to avoid modal confusion.

The present composition is in the key of **F** Lydian (no sharps or flats) with a modulation through intermediate Lydian and Dorian keys ending up in **D♭** Ionian with a return to **F** Lydian. Thus, unlike the M-P study composition, the work has a between-dyad modulation. As mentioned a number of times before, such between-dyad modulations need to be carefully considered and integrated into the structure of the work to avoid modal incoherence.

The L-D study composition is scored for seven clarinets instead of the six in the M-P composition. There are two changes though, since not only is a Contrabass Clarinet added, but also a third B♭ Clarinet replaces the second Bass Clarinet in M-P. This change was made to avoid an overly dark balance.

Section 1 Analysis: Measures 1-22

The work starts out with a low F1 in the Contrabass moving briefly to the A1 after the entry of the Basset-horn (Basset) on a trilling A3. In tonal works this beginning low note could be the tonic or perhaps the dominant. Thus, the listener probably expects to hear **B♭** Ionian or **F** Ionian. In m.2 the Bass Clarinet (Bass) enters on another **A** as the Contrabass returns to F1; however, the Bass unexpectedly moves to a **B♮**. This limits the key to **C** Ionian for the average (tonal) listener (although **a** minor is a slight possibility) since neither the **F** nor **B** of the scale is chromatically altered. This makes it reasonable that the extended **F1** is the subdominant rather than the dominant. The expectation then would be for the **G** major triad to follow. The entry of the C3 in the Bass in m.3 simply completes the **F** major triad, as does the descent in the Contrabass to A0. M.5 introduces the E♭ Clarinet on a pesky, sustained B5. The emphasis on **B** would be comprehensible if it was linked to the dominant triad, but here it occurs over a repeated occurrence of the **F** triad - this time announced in B♭ Clarinets 1 and 2 (1.B♭, 2.B♭) and the Basset. The emphasis on the **F** triad and the **B** make this a rather illogical opening for **C** Ionian. The one thing that might make the listener uncertain as to the meaning is the obvious preludial character of these measures.

While harmonically these opening measures are largely static, melodically somewhat more tension is present. Returning to the opening measure for the Bass Clarinet, we see a curiously cut off rising phrase. However, this was anticipated in m.1 with the figuration in the Contrabass contrasting an extended note with a brief note. Cutting off a phrase in that manner induces surprise, unlike the Contrabass phrase in m.1 where the brief note is completed by the following **F1**. Again, in mm.8 and 9 we see a repetition of the cutoff phrase in the Bass, E♭ and B♭ Clarinet 3 (3.B♭). The pattern is unmistakable at this point and creates a strong forward anticipation despite the static harmony.

Although in m.8 the Contrabass finally reaches a **C1** it is disconfirmed as a tonic note by the (**d** minor) harmony at variance with **C** Ionian. In m.9 the 2.B♭ introduces a rapid wide-ranging figuration still based on the **F** triad, this time in the as yet undeveloped central octaves. Note that the preceding entries have been mostly in high or low registers. The 1.B♭ confirms the quickening movement in m.10, but in disconcerting fashion, due both to the extreme range of the figuration and also the surprising introduction of the **F♯**. This time the figure is clearly based on the **C** triad which seems to rule out **C** Ionian as a possible modal key. The listener now has to seriously consider the possibility of the Lydian mode since **F** Lydian has no sharps or flats while **C** Lydian has one sharp. While the Lydian mode is far from established, it is the mode at this point which best fits the music in any given part.

The Bass in m.12 begins the sustained triplet figures which signal to the listener that the piece is finally getting underway. The static character is definitely diminished in the ensuing measures although the preludial feel doesn't fully vanish until m.22 (at least to my ears). In m.13, the first instance of melodic bitonality occurs in the modal context. The Bass figure is based on **C** Lydian while the 3.B♭ is in **G** Lydian (two sharps). The E♭ Clarinet remains in **F** Lydian as does the Basset. Note that in the succeeding measures the E♭ Clarinet, 1.B♭ and 2.B♭ and the Contrabass all remain locked in **F** Lydian. In contrast, the 3.B♭, the Basset and the Bass can be in **F**, **C** or **G** Lydian or the dyad complement **D**, **E** or **A** Dorian. The stratified nature of the lines makes the melodic bitonality rather clear and direct and the rapid figuration reduces the chance of harmonic muddiness. Note also that while bitonality may raise questions about the current key, it actually serves to solidify the <u>mode</u> through multiple confirmations. In addition, melodic bitonality is easier to integrate into the modal system than more harmonically conceived bitonality since the latter approach makes it harder to maintain modal stability. The harmonies would have to be more vertically organized, but then would introduce a greater possibility of (apparent) amodality.

Melodically there are several things worth noting or clarifying. First, the mode and key are justified by the prominence of the given notes in these running figures; for example, in m.14 the Bass is said to be in **E** Dorian since the melodic figure has two sharps, begins and ends on **E** and has **B** for the high point. Similarly, the Basset part in m.15 is said to be in **F** Lydian since the figure has no sharps and flats and begins and ends on **F** with **C** linked to it at the end. Second, the keys used are all interpretable within **F** Lydian and its parenthetic harmonies. More distant keys could give a greater impression of chromatic contrast, but at the expense of coherence. (This is a stylistic issue rather than a mandate.) Third, note that the running triplet eight figures all end in a run of sixteenth notes. This serves not only as a way to close the phrase, but also as a variant of the cutoff figuration. Thus, there is a melodic and thematic integration across seemingly disparate parts.

In m.18 the cutoff figure becomes more sustained by the simple expedient of pairing one occurrence with a second and reversing the short note so that it comes first. Note how the C6 peak in m.21 is still undercut by an F♯ in the Basset. To my ears, the C6 does not sound like a potential tonic at this point anyway, perhaps in part because of the continuing prominence of the **B** (the ostensible leading tone). The chord which follows in m.22 is the first Lydian parenthetic chord in the piece, namely, a {V of V}. Since the key is F Lydian, the dominant is C and, as we know, C Lydian has one sharp.

It is important to remember that the position of the chromatic note(s) in parenthetic harmonies varies by mode. In this case the Lydian {V of V} has the chromatic note in the seventh. Thus, the chord in m.22 is actually the {V^{M7} of V} which is rather 'daringly' followed by the tonic **F** in first inversion. The term 'daringly' is only half-facetious since the listener does not have a couple of centuries of history to make the shortcut clear. In tonal works, this abbreviated progression for the standard {V of V} - V - I occurred sufficiently often to not baffle the experienced listener. In a modal work, it may be asking a bit much for the listener to understand the nature of the relation, particularly where the chromatic alteration is of the tonic itself. To make sure the F♮ is not missed, however, it is in the form of a sustained trill.

Section 2 Analysis: Measures 23 - 50

Measure 23 restarts the rising motive with a progression of Lydian I - V - IV - I which keeps the dominant in its place. The passage through the subdominant is a useful Lydian progression since the tritone is absorbed, so to speak, in the larger movement of the fifth. In addition, the harmonic and melodic motion aids the definition of the Lydian tonic and diminishes the tonic quality of the dominant. The hint of imitation provides a contrast compared to the more obvious ascent in mm.16-21. In this connection, imitation is better suited to modal music than the sequences that the tonal composers used (unless with the Ionian mode possibly). Without the support of the tonal armory, the harmonically-based sequence can sound somewhat empty.

M.24 starts another parenthetic harmony based on III (which is the tonic of **A** Dorian, having one sharp). The movement of {II of III} to {V of III} to III highlights the basic Lydian and Dorian mode progression. At this point there is no danger that this would be interpreted as the Aeolian (or **a** minor) tonic progression and the III occurs as a III² chord anyway. But this does point out the attention the composer must pay to such matters when dealing with the six (or seven modes). Note that the E♭ Clarinet rises to the recurring **B5** again in m.24 and immediately afterwards, but goes no higher until m.32. The music more energetically rises in m.25 but the downward sliding chords VII - VI - V – IV work against this motion. This progression probably could not work in a tonal piece without calling attention to itself, but in a modal context the effect is less obvious. The harmonic movement does presage some musical conflict because what ensues is a series of parenthetic chords based on II, III and VII respectively.

In m.27, the first parenthetic progression is actually an extended sequence ending in the Lydian key of **G** (based on F:II), moving from {IV of V of II} to {VII of V of II} to {V of II} and then to II. The next parenthetic progression moves from IV to VII in **A** Dorian (III) and the final one is a standard II to V progression in **E** Dorian (VII). These progressions are juxtaposed against two competing movements, a variant of mm.19-22 in the three high instruments and a syncopated triplet figure in the lower instruments. The contrary forces signal some manner of resolution or else the musical flow will be seriously impeded at this point. The intrusive C♯ (an appoggiatura?) in the VII (m.31) is the precursor. Although it technically resolves to the D5, it will appear enharmonically in the next measure as part of the augmented sixth chord based on IV. The high trill eases the way slightly into this chord.

One thing should be pointed out immediately about this augmented sixth chord. Since this is the Lydian mode, the IV is already raised (so to speak, given a tonal reference) so the only chromatic change is the lowered VI step D♭ (or C♯). Its effect though is amplified here by the preceding F♯s in the parenthetic progressions. The purpose of the augmented sixth chord is to point to the dominant and that is what follows. (Note also that the D♭ in the chord is the goal of the main modulatory movement in the piece.) Needless to say, the C triad sounds nothing like the tonic; in fact, to my ears it almost sounds dissonant itself in this context. This may be due to the unorthodox voice leading. The next chord is the tonic I (F Lydian!) whose appearance resolves the parenthetic and chromatic progression.

Now that the existence of the Lydian tonic has been verified, the introduction of the B♭ in m.34 suggests a modulation rather than the erstwhile key of F Ionian. A short excursion to B♭ Lydian does ensue, pivoting on the F:VI chord in m.33 and pivoting back on the B♭ Lydian VII in m.37. For the record, the progression would be more atypical if interpreted in the key of F Ionian (VI - II - I - IV) rather than in B♭ Lydian (III - VI -V - I).

This quickly leads to a flowing rising phrase which seems to be a smoother, less energetic version of the running triplet phrase at the beginning. This time the modulation to B♭ Lydian is more definite and is the start of the long movement towards D♭ Ionian. In m.44 we see the first parenthetic harmonies in B♭ Lydian, in this case based on II.

The final measures covered in this section, mm.47 - 50 are an example of a diatonic dissonant cadence discussed in Chapter 5. In this case, the cadence is extended and harmonically varied, but retains its cadential form through the even rhythm of successive half-notes and the consistent dissonant seconds between the 2.B♭ and 3.B♭ Clarinets. The reader can judge whether this is effective as a (tonal) cadence substitute and should try different solutions here to see their effect.

Section 3 Analysis: Measures 51 - 88

An important point to remember about Lydian progressions (and modulations) is that the parenthetic harmonies of the Lydian-Dorian scalar dyad are unbalanced in the direction of the dominant (one or two sharps). Thus, progressions are more easily accomplished in the ascending (sharper) direction than descending (flatter) direction. Conversely, the Mixolydian-Phrygian parenthetic harmonies are unbalanced in the direction of the subdominant (one or two flats). It is only the Ionian-Aeolian scalar dyad which has symmetrical parenthetic harmonies across the dominant and subdominant.

Since the current modulation is in the direction of flatter keys, the parenthetic harmonies work against that movement. However, we don't always need to be in a hurry and some help is available through using the other scalar dyad member, in this case, Dorian. Dorian has the advantage of a more easily usable subdominant and also greater harmonic stability, so that modulations don't need as much confirmation to be accepted. This technique was used here to ease the prepared modulation to the flatter keys in a reasonably short space of time.

The section starts in the **B♭** Lydian key established at the end of the previous section. The end of the cadence is announced in m.51 by the rapid figure in the Basset. Note the difference between the earlier triplet eight figures and this figuration in standard duple rhythm. The figure is clearly in **G** Dorian, the relative key to **B♭** Lydian, and a short but definite sequence in **G** Dorian ensues for the next 3 measures.

In m.56 a pivot occurs on the **G** Dorian tonic chord which is reinterpreted as the **C** Dorian subdominant. This immediately leads to a similar flowing ascending phrase, this time in **C** Dorian (two flats). The high melody is now taken over by the 3.B♭ which also reinforces the new key. In m.61 the 1.B♭ plays a rapid phrase in **C** Lydian reminiscent of those in the preludial outset, again melodically bitonal, which fortuitously happens to be the parallel key to **C** Dorian. Another bitonal phrase appears in the E♭ Clarinet which is in the original key of **F** Lydian, which happens to be the parallel key to **F** Dorian.

As it turns out, in the next measure a pivot chord on **C** Dorian: V (**F** Dorian: II) ushers in an ascending phrase in **F** Dorian for the 1.B♭ and 2.B♭ which evolves into the triplet eight phrase (mm.66-71). As it does so, however, it modulates into A♭ Lydian. This is the relative key to F Dorian and the tonic note has the useful property of being the dominant of D♭, the goal of this motion (albeit in a different mode). Notice that the interval of the instrumental doubling is not uniform, varying between thirds, sixths, fourths or seconds. In the tonal system this kind of variability would play havoc with tonal harmony. In a modal context, however, where the scale is the dominant force, the variability merely adds coloristic harmony to the lines as long as it doesn't deviate overmuch from the key (mode).

A new rhythmic variant of the cutoff figure also enters in these measures (see, for example, the Bass part starting in m.67). The variant consists of the short note in both preceding and following position appended to each other. This rhythmic variant will play a significant role in the next section. The music solidifies in A♭ Lydian in the measures between 71 and 86 while the melodic motion starts to fragment slightly with frequent changes of grouping or rhythmic independence.

A bitonal figuration appears in m.84, this time in G Lydian before suddenly veering back into A♭ Lydian. G Lydian represents the furthest pole of F Lydian (through its parenthetic harmonies) since it has two sharps. Interestingly, the C♯ (D♭) is the goal of the present movement. In mm.85-86, the music modulates into D♭ Ionian through a slowed down variant of the triplet figure.

Section 4 Analysis: Measures 89 - 124

The start of the D♭ section is clear-cut with two <u>tutti</u> chords, first on the pivot A♭ VI (D♭ III) and then on D♭ VI⁹. Placing the tutti on these lesser (non-agreement) chords of the Ionian scale keeps them from becoming too important in the context. There have been few tutti chords and these two are supposed to lead in to a new section rather than end the piece. The second tutti chord leads to the dominant and subdominant of D♭ Ionian and then a sequence of parenthetic chords on II in mm.92-3. Since II is a minor chord, the harmonies are Aeolian in nature (E♭ Aeolian with six flats). Remember that the modal system does not alter their form as the tonal system

230

does. The parenthetic sequence of IV - II - V in the key of E♭ Aeolian closes on II in m.94.

A mild cadence on the tonic occurs in mm.95-6 with the VII - I (leading-tone) progression. Ironically, the tonal system made modest use of this progression. In m.97, another parenthetic sequence based on III begins in the key of F Aeolian. In m.103, a parenthetic sequence on IV commences a progression of V - VI - III in the key of G♭ Ionian, which has six flats (or sharps) of course.

The gentler melodic texture is matched by a slower harmonic pace where chordal movement occurs more from measure to measure rather than within a measure. A short sequence in D♭ occurs in mm.106-10 after the subdominant closes the parenthetic sequence. To provide a bit more impetus, a final parenthetic sequence on V starts in m.111 with a IV - V progression in the key of A♭ Ionian. The dominant activity triggers a return of the urgent melodic figure which occurred leading up to the augmented sixth chord in m.32. The insertion of a parenthetic harmony in m.118 provides a structured chromatic ascent to the D♭6 in m.119.

Rather than repeating that earlier sequence (around m.32), which would be a bit obvious, the music retreats into a softer passage (mm.120-23). Note that the high placement of the melody maintains tension by registral effects. Concurrently, the key and mode modulate in m.123 back to F Dorian pivoting on D♭ Ionian III which is actually the F Dorian tonic. However, here it is in double inversion. As the texture simplifies in m.124, a clear cadence in F Dorian commences.

Section 5 Analysis: Measures 125 - 158

The abrupt chords completing the cadence in F Dorian set in motion the conclusion of the work, although a number of intervening events are still to be played out. The lengthy modulation to D♭ Ionian from F Lydian of course moved to the subdominant side, which has no representation in the parenthetic harmonies of the Lydian-Dorian scalar dyad, as noted above. Now it is certainly possible to modulate to the dominant side in leisurely manner and quickly to the subdominant side, but the general tendency of the scalar dyad can't be ignored. In this case, the reader should consider the justification for the slow modulation away from F Lydian and the quick modulation back to it.

231

To return to the specific analysis, the chords in m.127 initiate a softer modal cadence, II - VII - I, in **F** Dorian which key has the benefit as noted of being the parallel key to **F** Lydian. A variation on the falling and rising phrase, this time a bit faster, appears starting in m.129. Parenthetic harmonies on IV (this is Dorian) appear which echo the progression in m.127.

While simultaneous ascents and descents are going on, another modulation occurs, this time to **B♭** Lydian in m.131, pivoting on **F** Dorian II (**B♭** Lydian VI). The running triplet figure makes a sudden reappearance in mm.134-39 although this time transformed into a spiky version with quite a bit of diatonic dissonance throughout this short section. The reader can analyze the exact nature of the harmonies and their variation from note to note. The terraced dynamics resolve (I think) some of the darker elements that have disturbed the piece on occasion (e.g. before the augmented sixth in m.32 and at the end of the **D♭** section). The use of the familiar triplet rhythm, however, serves to integrate it at least somewhat with what has gone on before.

Harmonically, the section covers the modulation back to the original key of **F** Lydian. This section begins on the **B♭** VI in m.134 moving to IV and then I. In m.135 a parenthetic harmony {V of II} introduces the **F♯** before returning to **B♭** Lydian II in m.136. The pivot chord occurs in the same measure **B♭** VII (**F** III). Measure 137 begins an initial cadence in **F** while the melodic cutoff phrase is shrilly announced in the top two parts. The progression moves from {V of V} - V - I in mm.138-139 before mildly returning to the more flowing triplet figure.

Parenthetic harmonies on III and VII enliven this ascent in mm.140-41 before ending abruptly at the entrance of the **F6** in the **E♭** part. The high note makes definite the return of **F** Lydian and re-initiates the sustained falling phrase heard in the opening measures but this time only the tonic triad is heard, without the intruding **B** representing Lydian IV. This small detail defines the difference between an opening and closing phrase and I think is quite audible to the listener. These sustained notes initiate the closing passage that displays a more 'normal' sequence of low to high registers. The reader should compare this with the opening in which the lowest and highest registers were announced first and only then followed by the rather erratically introduced midrange. Note the use of flutter-tongue on some of the longer notes to maintain momentum.

232

While no more modulations are heard, there are several parenthetic harmonies in this concluding section. In fact, this section begins on {V of VII} before progressing in modal fashion to the tonic in m.147, avoiding the dominant. The echo of the sustained note pattern appears, again avoiding the dominant. However, by m.149-150, the harmony is now firmly in **F** Lydian and the Contrabass part sticks to the tonic triad more closely. When the E♭ part enters in m.153, the music moves to the final cadence VI - {V of V} -V - IV - I. Note the appoggiatura in the final measure which creates a bit more momentum to the Lydian tonic note.

Study Composition 2
Lydian-Dorian

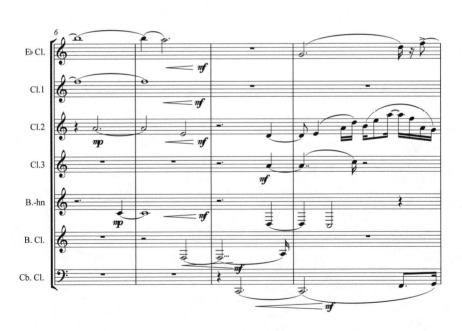

L-D

L-D

L-D

L-D

L-D

L-D

L-D

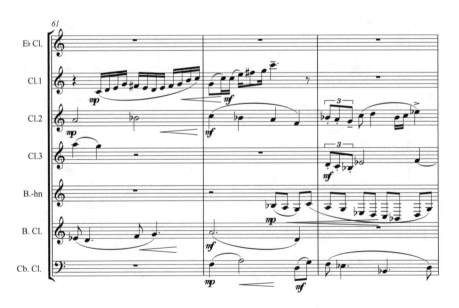

L-D

L-D

L-D

L-D

246

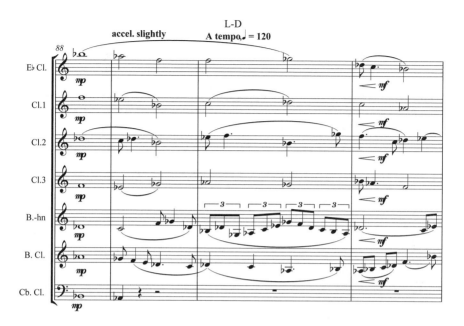

247

L-D

L-D

L-D

L-D

L-D

L-D

L-D

L-D

L-D

L-D

L-D

Study Composition in the Ionian-Aeolian Scalar Dyad

The Ionian-Aeolian Study Composition (hereafter I-A) is displayed in this chapter. The work is scored for six part clarinet choir in order to minimize issues related to orchestration and timbre, but also to provide more flexibility for part writing compared to keyboards. To assist the reader, a detailed analysis is provided here of significant aspects of the work.

This composition is mainly in the Aeolian mode in order to illustrate the significant differences between it and the more familiar minor scale. As noted, the Ionian mode is indistinguishable from the major scale in terms of its scale properties and differs only in the characteristic progressions (and melodic structures) commonly employed. The I-A begins and ends in **D** Aeolian, which has one flat as does **d** minor. There is a prepared modulation to **A** Aeolian which occurs halfway through the piece and then a more irregular return to **D** Aeolian. In addition to this fundamental modulatory progression, the piece has frequent transient modulations, either unprepared or prepared melodically, which traverse the keys related to the scale steps of **D** Aeolian. For example, **B♭** is the sixth step of **D** Aeolian. It also is the tonic note of **B♭** Aeolian which has 5 flats. For this kind of (transient) modulation to be comprehensible, the tonic note and perhaps the dominant (or scale degrees in agreement in the scalar dyad) have to be emphasized in some way.

In the current composition, the tonic note (of whatever key is active) is often the starting note of the phrase or passage and the harmony straightforwardly supports it. The point of the melodic modulations is to reinforce the scale notes of the key and also to reinforce the (Aeolian) mode.

A rather arbitrary metrical scheme underlies the piece as duple (4/4) and ternary (3/4) measures alternate first every measure, then every two measures, then every three measures at which point they reverse course back to single measure alternation. The coda, however, is duple meter exclusively. The goal is not to display compositional whim or virtuosity but to more concretely illustrate the inherent flexibility of modal rhythm and harmonic movement. Thus, metrical shifts are fluidly navigated that would create difficulties in a tonal framework. In fact, compositional virtuosity would be a greater necessity in a tonal composition with such metrical schemes than it is in the current modal system.

Section 1 Analysis: Measures 1 - 12

In contrast to the previous two study compositions, I-A begins with a more chordal introduction, although there is some modest polyphonic movement in the parts. In the duple m.1 (4/4 or 8/8), the key of **D** Aeolian is established directly, if not forcefully, due to the incomplete harmonies of Aeolian V and IV. The absence of the raised VII step (in the B♭ Clarinet part) does not decisively rule out the minor scale when the tutti I^7 chord occurs in root position. However, the movement from **C** to **D** in mm. 1-2 does not suggest the minor scale either. The I chord quickly shifts into first inversion, carrying over into m.2 which has a different meter (3/4 or 6/8). The second beat of m.2 introduces a rhythmically strong Aeolian parenthetic harmony {V of VII}, followed weakly by VII.

M.3 returns to duple meter with another parenthetic harmony {IV^7 of IV} followed by the more standard progression of IV – V - I in mm. 3-5. Again, the unraised VII moves to the tonic and the V - I progression in mm. 4 and 5 is Aeolian, not minor scale in nature. The raised scale degree six in m.4 functions more as an appoggiatura than a change in the harmony in this instance. Then the IV - V progression is repeated in a quite different form, leading not to I again, but to a more complex harmony based on VI in m.6. This is followed perhaps predictably by another parenthetic harmony {VII^7 of V} leading to a V - I^6 progression in mm.7-8. Another variant of the IV - V progression follows (with an interpolation of a parenthetic harmony {IV of VI} - VI – V) before landing on I in first inversion in m.12.

As argued repeatedly in this book, musical analysis should not be limited to harmonic sequences, so we should devote some attention to melodic, textural and rhythmic characteristics in this opening passage as well. These measures move from a primarily chordal texture to the thinner scored continuation in mm.13-52, which form a modal translation of what would be a conventional melody-accompaniment in tonal music. Melodically, the passage is characterized by 3 short forceful ascents followed by more extended descents. Each is based more on family resemblance than rote repetition, as has been seen in the other Study Compositions.

In the first ascent-descent, the parenthetic harmonies are emphasized melodically by the within-voice chromatic change (1.B♭ and Basset). With the slow tempo, the chromatic change is quite prominent, particularly with the {IV of IV} chord. Also slightly surprising is the I^7 chord in m.1 in terms of its placement and scoring: placement, because the slow tempo reduces the tendency of the first two chords to function as a standard upbeat short measure; scoring, because the first two chords are thinly scored incomplete harmonies immediately followed by a root position 5-part seventh chord. The descent in m.3 gives way to an ambiguous m.4 in which the melodic line seems to reverse course. In addition, the rhythm is off since it is now a ternary meter instead of the opening duple meter.

The second ascent begins in earnest in m.5 which does have a fairly direct correspondence with m.1, except that the harmony moves from I to V rather than V to I, but this is quite classical in nature. What is slightly odd is that the ascent here has as much downward as upward movement in the parts. The melodic line sinks lower in mm. 6 and 7. Measure 8 parallels m.4 but the harmony again moves from I to V rather than V to I. The downward tendency of the melody is confirmed in m.9 which despite its correspondence to m.1 and m.5 cannot sustain an upward ascent and sinks back onto a parenthetic harmony {IV of VI}. The next few measures continue the conflict between ascent and descent in a more melodic than chordal context. They serve as the transition to a texture closer to melody and accompaniment than in the introduction. Measure 12 has the entry of a more definite ascending line which leads into the first extended harmonic excursion to a distant Aeolian key.

Section 2 Analysis: Measures 13 - 52

The ascending line in the E♭ Clarinet, which started in m.12, picks up momentum when the 1.B♭ joins it in m.13. Harmonically, this begins the 'melodic modulation' into B♭ Aeolian. As discussed, melodic modulation differs from typical harmonic modulation since smooth melodic continuation controls the modulatory sequence rather than typical harmonic progressions of the kind seen in harmony texts. Smooth melodic continuation is defined as the introduction of chromatic notes (relative to the initial key) by consonant melodic movement, avoiding diminished and augmented intervals not found within the key.

Examining mm.13-17 shows how this process can work. The E♭ has already been introduced in parenthetic harmonies. In m.14 the G♭ is reached through a semitone movement (as is the D♭ in the 1.B♭ part). Attaining the G♭, the defining chromatic note of the key of B♭ Aeolian, provides a fulcrum for the melodic modulation since all the other chromatic alterations to fill in the key are now in a sense expected. Thus, in the E♭ Clarinet part, the G♭ is followed by the D♭, E♭ and B♭ in succession. The A♭ is sounded in two other parts in m.14. The harmony which was indeterminate in m.13 now becomes solidified in B♭ Aeolian by the VI - IV - V - I progression.

Once the B♭ tonic triad occurs in m.15, the return movement to D Aeolian rapidly unwinds the chromatic alterations. As mentioned, this composition approximates a melody and accompaniment type of texture in significant sections starting in m.17. The melody is spread among the parts, but is generally indicated by Solo above the part. The end of the solo for that part is indicated by 'ord.' (ordinario), which means to return to the customary manner of ensemble playing. The first phrase of the melody in mm.17-18 is a significant thematic motive that recurs in more or less varied form in much of the composition. The melodic continuation cadences modally on I with a modestly unorthodox V^2-I^7 progression in m.20 before a slightly more orthodox V^7-I cadence in mm.21-24. The word 'slightly' is used since the V chord is Aeolian rather than a major or altered minor dominant chord. In addition, the rhythmic independence of the parts, modest as it is here, further mitigates the strength of the cadential pause.

This point is worth a little more analysis to bring out some distinctions in the musical texture. Musical texture can vary from completely homophonic to completely polyphonic, the true distinction resting not on similar or contrary motion, but on a rhythmic differentiation. In m.21 the 2.B♭ and Basset exhibit a basically homophonic relation with each other. The 2.Bass has a mildly polyphonic relation with both parts, although the basis for this lies in the nature of the phrasing (which is a subspecies of rhythm). However, the 2.B♭ and Basset phrasing is distinctly different. They have the eighth note tied to the preceding notes while the Bass has it tied to the succeeding notes. In the latter case, an attack occurs on the eighth note which is not present in the two upper parts. In addition, the phrasing will alter subtly the duration and stress accorded to the note and those that immediately follow. To reiterate, modal melody should be carefully written in order to better shape the musical flow and this is more of a requirement than in the tonal system. The reader can do the analysis of musical texture in the remainder of the piece.

Returning to the main discussion, the first melodic phrase is presented in varied form in mm.23-26. The harmony modulates into **A** Aeolian rather abruptly but this is a closely related key. Another phrase is introduced in m.27 which leads off in a somewhat different direction, although the parenthetic harmonies lead back to the dominant in m.29 for a moment. Then another melodic modulation begins towards **C** Aeolian, followed immediately by **C** Ionian, before returning to **A** Aeolian with a VII - V - I progression in mm.32-33.

A climax is reached in m.33 although the build-up is rather restrained. From the start of the melody in m.17 to m.32, three different keys, two Aeolian and one Ionian, have been touched upon in addition to parenthetic harmonies referring to the main key of **D** Aeolian. In the two measures prior to m.32, the texture becomes simpler allowing the foreign keys to sound more clearly in the melody. The initial chord in m.32 could be the dominant in relation to the **C** Ionian suggested in the previous measure, although the harmony soon turns to **A** Aeolian and then **D** in m.35. The melody also rises suggestively in m.31. All of these factors taken together undoubtedly contribute to the effect, which should be kept in mind in analyses of music.

Just as soon as **D** Aeolian returns, a parenthetic harmony in m.37 serves as the initiator of another modulation, this time to E♭

Aeolian. This is a somewhat bolder move since it is the chromatic note in the parenthetic chord which serves as the basis for the progression. This emphasizes the remoteness of the modulation. The modulation quickly unwinds back to **D** Aeolian briefly, after touching on the dominant and subdominant of **E♭** Aeolian, before settling on **A** Aeolian as it moves leisurely towards a clear cadence.

The high **D** in the E♭ part perhaps is the most decisive indication of an approaching cadential pause, but it undoubtedly is only one factor. No confident analytical explanation is provided as to why this sensation exists (at least to me). There is a transformation of melodic activity from irregularity and arabesque to a considerably more regular motion starting in m.43. The accompaniment also becomes a variation on the opening rhythms in m.47 and the melody moves to the higher register of the Basset and Bass Clarinets creating a slight sense of strain. In terms of harmonic progression, there is little in the way of tonal cadential formulas with the exception of a {V of V} parenthetic chord in m.50 right before the half cadence in m.52. Note how unforcefully this chord is presented: inverted, in modal form (no raised third), arpeggiated, with not a single vertical presentation of the triad. Nevertheless, the progression stands out clearly because of the modal context in which it appears.

Section 3 Analysis: Measures 53 - 73

The pickup after the half cadence avoids a strong feeling of sectionality by the immediate appearance of the melodic sixteenth note pattern that appeared frequently in the preceding measures. Momentum is gained by pushing past the G5 ceiling (m.54) that has remained since m.46. This turns out to be a modulation to **E** Aeolian, a key not previously touched upon. The initial melodic fragment reappears along with a suggestion of the chordal beginning. The on-beat <u>sforzando</u> followed quickly by the off-beat <u>sforzando</u> provide a significant push to the ensuing measures (58-67) which are somewhat static in underlying flow (intentionally so, to permit the resumption of movement to sound more conclusive). Note that the meter changes are also less frequent here than earlier which tends to complement the slower harmonic movement.

The texture has two main elements: a slow moving cantus firmus based on the melodic line of the opening chordal section, the second an ascending, melodic variation on the initial figuration which rises to **F6**. The harmony moves into the Ionian mode for the first time (apart from the measure in **C** Ionian earlier), first to **A** and then **D** (of course, the parallel key to **D** Aeolian). The modulations are prepared but rather abrupt.

Since the melody returns to balance the piece, the increasing intensity of the melodic movement in this section, climaxing in m.66, needs to unwind to better prepare for it. The duet in mm. 68-71 accomplishes this (I think) by again reintroducing a more lyrical mood but one that is not overly close to the melody that began in m.17. The mode is Ionian rather than Aeolian and the accompaniment is the slow cantus firmus rather than the more varied accompaniment in the previous section. The harmony is also distinct. Although a conventional dominant seventh chord occurs at the start of the duet melody, it is followed by a modal parenthetic harmony {IV of IV}. After IV, two more parenthetic chords appear, {VI of V} and {V of V}. However, instead of resolution to V, the {V of V} moves to a six-four chord and then to a rather complex chord which could be analyzed as a (Ionian inflected) dominant ninth in second inversion (m.71). At this point (m.72-3), a melodic semitone sequence in the Basset slips the key over to **D** Aeolian through the melodic introduction of the **B♭** in the next measure.

Section 4 Analysis: Measures 74 - 92

The initial chord of m.74 faintly mimics the chordal introduction as does the melody, briefly modulating to **A** Aeolian in mm.80-4. In m.83 a pair of parenthetic harmonies on the dominant of A re-introduce the **F♯** before **D** Aeolian returns decisively in mm.85-93.

This section has a somewhat simpler texture and harmonic movement than the first melody-accompaniment section, although parenthetic harmonies on IV and V are quite prominent. Unisons or simple parallel movements between two parts are seen in every measure between 82 and 92. There is a bit more open space between parts as well. The melody is not obviously based on that in the first section but has a similar mood to my ears. (The reader is invited to analyze why they agree or disagree.) The sixteenth note figuration provides the most direct relation between the melodic lines.

Section 5 Analysis: Measures 93 - 107

Measure 93 is a direct reprise of the opening measure but the next measure departs into a more rhapsodic blend of the qualities of the opening and the measures 55 to 72. An immediate modulation to B♭ Aeolian occurs in m.94 which starts a series of such references to keys touched upon previously, first with A Aeolian, then E Aeolian before returning to D Aeolian in m.100. The harmonic progressions are generally more straightforward with few parenthetic harmonies within each of these keys. In compensation, the voice leading is unorthodox, with voices moving by large, sometimes dissonant intervals. Measure 95, for example, shows leaps of a fifth and minor seventh in a garden variety I-V progression. This creates a sense of movement and energy that would be lacking otherwise. This is a useful way of enriching the somewhat blander progressions of modal music without destroying their vital character.

The topmost melody, played by the E♭ and 1.B♭, also has a wider range and more frequent intervallic leaps than before, although the disjunct intervals are typically limited to a sixth or minor seventh. These intervals were used in the prior melodic sections and thus provide a degree of correspondence between the different sections. Rhythmically this section has a much more regular melodic character. The flowing sixteenth note pattern, on the other hand, is asymmetrically organized because of the offbeat placement of the longer duration note in the sequence.

The irregularity is by no means consistently applied as there is one pattern which first appears in m.100 that serves as a melodic and, to a lesser extent, harmonic guidepost. Although it technically has a range of a major sixth, the principal ambit is a fifth since that is the interval between the first note and the extended high note of the pattern, at least in its initial occurrences. The pattern is briefly interrupted in m.103 to avoid over emphasis, but it resumes in m.104 rising to the mediant F5.

266

The pattern resumes in m.105 with one subtle but important difference. The pattern starts out the same as m.100 on the **G** and rises to the **D**, however, this time the phrase rises to the extended **F5**. In this case, the high note is an eighth note in duration, unlike the dotted eighth of the other measures with this pattern. This unexpected but shortened high note provides a feeling of anticipation. This is confirmed by a novel pattern, also starting on the **G** and more strongly pointing to an impending end, which occurs in the next measure on a tonic ninth chord. Note how the arrangement, spacing and doubling of the tonic note contributes stability to what typically is an unstable chord. The stability is enhanced by the context as well since the relative minimization of strong cadences makes this chordal structure stand out.

Study Composition 3
Ionian-Aeolian

I-A

I-A

I-A

I-A

I-A

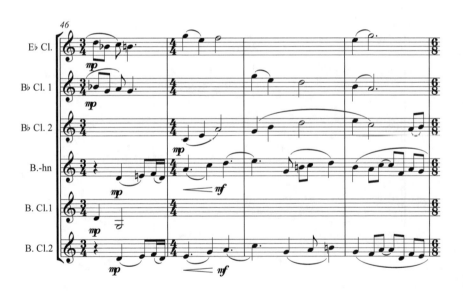

I-A

I-A

I-A

I-A

I-A

I-A

I-A

I-A

I-A

I-A

I-A

References

Antokoletz, E. (1984) *The music of Bela Bartok.* U. of Calif. Press: Berkeley, CA.

Aubrey, E. (1996) *Music of the troubadours.* Indiana U. Press: Bloomington, IN

Cogan, R. & Escot, P. (1976) *Sonic design.* Prentice Hall: Englewood Cliffs, NJ.

Cook, N. (1990) *Music, imagination and culture.* Oxford U. Press: Oxford, G.B.

Hoppin, R.H. (1978) *Medieval music.* W.W. Norton Music: NY.

Jones, G.T. (1963) *Music composition: A manual for training the young composer.* Summy-Birchard: Evanston, IL

McHose, A.I. (1947) *The contrapuntal harmonic technique of the 18th century.* F.S. Crofts: NY

Meyer, L.B. (1956) *Emotion and meaning in music.* U. of Chicago: Chicago IL.

Meyer, L.B. (1973) *Explaining music.* U. of Calif. Press: Berkeley, CA.

Miller, R. (1996/7, vol. 1 & 2) *Modal Jazz Composition and Harmony.* Advance Music: Rottenburg, Germany.

Owen, H. (1992) *Modal and tonal counterpoint: From Josquin to Stravinsky.* Schirmer:NY

Pike, L. (1978) *Beethoven, Sibelius and the Profound Logic.* Athlone Press (U. Of London): London, G.B.

Piston, W. (1941) *Harmony.* W.W. Norton: NY.

Schenker, H. (1913) *Harmony.* (Trans. E. Borgese: 1954) U. of Chicago: Chicago, IL.

Schenker, H. (1935) *Free composition.* (Trans. E. Oster: 1979) Longman: NY

Schoenberg, A. (1911) *Theory of harmony.* (Trans. R.E. Carter:1978) U. of Calif.: Berkeley, CA.

Schoenberg, A. (1969) *Structural functions of harmony.* (Ed. L. Stein) 2nd ed. Benn: London, G.B.

Schubert, P. (1999) *Modal counterpoint: Renaissance style.* Oxford U. Press: NY

Sloboda, J. (1985) *The musical mind.* Oxford U. Press: Oxford, G.B.

Wade, B.C. (1979) *Music in India.* Manohar Publishers: New Delhi, India.

Appendix 1

The Mixolydian-Phrygian Dyad

In this and the next two appendices, specific attention is devoted to the modal scalar dyads, concentrating more on the practical aspects of their use in composition. The aim is to provide the necessary information in accessible form that would otherwise have to be generated by the reader in order to compose readily in this system. Each appendix will first cover the melodic character of the scalar dyad and its constituent scales. Then the character of cadences in the scalar dyad is examined followed by the pattern of the parenthetic harmonies and their usage. Finally, various modulatory strategies are presented. To illustrate the techniques and procedures discussed, Study Compositions and analyses relevant to this and the following Appendices were provided earlier in the text.

Melodic Character of the Mixolydian-Phrygian Dyad

As noted previously, this scalar dyad has a subdominant tilt, due to the location of the diminished triad in the Mixolydian and Phrygian scales on the dominant side, III and V respectively. The Mixolydian mode has the tritone out of the way of melodic cadences since it rests on neither the Final, dominant or subdominant steps with ascending half-steps to the fourth and seventh scale degrees. The lack of significant ascending and descending relationships does produce a reduced melodic tension in this mode. The Phrygian has the tritone positioned between I and V. The prominent tritone and descending half-step to the Final and fifth scale degree combined with the lack of prominent ascending relations produces a melodically tense mode with strong downward tendencies. This Mixolydian-Phrygian pattern of melodic tension represents a modest intensification of the Ionian-Aeolian pattern between its major and minor scales in the opposite direction of the Lydian-Dorian dyad. Phrygian is the most melodically tense minor scale (leaving Locrian aside) and Mixolydian is the most relaxed major scale.

Given the prominent tritone in Phrygian between II and V, the Mixolydian mode provides a means of restoring some freer melodic movement between these two steps. The Mixolydian tritone between III and VII is not nearly as prominent and Phrygian has no restriction in this particular melodic movement. There is no significant ascending leading-tone in either mode. Although the Phrygian half step from II to I does impart some melodic strength to the tonic, it does not have quite the same importance as the Ionian V - I. Since Phrygian II forms the root of a major rather than the diminished triad, its tendency for resolution is reduced. Nevertheless, since the Phrygian dominant is weakened, the Phrygian tonic is in a struggle with the subdominant. The downward leading-tone helps to maintain the Phrygian tonic in this circumstance. Mixolydian has a similar problem with the subdominant, but no comparable counterforce.

Both modes have the I, IV, VII harmonies in agreement with the tonic, but the Phrygian melodic movement around the dominant, particularly if it has harmonic confirmation, needs to be more carefully weighed than in the Mixolydian. Of course, it is possible to use this melodic movement and not confirm it harmonically or provide it with ambiguous harmonic support.   Conversely, the Mixolydian lack of tension makes progressions involving IV more of a threat to the tonic.

Cadential Character of the Mixolydian-Phrygian Dyad

Effective cadences that are shared by both modes of the Mixolydian-Phrygian dyad are the IV - I and VII - I progressions. The V - I progression is relatively weak in both modes but usable. The Mixolydian V - I moves from minor to major while the Phrygian has the diminished V. The Phrygian does have the relatively strong II - I cadence. The III - I progression is possible in Phrygian, but Mixolydian has a diminished III which further weakens the softer cadence.

Mixolydian-Phrygian Parenthetic Harmonies

In Table 13 in the previous chapter, the differing chromatic relations of secondary dominant {V of V} to dominant were displayed in the various modes. The Mixolydian {V of V} has an altered fifth (rather than sixth) because the V is not in agreement with the tonic and follows the Phrygian mode, while the Phrygian {V of V} has an altered root. However, in the modal system, the parenthetic harmonies go beyond the secondary dominant to apply to all the triads in a given key (excepting the diminished triad). Apart from the scale degree (Mixolydian VI, Phrygian III) which forms the relative minor or major key, the scales based on the different scale degrees have chromatic notes in relation to the given scale. The parenthetic key harmonies for each Mixolydian and Phrygian key necessarily vary as can be seen in Table 15a and b. (Table 15b shows the contents of Table 15a in a Phrygian context for convenience.)

Parenthetic harmonies are not provided for the step on the diminished triad (e.g., b°) nor on the step of the relative minor of G Mixolydian (E Phrygian) which does not have the harmonically altered tonal form. Since the modern modal system presented here does not make use of chromatic alterations to the minor mode to emulate the major mode, the relative Mixolydian and Phrygian keys are not chromatically distinguishable in their ordinary parenthetic harmonies.

Table 15a: The Mixolydian (and Phrygian) Keys and their Parenthetic Harmonies (Scales)

Mixoly.	Phryg.	-	Mixoly.	Phryg.	Phryg.	Mixoly.
G/0	a/1♭	b*	C/1♭	d/2♭	e/0	F/2♭
D/1♯	e/0	f♯*	G/0	a/1♭	b/1♯	C/1♭
A/2♯	b/1♯	c♯*	D/1♯	e/0	f/2♯	G/0
E/3♯	f♯/2♯	g♯*	A/2♯	b/1♯	c♯/3♯	D/1♯
B/4♯	c♯/3♯	d♯*	E/3♯	f♯/2♯	g♯/4♯	A/2♯
F♯/5♯	g♯/4♯	a♯*	B/4♯	c♯/3♯	d♯/5♯	E/3♯
C/1♭	d/2♭	e*	F/2♭	g/3♭	a/1♭	B♭/3♭
F/2♭	g/3♭	a*	B♭/3♭	c/4♭	d/2♭	E♭/4♭
B♭/3♭	c/4♭	d*	E♭/4♭	f/5♭	g/3♭	A♭/5♭
E♭/4♭	f/5♭	g*	A♭/5♭	b♭/6♭	c/4♭	D♭/6♭
A♭/5♭	b♭/6♭	c*	D♭/6♭	e♭/5♯	f/5♭	G♭/5♯
D♭/6♭	e♭/5♯	f*	G♭/5♯	a♭/4♯	b♭/6♭	C♭/4♯

Table 15b: The Phrygian (and Mixolydian) Keys for Parenthetic Harmonies (Scales)

Phryg.	Mixoly.	Mixoly.	Phryg.	-	Mixoly.	Phryg.
e/0	F/2♭	G/0	a/1♭	b*	C/1♭	d/2♭
b/1♯	C/1♭	D/1♯	e/0	f♯*	G/0	a/1♭
f/2♯	G/0	A/2♯	b/1♯	c♯*	D/1♯	e/0
c♯/3♯	D/1♯	E/3♯	f♯/2♯	g♯*	A/2♯	b/1♯
g♯/4♯	A/2♯	B/4♯	c♯/3♯	d♯*	E/3♯	f♯/2♯
d♯/5♯	E/3♯	F♯/5♯	g♯/4♯	a♯*	B/4♯	c♯/3♯
a/1♭	B♭/3♭	C/1♭	d/2♭	e*	F/2♭	g/3♭
d/2♭	E♭/4♭	F/2♭	g/3♭	a*	B♭/3♭	c/4♭
g/3♭	A♭/5♭	B♭/3♭	c/4♭	d*	E♭/4♭	f/5♭
c/4♭	D♭/6♭	E♭/4♭	f/5♭	g*	A♭/5♭	b♭/6♭
f/5♭	G♭/5♯	A♭/5♭	b♭/6♭	c*	D♭/6♭	e♭/5♯
b♭/6♭	C♭/4♯	D♭/6♭	e♭/5♯	f*	G♭/5♯	a♭/4♯

Looking at Table 15a, we see the Mixolydian-Phrygian pattern of chromatic notes introduced by parenthetic harmonies. A few specific examples should be helpful in clarifying the relationships displayed in Tables 15a (and b). G Mixolydian (first row in Table 15a) has parenthetic harmonies derived from **A** Phrygian, **D** Phrygian, **C** Mixolydian and **F** Mixolydian. These keys introduce one or two chromatic notes as mentioned in previous chapters. Unlike the major-minor scale (or the Ionian-Aeolian dyad), parenthetic harmonies are unbalanced toward the flat keys in the Mixolydian-Phrygian dyad. Whether a particular parenthetic triad introduces a chromatic note depends on its root but this is no different from the major-minor system (e.g. the tonic triad acting as the dominant for IV). Of course, in a contrapuntal texture, the chromatic notes can easily be introduced outside of a vertical chord.

Steps II, IV, V and VII have parenthetic harmonies which introduce chromatic alterations into the primary key (e.g. G Mixolydian.) (The parenthetic harmonies are Mixolydian, if based on IV and VII, and Phrygian, if based on II and V.) However, the particular point of introduction of the chromatic change varies in chordal position and may not occur within a given triad. Looking at parenthetic harmonies based on G Mixolydian II (**A**) and IV (**C**), one chromatic note, **B**♭, is introduced. Mixolydian II can serve as the tonic of **A** Phrygian, which would thus have **B**♭, instead of **B**, as its second degree. (Obviously, any chord in **A** Phrygian containing its second degree will introduce a chromatic note in relation to G Mixolydian.) As for the parenthetic harmonies for Mixolydian IV acting as C Mixoldian, the chromatic note, **B**♭, occurs on the sixth of {II of IV} (**d** minor triad) and sequentially down to the root of {VII of IV} (**B**♭ major triad).

Mixolydian parenthetic harmonies based on V and VII have two chromatic alterations in the key compared with the primary key. For example, the V of G Mixolydian is the tonic of D Phrygian, which has two flats. Looking at the row for **D** Phrygian in Table 15b, we can see that a triad built on {II of V} would be **E**♭ and thus would have chromatic alterations of the root and fifth of the chord relative to G Mixolydian. Similarly, the G Mixolydian VII is also the tonic for **F** Mixolydian, which has two flats. A triad built on {II of VII} (**g** minor triad) would introduce one chromatic note at the third, but to introduce the other chromatic note, the chord would have to include

293

as an added sixth the seventh degree of **F**, namely, **E♭**. (Chords based on the other steps obviously have the two changed notes at different positions of the chord.)

The first row of Table 15b displays the pattern for the Phrygian key of **E** within the dyad. For the Phrygian mode, the parenthetic harmonies are built on II, IV, VI and VII since V is the diminished triad and III is the Mixolydian relative major **key of G**. Steps II and VI have Mixolydian parenthetic harmonies while IV and VII are Phrygian in form. The parenthetic harmonies based on IV and VI potentially introduce one chromatic change while those based on II and VII potentially introduce two chromatic changes.

To carry forward the previous Mixolydian example, the VII of **E** Phrygian is **D** Phrygian, which has two flats. Looking at the row for **D** Phrygian in Table 15b, we can see that a **E♭** major triad would be built on {II of VII} and thus would have chromatic alterations of the root and fifth of the chord relative to **E** Phrygian. In this case, the tonic note itself is chromatically altered. Similarly, the **E** Phrygian II is also the tonic for **F** Mixolydian, which has two flats. A triad built on {VI of II} (**d** minor triad) would have no chromatic notes, unless the ninth (second) **E♭** was added. To introduce the other chromatic note, the chord would have to include as an added sixth the fourth degree of **F**, namely, **B♭**.

Modulation in the Mixolydian-Phrygian Dyad

The two tables below (Tables 16a and b) display the set of transposed scales for the Mixolydian and Phrygian scales respectively. Obviously, the keys with six flats (**D♭** Mixolydian and **B♭** Phrygian) are equivalent to keys with six sharps (**C♯** Mixolydian and **A♯** Phrygian) and keys with five flats (sharps) are equivalent to keys with seven sharps (flats).

Table 16a: Mixolydian Key Scales

G	A	B	C	D	E	F
D	E	F♯	G	A	B	C
A	B	C♯	D	E	F♯	G
E	F♯	G♯	A	B	C♯	D
B	C♯	D♯	E	F♯	G♯	A
F♯	G♯	A♯	B	C♯	D♯	E
C	D	E	F	G	A	B♭
F	G	A	B♭	C	D	E♭
B♭	C	D	E♭	F	G	A♭
E♭	F	G	A♭	B♭	C	D♭
A♭	B♭	C	D♭	E♭	F	G♭
D♭	E♭	F	G♭	A♭	B♭	C♭

Table 16b: Phrygian Key Scales

E	F	G	A	B	C	D
B	C	D	E	F♯	G	A
F♯	G	A	B	C♯	D	E
C♯	D	E	F♯	G♯	A	B
G♯	A	B	C♯	D♯	E	F♯
D♯	E	F♯	G♯	A♯	B	C♯
A	B♭	C	D	E	F	G
D	E♭	F	G	A	B♭	C
G	A♭	B♭	C	D	E♭	F
C	D♭	E♭	F	G	A♭	B♭
F	G♭	A♭	B♭	C	D♭	E♭
B♭	C♭	D♭	E♭	F	G♭	A♭

Within-Mode Prepared Modulation

For the purposes of prepared modulation, the next two Tables, 17a and b, display the pattern of pivot chord (triads) occurrences across the various Mixolydian and Phrygian keys for use in prepared within-mode modulation. (The pivot chord relations for within-dyad and between-dyad modulation are discussed later.) In Table 17a, each scale step triad (shown in bold, with major triads in uppercase and minor triads in lowercase) is followed by the Mixolydian keys in which it occurs. The same relations for Phrygian pivot chords are shown in Table 17b.

296

Table 17a: The Key Relations of Mixolydian Pivot Chords (Within-Mode)

I	II	III	IV	V	VI	VII
G/A,D,G	a/C,D,G	b*/G	C/C,D,G	d/C,F,G	e/A,D,G	F/C,F,G
D/A,D,E	e/A,D,G	f♯*/D	G/A,D,G	a/C,D,G	b/A,D,E	C/C,D,G
A/A,B,E	b/A,D,E	c♯*/A	D/A,D,E	e/A,D,G	f♯/A,B,E	G/A,D,G
E/B,E,F♯	f♯/A,B,E	g♯*/E	A/A,B,E	b/A,D,E	c♯/B,E,F♯	D/A,D,E
B/B,D♭,F♯	c♯/ B,E,F♯	d♯*/B	E/B,E,F♯	f♯/A,B,E	g♯/B,D♭,F♯	A/A,B,E
F♯/A♭,D♭,F♯	g♯/B,D♭,F♯	a♯*/F♯	B/B,D♭,F♯	c♯/ B,E,F♯	d♯/A♭,D♭,F♯	E/B,E,F♯
C/C,D,G	d/C,F,G	e*/C	F/C,F,G	g/B♭,C, F	a/C,D,G	B♭/B♭,C,F
F/C,F,G	g/B♭,C,F	a*/F	B♭/B♭,C,F	c/Bb,E♭,F	d/C,F,G	E♭/B♭,E♭,F
B♭/B♭,C,F	c/B♭,E♭,F	d*/B♭	E♭/B♭,E♭,F	f/A♭,B♭,E♭,	g/B♭,C,F	A♭/A♭,B♭,E♭
E♭/ B♭,E♭,F	f/A♭,B♭,E♭	g*/E♭	A♭/A♭,B♭,E♭	b♭/A♭,D♭,E♭	c/B♭,E♭,F	D♭/A♭,D♭,E♭
A♭/A♭,B♭,E♭	b♭/A♭,D♭,E♭	c*/A♭	D♭/A♭,D♭,E♭	e♭/A♭,D♭,F♯	f/A♭,B♭,E♭	G♭/A♭,D♭,F♯
D♭/A♭,D♭,E♭	e♭/A♭,D♭,F♯	f*/D♭	G♭/A♭,D♭,F♯	a♭ /B,D♭,F♯	b♭/A♭,D♭,E♭	C♭/B,D♭,F♯

The within-mode prepared modulations in Mixolydian and Phrygian were touched upon previously, but here the possibilities are presented more systematically. The discussion centers around the use of the triad as interpreted in the destination (second) key, although in some cases the role of the triad in the source (first) key has some bearing on the effect of the modulatory sequence.

In the associated music examples, the use of each scale step (as interpreted in the first key) in modulation will be presented for related keys (shared triads) starting with the tonic chords. All progressions, without reference to their subjective 'goodness' or utility, are shown from a given pivot triad to the triads in the second key which introduce a chromatic change. However, the repetition of the given pivot triad also shows at the same time modulations back to that triad from the respective second keys. Thus, a relatively complete picture of each triad's voice leading as a first and second key pivot can be gleaned from these examples.

The Mixolydian pivot chords are restricted to keys a major second, perfect fourth, perfect fifth and minor seventh above the tonic. It is important to note that the Mixolydian V can be more easily used as pivot (in the destination key) since it is a minor chord not in agreement with the mode. On the negative side, modulations to the key of the subdominant or using the IV step of the second (destination) key as pivot chord are problematic due to the enhanced strength of the Mixolydian subdominant.

Table 17b: The Key Relations of Phrygian Pivot Chords (Within-Mode)

I	II	III	IV	V	VI	VII
e/B,E,F♯	F/A,D,E	G/B,E,F♯	a/A,B,E	b*/e	C/A,B,E	d/A,D,E
b/B,C♯,F♯	C/A,B,E	D/B,C♯,F♯	e/ B,E,F♯	f♯*/b	G/B,E,F♯	a/A,B,E
f♯/C♯,F♯,G♯	G/B,E,F♯	A/C♯,F♯,G♯	b/B,C♯,F♯	c♯*/f♯	D/B,C♯,F♯	e/B,E,F♯
c♯/C♯,D♯,G♯	D/B,C♯,F♯	E/C♯,D♯,G♯.	f♯/C♯,F♯,G♯	g♯*/c♯	A/C♯,F♯,G♯	b/B,C♯,F♯
g♯/B♭,D♯,G♯	A/C♯,F♯,G♯	B/B♭,D♯,G♯	c♯/C♯,D♯,G♯	d♯/g♯	E/C♯,D♯,G♯.	f♯/C♯,F♯,G♯
d♯/D♯,F,G♯	E/C♯,D♯,G♯.	F♯/D♯,F,G♯	g♯/B♭,D♯,G♯	a♯*/d♯	B/B♭,D♯,G♯	c♯/C♯,D♯,G♯
a/A,B,E	B♭/A,D,G	C/A,B,E	d/A,D,E	e*/a	F/A,D,E	g/A,D,G
d/A,D,E	E♭/C,D,G	F/A,D,E	g/A,D,G	a*/d	B♭/A,D,G	c/C,D,G
g/A,D,G	A♭/C,F,G	B♭/A,D,G	c/C,D,G	d*/g	E♭/C,D,G	f/C,F,G
c/C,D,G	D♭/B♭,C,F	E♭/C,D,G	f/C,F,G	g*/c	A♭/C,F,G	b♭/B♭,C,F
f/C,F,G	G♭/B♭,D♯,F	A♭/C,F,G	b♭/B♭,C,F	c*/f	D♭/B♭,C,F	e♭/B♭,D♯,F
b♭/B♭,D♯,F	C♭/B♭,D♯,G♯	D♭/B♭,D♯,F	e♭/B♭,D♯,F	f*/b♭	G♭/B♭,D♯,F	a♭/B♭,D♯,G♯

Mixolydian Tonic.

The Mixolydian tonic of the first (source) key can be a useful pivot in some cases, but is best used carefully in modulations to the key of the dominant where it would stand as IV. The main factor to consider with the (first key) tonic is the frequent presence of some partial or full cadence that does affect the context of the modulation.

The tonic chord is shared in the Mixolydian keys a major second and perfect fifth above, acting as the VII and IV respectively. In the case of G Mixolydian, that would be **A:VII** and **D:IV**. In Ex. 56a, the progressions to and from **G:I** to each chord of **A** and **D** that introduces a chromatic change are shown.

Ex.56a: Mixolydian Tonic Triad as Within-mode Pivot

G:I A:I G:I A:II G:I A:III G:I A:IV G:I A:VI G:I D:I G:I D:III G:I D:VI

Phrygian Tonic.

The Phrygian tonic (of the first key) can be used as pivot chord to the Phrygian keys a major second and perfect fifth above. In the case of E Phrygian, that would be **F♯:VII** and **B:IV** Phrygian. The subdominant pivot is not a problem in the Phrygian mode. In Ex. 56b, the progressions from **E:I** to each chord of **F♯** and **B** Phrygian that introduces a chromatic change are shown.

Ex.56b: Phrygian Tonic Triad as Within-Mode Pivot

E:I F♯:I   E:I F♯:III E:I F♯:IV E:I   F♯:V   E:I F♯:VI   E:I B:I   E:I B:III   E:I B:V

Mixolydian II.

The Mixolydian II is a minor chord and due to its neutral relations in both the first and second keys of the modulation can be a widely useful pivot. The II chord also occurs in the Mixolydian keys a perfect fourth and perfect fifth above. In the case of **G** Mixolydian, that would be **C:VI** and **D:V**. Use of the Mixolydian dominant as pivot chord in the second key does not pose an issue as it would in Ionian. In Ex. 57a, the progressions from G:II to each chord of **C** and **D** Mixolydian that introduces a chromatic change are shown.

Ex.57a: Mixolydian II Triad as Within-Mode Pivot

G:II   C:III   G:II   C:V   G:II   C:VII   G:II   D:I   G:II   D:III   G:II   D:VI

Phrygian II.

Because of the prominence of the Phrygian II – I cadence, the Phrygian II is a little trickier to use as pivot. This relation will affect the use of II as interpreted in the first key since it will make it a deceptive (or non-cadential) progression, but it will also affect its use as interpreted in the second key. The II chord is shared by the Phrygian keys a perfect fourth and minor seventh above. In the case of **E** Phrygian, that would be **A:**VI and **D:**III. In Ex. 57b, the progressions from **E:**II to each chord of **A** and **D** Phrygian that introduces a chromatic change are shown.

Ex.57b: Phrygian II Triad as Within-Mode Pivot

E:II A:II E:II A:V E:II A:VII   E:II D:II E:II D:IV E:II D:V E:II D:VI E:II D:VII

Mixolydian III.

The diminished Mixolydian III cannot be used as pivot since it is unique to a Mixolydian key.

Phrygian III.

The Phrygian III is a convenient first key pivot due to its neutrality. The III can be used as pivot chord to the Phrygian keys a major second and perfect fifth above. In the case of **E** Phrygian, that would be **F♯:**II and **B:**VI Phrygian. Note however, that the interpretation of III in the key of II is also II, which is a somewhat awkward second key pivot. In Ex. 58, the progressions from **E:**III to each chord of **F** and **B** Phrygian that introduces a chromatic change are shown.

301

Ex.58: Phrygian III Triad as Within-Mode Pivot

E:III F♯:I   E:III F♯:III E:III F♯:IV E:III F♯:V E:III F♯:VI E:III B:I E:III B:III E:III B:V

Mixolydian IV.

The Mixolydian IV can easily be used as a first key pivot, but less so if it is IV in the second key. The IV chord also occurs in the keys a perfect fourth and perfect fifth above. In the case of **G** Mixolydian, that would be **C:I** and **D:VII** Mixolydian. Note however that **G:IV** is the tonic for **C** Mixolydian and care would need to be taken to avoid an interpretation as **C** Ionian. In Ex. 59a, the progressions from **G:IV** to each chord of **C** and **D** that introduces a chromatic change are shown.

Ex.59a: Mixolydian IV Triad as Within-Mode Pivot

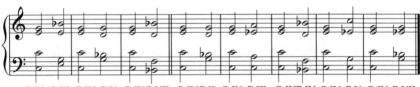

G:IV C:III G:IV C:V   G:IV C:VII G:IV F:II G:IV F:III G:IV F:IV G:IV F:V G:IV F:VII

302

Phrygian IV.

The Phrygian IV can be used freely due to its relative neutrality in the first and second keys. The IV chord appears in the keys a perfect fourth and perfect fifth above. In the case of E Phrygian, that would be **A:I** and **B:VII** Phrygian. Note however that **E:IV** is the tonic of **A** Phrygian and probably should be used only in inversion. In Ex. 59b, the progressions from **E:IV** to each chord of **A** and **B** that introduces a chromatic change are shown.

Ex.59b: Phrygian IV Triad as Within-Mode Pivot

E:IV A:II   E:IV A:V   E:IV A:VII   E:IV B:I   E:IV B:III   E:IV B:V

Mixolydian V.

The Mixolydian V can be more easily used as pivot (as interpreted in either the first or second key) since it is a minor chord not in agreement with the mode. The V chord appears in the keys a perfect fourth and minor seventh above. In the case of **G** Mixolydian, that would be **C:II** and **F:VI** Mixolydian. The V is a better pivot to the subdominant key since its minor character doesn't overaccentuate the inherently strong relation. In Ex. 60, the progressions from **G:V** to each chord of **C** and **F** that introduces a chromatic change are shown.

Ex.60: Mixolydian V Triad as Within-Mode Pivot

G:V C:III   G:V   C:V   G:VC:VII G:V F:II   G:V F:III G:V F:IVG:V F:V   G:V F:VII

Phrygian V.

The diminished Phrygian V cannot be used as pivot since it is unique to a Phrygian key.

Mixolydian VI.

The minor Mixolydian VI can be easily used as pivot. The VI chord appears in the Mixolydian keys a major second and perfect fifth above. In the case of **G** Mixolydian, that would be **A:V** and **D:II** **Mixolydian**. In Ex. 61a, the progressions from G:VI to each chord of **A** and **D** that introduces a chromatic change are shown.

Ex.61a: Mixolydian VI Triad as Within-Mode Pivot

G:VI A:I   G:VI A:II   G:VI A:III G:VI A:IV   G:VI A:VI   G:VI D:I   G:VI D:III   G:VI D:VI

Phrygian VI.

The Phrygian VI is a convenient first key pivot due to its neutrality. The VI chord appears in the keys a perfect fourth and perfect fifth above. In the case of **E** Phrygian, that would be **A**:III and **B**:II Phrygian. Note that the interpretation of VI in the key of V is the cadentially important II. In Ex. 61b, the progressions from **G**:VI to each chord of **A** and **B** that introduces a chromatic change are shown.

Ex.61b: Phrygian VI Triad as Within-Mode Pivot

```
E:VI  A:II   E:VI  A:V   E:VI  A:VII   E:VI  B:I   E:VI  B:III   E:VI  B:V
```

Mixolydian VII.

The Mixolydian VII is a somewhat awkward within-mode pivot due to its second key interpretation. The VII chord occurs in the keys a perfect fourth and minor seventh above. In the case of **G** Mixolydian, that would be **F**:I and **C**:IV Mixolydian. It is not as good a pivot choice for modulations to the subdominant key as V and it is the tonic of **F** Mixolydian. In Ex. 62a, the progressions from **G**:VII to each chord of **C** and **F** that introduces a chromatic change are shown.

Ex.62a: Mixolydian VII Triad as Within-Mode Pivot

G:VIIC:III G:VII C:V G:VIIC:VII G:VII F:II G:VIIF:III G:VIIF:IV G:VII F:V G:VIIF:VII

Phrygian VII.

The Phrygian VII can be easily used as pivot. The VII chord occurs in the keys a perfect fourth and minor seventh above. In the case of **E** Phrygian, that would be **A:IV** and **D:I** Phrygian. Note that **E:VII** is the tonic for **D** Phrygian. In Ex. 62b, the progressions from **E:VII** to each chord of **A** and **D** that introduces a chromatic change are shown.

Ex.62b: Phrygian VII Triad as Within-Mode Pivot

E:VII A:II E:VII A:V E:VIIA:VIIE:VII D:II E:VIID:IV E:VII D:V E:VII D:VI E:VIID:VII

306

Within-Dyad Prepared Modulation

Tables 18a and b display the relations of steps for within-dyad and between-dyad prepared modulation. Although the possibilities inherent in within-dyad modulation are greater than within-mode obviously, the available pivots don't change with the exception of the diminished chord. (Since within the scalar dyad, two keys share the same diminished chord, e.g. b° in G Mixolydian and E Phrygian, it can be used as a pivot.) However, their particular role or utility in the modulation may vary since the chords play a different role depending on the mode. For example, the V - VI progression in G Mixolydian would become a VII - I progression in E Phrygian.

Table 18a: The Relations of Mixolydian Scale Degrees with the Other Modes (Within-Dyad and Between-Dyad Modulation)

Mixolyd.	I	II	III	IV	V	VI	VII
Phrygian	III	IV	V	VI	VII	I	II
Lydian	II	III	IV	V	VI	VII	I
Dorian	IV	V	VI	VII	I	II	III
Ionian	V	VI	VII	I	II	III	IV
Aeolian	VII	I	II	III	IV	V	VI

Table 18b: The Relations of Phrygian Scale Degrees with the Other Modes (Within-Dyad and Between-Dyad Modulation)

Phrygian	I	II	III	IV	V	VI	VII
Mixolyd.	VI	VII	I	II	III	IV	V
Lydian	VII	I	II	III	IV	V	VI
Dorian	II	III	IV	V	VI	VII	I
Ionian	III	IV	V	VI	VII	I	II
Aeolian	V	VI	VII	I	II	III	IV

The tricky part of within-dyad modulation, and between-dyad modulation for that matter, is the differentiation of relative keys in different modes. This is the reason for the extensive examination in previous chapters on characteristic progressions for each of the modes. As was also noted, the establishment of a mode is a lengthier process outside of the Ionian mode since there is nothing as decisive as the V^7 - I progression.

Mixolydian Tonic to Phrygian.

The Mixolydian tonic is the Phrygian III, which is a generally neutral chord, without pronounced upward or downward tendencies (Ex. 63a).

Phrygian Tonic to Mixolydian.

The Phrygian tonic is the Mixolydian VI, which is a neutral chord (Ex. 63b).

Ex.63: Mixolydian and Phrygian Tonic Triads as Within-Dyad Pivot

Mixolydian II to Phrygian.

The Mixolydian II is Phrygian IV, which is an important step of that mode. It can be a useful pivot in many cases, particularly where a more direct modulation is sought. Although it cannot be easily used as a second key pivot in Mixolydian modulations, it can easily take this route through Phrygian (Ex. 64a).

308

Phrygian II to Mixolydian.

The Phrygian II is Mixolydian VII, which is an important step of the mode due to its agreement with the tonic. It has a mild cadential relation to I (Ex. 64b).

Ex.64: Mixolydian and Phrygian II Triads as Within-Dyad Pivot

Ex. 64a Mixolydian II - Phrygian			Ex. 64b Phrygian II - Mixolydian		
G:II/E:IV E:I⁶	E:VII⁶	E:I	E:II/G:VII⁶₄	G:IV⁶	G:V G:I

Mixolydian III to Phrygian.

The diminished Mixolydian III is the Phrygian V, which despite its harmonic nature has some importance due to its position as dominant. Although the III (V) is an unorthodox, but viable pivot, it requires some care since the V often moves to the Phrygian I (Ex. 65a).

Phrygian III to Mixolydian.

The Phrygian III is the Mixolydian tonic. The triad is slightly awkward but usable as a pivot, particularly in single or double inversion (Ex. 65b).

309

Ex.65: Mixolydian and Phrygian III Triads as Within-Dyad Pivot

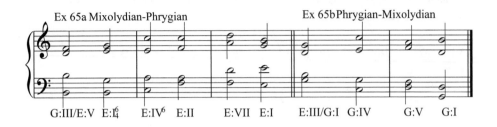

Ex 65a Mixolydian-Phrygian

Ex 65b Phrygian-Mixolydian

G:III/E:V E:I$^6_4$ E:IV^6 E:II E:VII E:I E:III/G:I G:IV G:V G:I

Mixolydian IV to Phrygian.

The Mixolydian IV is the Phrygian VI, which has some downward tendencies to the Phrygian V. (Ex. 66a).

Phrygian IV to Mixolydian.

The Phrygian IV is Mixolydian II, which is a convenient pivot due to its neutrality (Ex. 66b).

Ex.66: Mixolydian and Phrygian IV Triads as Within-Dyad Pivot

Ex. 66a Mixolydian IV - Phrygian

Ex. 66b Phrygian IV - Mixolydian

G:IV/E:VI E:II E:V$^6_4$ E:I E:IV/G:II G:IV^6 G:V G:I

310

Mixolydian V to Phrygian.

The Mixolydian V is Phrygian VII, which has a mild tendency to ascend to the tonic in cadences, but not as strongly as the Phrygian II – I progression (Ex. 67a).

Phrygian V to Mixolydian.

The Phrygian V is the diminished Mixolydian III, which is not a convenient pivot, but can be used if progressing to VI (Ex. 67b).

Ex.67: Mixolydian and Phrygian V Triads as Within-Dyad Pivot

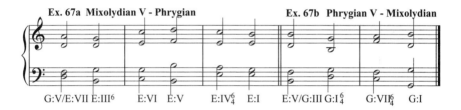

Mixolydian VI to Phrygian I.

The Mixolydian VI is Phrygian I. This is slightly awkward as a pivot unless in an inversion (Ex. 68a).

Phrygian VI to Mixolydian.

The Phrygian VI is Mixolydian IV, which is a key step of the mode and also a threat to its tonic. Therefore, this pivot has to be used carefully (Ex. 68b).

Ex.68: Mixolydian and Phrygian VI Triads as Within-Dyad Pivot

G:VI/E:I⁶ E:VI E:V⁶ E:VII⁶ E:IV⁶₄ E:I   E:VI/G:IV G:V G:I⁶₄ G:VII G:II⁶ G:I

Mixolydian VII to Phrygian.

The Mixolydian VII is Phrygian II, which has a strong downward tendency to the tonic. It is a somewhat awkward pivot (Ex. 69a).

Phrygian VII to Mixolydian.

The Phrygian VII is Mixolydian V and a convenient pivot, unlike in Ionian. Due to its lack of agreement with the tonic, it does not have as strong a dominant tendency (Ex. 69b).

Ex.69: Mixolydian and Phrygian VII Triads as Within-Dyad Pivot

G:VII/E:I⁶ E:I⁶₄ E:IV⁶ E:VII E:II   E:I   E:VII/G:V G:I⁶ G:VII⁶ G:I

Between-Dyad Prepared Modulation

Even more so than within-dyad prepared modulation, between-dyad prepared modulation has enough different possibilities to fill several chapters describing them. Again the major difficulty is establishing the mode given the existence of the competing relative keys. Between-dyad modulation is more difficult to accomplish successfully in the modern modal system since it goes against the procedures designed to establish and maintain the dyad. Its use requires care also because of its centrifugal effect on the musical form of modal compositions. On the other hand, it can provide more varied and complex harmonic structures while maintaining a modal framework. Generally, between-dyad modulation has to be made an integral part of a work's structure and sufficient repetition or musical space should be allowed to establish the new dyad. Music examples are already found in the within-dyad sections for each modal dyad since the same chords exist in each mode (see Tables 18a and b). For example, Myxolydian to Ionian can be assessed in the Aeolian to Ionian example progressions since Myxolydian I is Aeolian VII and so forth.

Mixolydian Tonic to Lydian/Dorian.
The Mixolydian tonic is the Lydian II. This is an important step of the mode, with prominent involvement in cadences, but is still usable. The Mixolydian I is the Dorian IV, which is a convenient pivot.

Phrygian Tonic to Lydian/Dorian.
The Phrygian tonic is the Lydian VII and Dorian II, both of which do have some cadential role.

Mixolydian II to Lydian/Dorian.
The Mixolydian II is Lydian III, which is a neutral step and Dorian V, an important chord in the tonic cadence that should be used carefully.

Phrygian II to Lydian/Dorian.
The Phrygian II is Lydian I which is generally not the best choice for pivot except in inversion. Phrygian II is Dorian III, which only has a mild cadential relation to I and makes a good pivot.

313

Mixolydian III to Lydian/Dorian.

The diminished Mixolydian III is the Lydian IV and the Dorian VI. With respect to Lydian, it can be an unorthodox but viable pivot, however, its use requires some care since the IV - V progression is a slight threat to the mode.

Phrygian III to Lydian/Dorian.

The Phrygian III is the Lydian II, which is important to modal cadences. It is Dorian IV, which is a useful pivot.

Mixolydian IV to Lydian/Dorian.

The Mixolydian IV is the Lydian V, which is not the best choice for pivot due to its strength in the mode. The IV is also Dorian VII, a neutral chord.

Phrygian IV to Lydian/Dorian.

The Phrygian IV is Lydian III, which is a convenient pivot due to its neutrality. It is the Dorian V, which is a somewhat less convenient pivot.

Mixolydian V to Lydian/Dorian.

The Mixolydian V is Lydian VI, a neutral chord, as well as Dorian I, which is best used in inversion.

Phrygian V to Lydian/Dorian.

The Phrygian V is the diminished Lydian IV and the Dorian VI. It is an awkward pivot, but can be used in certain limited progressions.

Mixolydian VI to Lydian/Dorian.

The Mixolydian VI is Lydian VII, a neutral chord, and Dorian II, usable but having a role in cadences.

Phrygian VI to Lydian/Dorian.

The Phrygian VI is Lydian V, which is a key step of the mode and also a threat to its tonic. Therefore, this pivot has to be used very carefully. It is also Dorian VII, which is a neutral chord.

Mixolydian VII to Lydian/Dorian.
The Mixolydian VII is Lydian I, which should be used in inversion as pivot, as well as Dorian III, a convenient pivot.

Phrygian VII to Lydian/Dorian.
The Phrygian VII is Lydian VI and a convenient pivot. It is also Dorian I, which is usable in inversion as a pivot.

Mixolydian Tonic to Ionian/Aeolian.
The Mixolydian tonic is the Ionian V. This is an important step of the mode, with prominent involvement in cadences and should be used carefully. The Mixolydian I is the Aeolian VII, which is a convenient pivot.

Phrygian Tonic to Ionian/Aeolian.
The Phrygian tonic is the Ionian III, a neutral chord and Aeolian V, not as usable.

Mixolydian II to Ionian/Aeolian.
The Mixolydian II is Ionian VI, which is a neutral step and Aeolian I, best used in inversion.

Phrygian II to Ionian/Aeolian.
The Phrygian II is Lydian I, which is not a good choice for pivot except inverted. Phrygian II is Aeolian VI, which is a neutral pivot.

Mixolydian III to Ionian/Aeolian.
The diminished Mixolydian III is the Ionian VII and the Dorian II. Ionian VII is difficult to use, but Aeolian II can be an unorthodox, yet viable pivot.

Phrygian III to Ionian/Aeolian.
The Phrygian III is the Ionian V, which is important to the cadence and not easily usable. It is also Aeolian VII, which is a useful pivot, unlike its minor scale counterpart.

Mixolydian IV to Ionian/Aeolian.

The Mixolydian IV is the Ionian tonic, which is best used in inversion for a pivot. The IV is also Aeolian III, which is a neutral chord.

Phrygian IV to Lydian/Dorian.

The Phrygian IV is Ionian VI, which is a convenient pivot due to its neutrality. It is the Aeolian tonic, which is a less convenient pivot.

Mixolydian V to Ionian/Aeolian.

The Mixolydian V is Ionian II, which is a fairly neutral chord, although it is often used in cadential progressions. It is also Aeolian IV, which is about as usable.

Phrygian V to Ionian/Aeolian.

The Phrygian V is the diminished Ionian VII and Aeolian II.

Mixolydian VI to Ionian/Aeolian.

The Mixolydian VI is Ionian III, a neutral chord, and Aeolian V, which has an important role in cadences, and should be used carefully.

Phrygian VI to Ionian/Aeolian.

The Phrygian VI is Ionian I, which is preferably used in inversion. It is also Aeolian III, which is a neutral chord.

Mixolydian VII to Ionian/Aeolian.

The Mixolydian VII is Ionian IV, which is usable with some care as pivot, as well as Aeolian VI, which is a convenient pivot.

Phrygian VII to Ionian/Aeolian.

The Phrygian VII is Ionian II, a usable pivot. It is also a convenient pivot as Aeolian IV.

316

Appendix 2

The Lydian-Dorian Dyad

Melodic Character of the Lydian-Dorian Dyad

This dyad, due to the location of the diminished triad in the Lydian and Dorian scales on the subdominant side, IV and VI respectively, has a dominant tilt. The Lydian mode has the tritone prominently positioned between I and IV. The prominent tritone and ascending half-step to the Final combined with the lack of prominent descending relations produces a melodically tense mode with strong upward tendencies. The Dorian mode has the tritone out of the way of melodic cadences since it rests on neither the Final, dominant or subdominant steps with ascending half-steps to the third and seventh steps. The lack of significant descending relationships in Dorian combined with non-salient ascending relations does produce a reduced melodic tension in this mode.

This Lydian-Dorian pattern of melodic tension represents a modest intensification of the Ionian-Aeolian pattern between its major and minor scales. Lydian is the most melodically tense major scale and Dorian is the most relaxed minor scale. Ionian and Aeolian are in the middle with Ionian somewhat more relaxed and Aeolian slightly more tense than their Lydian-Dorian counterparts. Mixolydian and Phrygian reverse the pattern of melodic tension for major and minor compared with Lydian-Dorian since it is the minor (Phrygian) scale which is the most melodically tense.

Given the prominent tritone in Lydian between I and IV, the Dorian mode provides a means of restoring some freer melodic movement between these two steps. The Dorian tritone lies between III and VI, thus is not nearly as prominent, and Lydian has no restriction in this particular melodic movement. The leading-tone is present in Lydian and not in Dorian. Although the Lydian leading-tone does impart some melodic strength to the tonic, it does not have quite the same importance as in Ionian due to the existing strength of the dominant. Since it forms the root of a minor triad, rather than the diminished triad, its tendency for resolution is reduced. Nevertheless, since the Lydian subdominant is weakened, the Lydian tonic is in a struggle with the dominant. The leading-tone helps to maintain the Lydian tonic in this circumstance.

While both modes have the I, II, V steps in agreement, the Lydian melodic movement, particularly if it has harmonic confirmation, needs to be more carefully weighed than in the Dorian. Of course, it is possible to use this melodic movement and not confirm it harmonically or have ambiguous harmonic support. The Dorian has less melodic tension than Lydian and benefits from the direction provided from this strong movement and also can make easier use of countervailing movement involving IV.

It is useful to remember that the harmonic significance of the melody varies according to its position among the voices. As was discussed in Chapter 4 and 5, the use of inversions has a significant effect on the harmonic weight and effect of chords. Also, non-simultaneity of note attack in the different voices lessens the harmonic effect that simultaneity enhances. Such techniques should be used to mitigate or enhance particular modal attributes.

Cadential Character of the Lydian-Dorian Dyad

The more effective cadences common to both modes of the Lydian-Dorian dyad are the V - I and III - I progressions. The Dorian IV - I progression moves from major to minor and has moderate effectiveness while the Dorian VII - I has less definite character. The Lydian has a complementary character with a more effective leading-tone based VII - I progression and a minimally useful IV - I. The use of dissonant cadences as discussed earlier can also be employed both within the Lydian-Dorian dyad and outside of it.

The modal tonic is best confirmed through a variety of cadences since none match the definiteness of the Ionian V - I. Additionally, the modal cadence should be prepared through melodic

318

motion (or stasis) and rhythm. Instead of providing short examples devoid of context, the reader should review the Lydian-Dorian Study Composition. Different types of cadences are demonstrated there in a more realistic manner, leaving aside the aesthetic effect of this particular realization.

Parenthetic Harmonies

In Table 13 (Chapter 5), the differing chromatic relations of secondary dominant {V of V} to dominant were displayed in the various modes. The Dorian {V of V} has an altered ninth (second), while Lydian has an altered seventh. However, as noted in the modern modal system, the parenthetic harmonies go beyond the secondary dominant to apply to all the steps in the same key as the given scale step.

The relation of various parenthetic harmonies to the original key and mode necessarily varies as can be seen in Table 19a and b. (Table 19b restates the contents of Table 19a in a Dorian context for convenience.) It should be emphasized that the notes are chromatic in relation to **F** Lydian since they are diatonic to the tonic key formed on that step. This is in contrast to the major-minor system practice of chromatically raising notes in secondary dominant harmony which are foreign to both the primary and secondary keys, e.g. the raised third in the minor chord. Parenthetic harmonies are not provided for the step on the diminished triad (**B**) nor on the step of the relative minor **D** Dorian since the modal system proposed here doesn't use a harmonically altered form.

Table 19a: The Lydian (and Dorian) Keys and their Parenthetic Harmonies (Scales)

Lydian	Lydian	Dorian	-	Lydian	Dorian	Dorian
F/0	G/2♯	a/1♯	b*	C/1♯	d/0	e/2♯
C/1♯	D/3♯	e/2♯	f*	G/2♯	a/1♯	b/3♯
G/2♯	A/4♯	b/3♯	c♯*	D/3♯	e/2♯	f♯/2♯
D/3♯	E/5♯	f♯/4♯	g♯*	A/4♯	b/3♯	c♯/5♯
A/4♯	B/6♯	c♯/5♯	d♯*	E/5♯	f♯/4♯	g♯/6♯
E/5♯	F♯/7♯/5♭	g♯/6♯	a♯*	B/6♯	c♯/5♯	d♯/7♯/5♭
B♭/1♭	C/1♯	d/0	e*	F/0	g/1♭	a/1♯
E♭/2♭	F/0	g/1♭	a*	B♭/1♭	c/2♭	d/0
A♭/3♭	B♭/1♭	c/2♭	d*	E♭/2♭	f/3♭	g/1♭
D♭/4♭	E♭/2♭	f/3♭	g*	A♭/3♭	b♭/4♭	c/2♭
G♭/5♭	A♭/3♭	b♭/4♭	c*	D♭/4♭	e♭/5♭	f/3♭
C♭/6♭	D♭/4♭	e♭/5♭	f*	G♭/5♭	a♭/6♭	b♭/4♭

Table 19b: The Dorian (and Lydian) Keys and their Parenthetic Harmonies (Scales)

Dorian	Dorian	Lydian	Lydian	Dorian	-	Lydian
d/0	e/2♯	F/0	G/2♯	a/1♯	b*	C/1♯
a/1♯	b/3♯	C/1♯	D/3♯	e/2♯	f♯*	G/2♯
e/2♯	f♯/2♯	G/2♯	A/4♯	b/3♯	c♯*	D/3♯
b/3♯	c♯/5♯	D/3♯	E/5♯	f♯/4♯	g♯*	A/4♯
f♯/4♯	g♯/6♯	A/4♯	B/6♯	c♯/5♯	d♯*	E/5♯
c♯/5♯	d♯/7♯/5♭	E/5♯	F♯/7♯/5♭	g♯/6♯	a♯*	B/6♯
g/1♭	a/1♯	B♭/1♭	C/1♯	d/0	e*	F/0
c/2♭	d/0	E♭/2♭	F/0	g/1♭	a*	B♭/1♭
f/3♭	g/1♭	A♭/3♭	B♭/1♭	c/2♭	d*	E♭/2♭
b♭/4♭	c/2♭	D♭/4♭	E♭/2♭	f/3♭	g*	A♭/3♭
e♭/5♭	f/3♭	G♭/5♭	A♭/3♭	b♭/4♭	c*	D♭/4♭
a♭/6♭	b♭/4♭	C♭/6♭	D♭/4♭	e♭/5♭	f*	G♭/5♭

A few specific examples should be helpful in clarifying the relationships displayed in Tables 19a and b. F Lydian (first row in Table 19a) has parenthetic harmonies of G Lydian, A Dorian, C Lydian and E Dorian. These keys introduce one or two chromatic notes as mentioned in previous chapters. Unlike the major-minor scale (or the Ionian-Aeolian dyad), parenthetic harmonies are unbalanced toward the sharp keys in the Lydian-Dorian scalar dyad. Whether a particular parenthetic triad introduces a chromatic note depends on its root, but this is no different from the major-minor system (e.g. the Tonic triad acting as the dominant for IV). Of course, in a contrapuntal texture, the chromatic notes can easily be introduced outside of a vertical chord.

Steps II, III, V and VII have parenthetic harmonies which introduce chromatic alterations into the primary key (e.g. F Lydian.) (The parenthetic harmonies are Lydian, if based on II and V, and Dorian, if based on III and VII.) However, the particular point of introduction of the chromatic change varies in chordal position and may not occur within a given triad. Looking at parenthetic harmonies based on Lydian III (A) and V (C), one chromatic note, F♯, is introduced. Lydian III can serve as A Dorian (row 2 on Table 19b), which would thus have F♯ as its sixth degree, altered from F. (Obviously, any chord in A Dorian containing its sixth degree will introduce a chromatic note in relation to F Lydian.) As for the parenthetic harmonies for Lydian V acting as C Lydian, the chromatic note, F♯, occurs on the third of {II of V} (D major triad) and sequentially down to the fifth of {VII of IV} (b minor triad).

Lydian parenthetic harmonies based on II and VII have two chromatic alterations in the key compared with the primary key. For example, the II of F Lydian is G Lydian, which has two sharps. Looking at the row for G Lydian in Table 19a, we can see that a triad built on {VII of II} would be f♯ minor and thus would have chromatic alterations of the root and fifth of the chord relative to F Lydian. Similarly, the F Lydian VII is also the tonic for E Dorian, which has two sharps. A triad built on {V of VII} (b minor triad) would introduce one chromatic note at the fifth, but to introduce the other chromatic note, the chord would have to include the ninth (or second), namely, C♯. (Chords based on the other steps obviously have the two changed notes at different positions of the chord.)

The first row of Table 19b displays the pattern for the Dorian key of **D** within the dyad. For the Dorian mode, the parenthetic harmonies are built on II, IV, V and VII since VI is the diminished triad and III is the Lydian relative major key of **F**. Steps II and V have Dorian parenthetic harmonies while IV and VII are Lydian in form. The parenthetic harmonies based on V and VII potentially introduce one chromatic change while those based on II and IV potentially introduce two chromatic changes.

To carry forward the previous Lydian example, the VII of **D** Dorian is **C** Lydian, which has one sharp. Looking at the row for **C** Lydian in Table 19b, we can see that a **D** major triad would be built on {II of VII} and thus would have chromatic alteration of the third of the chord relative to **D** Dorian. Similarly, the **D** Dorian II is also the tonic for **E** Dorian, which has two sharps. A triad built on {VII of II} (**b** minor triad) would introduce one chromatic note at the fifth, but to introduce the other chromatic note, the chord would have to add the ninth (second), namely, **C♯**.

Modulation in the Lydian-Doran Scalar Dyad

The two tables below (Tables 20a and 20b) display the set of transposed scales for the Lydian and Dorian scales respectively. For the purposes of prepared modulation the next Tables (21a and b) display the pattern of pivot chords (triads) between these modal keys. The triad is displayed in bold, followed by the within-mode keys in which it appears.

Table 20a: Lydian Key Scales

F	G	A	B	C	D	E
C	D	E	F♯	G	A	B
G	A	B	C♯	D	E	F♯
D	E	F♯	G♯	A	B	C♯
A	B	C♯	D♯	E	F♯	G♯
E	F♯	G♯	A♯	B	C♯	D♯
B	C♯	D♯	E♯	F♯	G♯	A♯
B♭	C	D	E	F	G	A
E♭	F	G	A	B♭	C	D
A♭	B♭	C	D	E♭	F	G
D♭	E♭	F	G	A♭	B♭	C
G♭	A♭	B♭	C	D♭	E♭	F

Table 20b: Dorian Key Scales

D	E	F	G	A	B	C
A	B	C	D	E	F♯	G
E	F♯	G	A	B	C♯	D
B	C♯	D	E	F♯	G♯	A
F♯	G♯	A	B	C♯	D♯	E
C♯	D♯	E	F♯	G♯	A♯	B
G	A	B♭	C	D	E	F
C	D	E♭	F	G	A	B♭
F	G	A♭	B♭	C	D	E♭
B♭	C	D♭	E♭	F	G	A♭
E♭	F	G♭	A♭	B♭	C	D♭
A♭	B♭	C♭	D♭	E♭	F	G♭

324

Table 21a: The Key Relations of Lydian Pivot Chords (Within-Mode)

I	II	III	IV	V	VI	VII
F/Bb,Eb,F	G/C,F,G	a/Bb,C, F	b*/F	C/Bb,C, F	d/Bb,Eb,F	e/C,F,G
C/Bb,C, F	D/C,D,G	e/C,F,G	f♯*/C	G/C,F,G	a/Bb,C, F	b/C,D,G
G/C,F,G	A/A,D,G	b/C,D,G	c♯*/G	D/C,D,G	e/C,F,G	f♯/A,D,G
D/C,D,G	E/A,D,E	f♯/A,D,G	g♯*/D	A/A,D,G	b/C,D,G	c♯/A,D,E
A/A,D,G	B/A,Cb,E	c♯/A,D,E	d♯*/A	E/A,D,E	f♯/A,D,G	g♯/A,Cb,E
E/A,D,E	F♯/Cb,E,Gb	g♯/A,Cb,E	a♯*/E	B/A,Cb,E	c♯/A,D,E	d♯/Cb,E,Gb
Bb/Ab,Bb,Eb	C/Bb,C,F	d/Bb,Eb,F	e*/Bb	F/Bb,Eb,F	g/Ab,Bb,Eb	a/Bb,C, F
Eb/Ab,Db,Eb	F/Bb,Eb,F	g/Ab,Bb,Eb	a*/Eb	Bb/Ab,Bb,Eb	c/Ab,Db,Eb	d/Bb,Eb,F
Ab/Ab,Db,Gb	Bb/Ab,Bb,Eb	c/Ab,Db,Eb	d*/Ab	Eb/Ab,Db,Eb	f/Ab,Db,Gb	g/Ab,Bb,Eb
Db/Cb,Db,Gb	Eb/Ab,Db,Eb	f/Ab,Db,Gb	g*/Db	Ab/Ab,Db,Gb	bb/Cb,Db,Gb	c/Ab,Db,Eb
Gb/Cb,E,Gb	Ab/Ab,Db,Gb	bb/Cb,Db,Gb	c*/Gb	Db/Cb,Db,Gb	eb/Cb,E,Gb	f/Ab,Db,Gb
Cb/A,Cb,E	Db/Cb,Db,Gb	eb/Cb,E,Gb	f*/Cb	Gb/Cb,E,Gb	ab/A,Cb,E	bb/Cb,Db,Gb

Table 21b: The Key Relations of Dorian Pivot Chords (Within-Mode)

I	II	III	IV	V	VI	VII
d/C,D,G	e/A,D,E	F/C,D,G	G/A,D,E	a/A,D,G	b*/D	C/A,D.G
a/A,D,G	b/A,B,E	C/A,D,G	D/A,B,E	e/A,D,E	f♯*/A	G/A,D,E
e/A,D,E	f♯/B,E,F♯	G/A,D,E	A/B,E,F♯	b/A,B,E	c♯*/E	D/A,B,E
b/A,B,E	c♯/B,C♯,F♯	D/A,B,E	E/B,C♯,F♯	f♯/ B,E,F♯	g♯*/B	A/B,E,F♯
f♯/ B,E,F♯	g♯/A♭,C♯,F♯	A/B,E,F♯	B/A♭,C♯,F♯	c♯/B,C♯,F♯	d♯*/F♯	E/B,C♯,F♯
c♯/B,C♯,F♯	d♯/A♭,C♯,E♭	E/B,C♯,F♯	F♯/A♭,C♯,E♭	g♯/A♭,C♯,F♯	a♯*/C♯	B/A♭,C♯,F♯
g/C,F,G	a/A,D,G	B♭/C,F,G	C/A,D,G	d/C,D,G	e*/G	F/C,D,G
c/ B♭,C,F	d/C,D,G	E♭/ B♭,C,F	F/C,D,G	g/C,F,G	a*/C	B♭/C,F,G
f/B♭,E♭,F	g/C,F,G	A♭/B♭,E♭,F	B♭/C,F,G	c/B♭,C,F	d*/F	E♭/B♭,C,F
b♭/A♭,B♭,E♭	c/B♭,C,F	D♭/A♭,B♭,E♭	E♭/B♭,C,F	f/B♭,E♭,F	g*/B♭	A♭/B♭,E♭,F
e♭/A,C♯,E♭	f/B♭,E♭,F	G♭/A,C♯,E♭	A♭/B♭,E♭,F	b♭/A♭,B♭,E♭	c*/E♭	D♭/A♭,B♭,E
a♭/A♭,C♯,F♯	b♭/A♭,B♭,E♭	C♭/A♭,C♯,F♯	D♭/A♭,B♭,E♭	e♭/A,C♯,E♭	f*/A♭	G♭/A,C♯,E♭

Within-Mode Prepared Modulation

The within-mode prepared modulations in Lydian and Dorian were touched upon previously, but here the possibilities are presented more systematically. The use of each scale step in modulation will be presented for closer and more distant keys starting with the tonic chords. The Lydian and Dorian pivot chords are restricted to keys a major second, perfect fourth, perfect fifth and minor seventh above the tonic.

Lydian Tonic.

The Lydian tonic of the first (source) key can be a useful pivot in some cases, but unlike other modes, note that it cannot be used in modulations to the (altered) subdominant. The main other factor to consider with the (first key) tonic is the frequent presence of some partial or full cadence that does affect the context of the modulation. The tonic chord is shared by the Lydian key a perfect fourth and minor seventh above. In the case of **F** Lydian, that would be **E♭:II** and **B♭:V**. In Ex. 70a, the progressions from **F:I** to each chord of **E♭** and **B♭** Lydian that introduces a chromatic change are shown.

Ex.70a: Lydian Tonic Triad as Within-Mode Pivot

F:I E♭:I F:I E♭:III F:I E♭:IV F:I E♭:V F:I E♭:VI F:I B♭:I F:I B♭:IV F:I B♭:VI

Dorian Tonic.

The Dorian tonic of the first key can be used as pivot chord to the shared Dorian keys a perfect fourth and minor seventh above. In the case of **D** Dorian, that would be **G:V** and **C:II**. The dominant pivot is not as problematic in the Dorian mode, although Dorian V - I is still the predominant cadence. In Ex. 70b, the progressions from **D:I** to each chord of **G** and **C** Dorian that introduces a chromatic change are shown.

Ex.70b: Dorian Tonic Triad as Within-Mode Pivot

D:I C:I   D:I C:III D:I C:V D:I C:VI D:I C:VII D:I G:I   D:I G:III D:I G:VI

Lydian II.

The Lydian II is a major chord and its cadential relation to Lydian V requires more care in its use, particularly with progressions to V. Lydian II also has issues when used as a pivot. Note that in modulations to the dominant key, it is the dominant of the second key. The II chord occurs in the keys a major second and perfect fifth above. In the case of F Lydian that would be G:I and C:V. Lydian II is the tonic for G Lydian and should be used in inversion in this modulation. In Ex. 71a, the progressions from F:II to each chord of C and G Lydian that introduces a chromatic change are shown.

Ex.71a: Lydian II Triad as Within-Mode Pivot

F:II C:II   F:II C:IV F:II C:VII F:II G:II F:II G:III F:II G:IV F:II G:V F:II G:VII

Dorian II.

The Dorian II has the same issues as Lydian II used as a pivot due to its cadential relation to V and I and to its status in the second key. The II chord is shared by the key a perfect fifth and major second above. In the case of **D** Dorian that would be **E:I** and **A:V**. Note that Dorian II is the tonic for **E** Dorian. In Ex. 71b, the progressions from **D:II** to each chord of **E** and **A** Dorian that introduces a chromatic change are shown.

Ex.71b: **Dorian II Triad as Within-Mode Pivot**

D:II   A:II   D:II   A:IV   D:II   A:VI   D:II   E:II   D:II   E:IV   D:II   E:V   D:II E:VI   D:II   E:VII

Lydian III.

The Lydian III is a neutral chord and a very usable pivot chord. It is shared by the keys a perfect fourth and fifth above. In the case of **F** Lydian that would be C:VI and B♭:VII. In Ex. 72a, the progressions from **F:III** to each chord of **C** and **B♭** Lydian that introduces a chromatic change are shown.

Ex.72a: Lydian III Triad as Within-Mode Pivot

F:III C:II F:III C:IV F:III C:VII F:III Bb:I F:III Bb:IV F:III Bb:VI

Dorian III.

The Dorian III is a convenient pivot due to its neutrality in both the first and second keys. The III can be used as pivot chord to the shared Dorian keys a perfect fourth and minor seventh above. In the case of **D** Dorian, that would be **G:VII** and **C:IV** Dorian. In Ex. 72b, the progressions from **D:III** to each chord of **G** and **C** that introduces a chromatic change are shown.

Ex.72b: Dorian III Triad as Within-Mode Pivot

D:III G:I D:III G:III D:III G:VI D:III C:I D:III C:III D:III C:V D:III C:VI D:III C:VII

330

Lydian IV.

The Lydian IV is diminished and not useable as a within-mode pivot.

Dorian IV.

The Dorian IV can be used freely as a pivot to the destination key. The IV chord is shared by the key a major second and perfect fifth above. In the case of **D** Dorian, that would be **E**:III and **A**:VII. In Ex. 73b, the progressions from **D**:IV to each chord of **A** and **E** Dorian that introduces a chromatic change are shown.

Ex.73: Dorian IV Triad as Within-Mode Pivot

D:IV A:II   D:IV A:IV D:IV A:VI D:IV E:II   D:IV E:IV   D:IV E:V   D:IV E:VI D:IV E:VII

Lydian V.

The Lydian V should be very carefully used as pivot (as interpreted in the destination key) since it is a threat to the Lydian tonic. Even as interpreted in the first key the V is somewhat problematic. The V chord is shared by the key a perfect fourth and perfect fifth above. In the case of **F** Lydian that would be **B♭**:II and **C**:I. Note, however, that V is the tonic in **C** Lydian. In Ex. 74a, the progressions from **F**:V to each chord of **C** and **B♭** Lydian that introduces a chromatic change are shown.

Ex.74a: Lydian V Triad as Within-Mode Pivot

F:V   C:II   F:V   C:IV   F:V   C:VII   F:V   Bb:I   F:V   Bb:IV   F:V   Bb:VI

Dorian V.

The Dorian V should be sparingly used as pivot (in the destination key) since it is important to the cadence. It is not optimally neutral in the source key either due to its cadential role. The V chord is shared by the key a perfect fourth and perfect fifth above. In the case of **D** Dorian that would be G:II and A:I. Note that V is the tonic of **A** Dorian. In Ex. 74b, the progressions from **D**:V to each chord of **G** and **A** Dorian that introduces a chromatic change are shown.

Ex.74b: Dorian IV Triad as Within-Mode Pivot

D:V   A:II   D:V   A:IV   D:V   A:VI   D:V   G:I   D:V   G:III   D:V   G:VI

332

Lydian VI.

The minor Lydian VI can be easily used as pivot. The VI chord is shared by the Lydian key a perfect fourth and minor seventh above. In the case of **F** Lydian, that would be **B♭:III** and **E♭:VII**. In Ex. 75a, the progressions from **F:VI** to each chord of **B♭** and **E♭** that introduces a chromatic change are shown.

Ex.75: Lydian VI Triad as Within-Mode Pivot

F:VI   B♭:I   F:VI   B♭:IV   F:VI   B♭:VI   F:VI   E♭:I   F:VI   E♭:III   F:VI   E♭:IV   F:VI   E♭:V   F:VI   E♭:VI

Dorian VI.

The Dorian VI is the diminished triad and not usable as a within-mode pivot.

Lydian VII.

The Lydian VII is a neutral pivot. The VII chord is shared by the key a major second and perfect fifth above. In the case of **F** Lydian, that would be **G:VI** and **C:III**. In Ex. 76a, the progressions from **F:VII** to each chord of **C** and **G** Lydian that introduces a chromatic change are shown.

Ex.76a: Lydian VII Triad as Within-Mode Pivot

F:VII C:II   F:VII C:IV F:VII C:VII F:VII G:II F:VII G:III F:VII G:IV F:VII G:V F:VII G:VII

Dorian VII.

The Dorian VII can be easily used as pivot. The VII chord is shared by the key a perfect fourth and perfect fifth above. In the case of **D** Dorian, that would be **G:IV** and **A:III**. In Ex. 76b, the progressions from **D:VII** to each chord of **G** and **A** Dorian that introduces a chromatic change are shown.

Ex.76b: Dorian VII Triad as Within-Mode Pivot

D:VII G:I   D:VII G:III   D:VII G:VI   D:VII A:II   D:VII A:IV D:VII A:VI

334

Within-Dyad Prepared Modulation

Although the possibilities inherent in within-dyad modulation are much greater than with within-mode obviously, the additional keys relevant to pivot chords are all relative keys in the sense noted in the previous chapter. Thus, the basic nature of the available progressions don't change. However, their particular role in the modulation may vary since the chords play a different role depending on the mode. For example, the V - VI progression in **F** Lydian would become a III - IV progression in **D** Dorian (see Tables 22a and b).

Table 22a: The Relations of Lydian Scale Degrees with the other Modes (Within-Dyad and Between-Dyad Modulation)

Lydian	I	II	III	IV	V	VI	VII
Dorian	III	IV	V	VI	VII	I	II
Mixolyd.	VII	I	II	III	IV	V	VI
Phrygian	II	III	IV	V	VI	VII	I
Ionian	IV	V	VI	VII	I	II	III
Aeolian	VI	VII	I	II	III	IV	V

Table 22b: The Relations of Dorian Scale Degrees with the other Modes (Within-Dyad and Between-Dyad Modulation)

Dorian	I	II	III	IV	V	VI	VII
Lydian	VI	VII	I	II	III	IV	V
Mixolyd.	V	VI	VII	I	II	III	IV
Phrygian	VII	I	II	III	IV	V	VI
Ionian	II	III	IV	V	VI	VII	I
Aeolian	IV	V	VI	VII	I	II	III

The tricky part of within-dyad modulation, and between-dyad modulation for that matter, is the differentiation of relative keys in different modes. This is the reason for the extensive examination in previous chapters on characteristic progressions for each of the modes. As was also noted, the establishment of a mode is a lengthier process outside of the Ionian mode since there is nothing as decisive as the V^7 - I progression. Therefore the focus again in the examples will be on such modulations to relative keys.

Lydian Tonic to Dorian. The Lydian tonic is the Dorian III, which is a generally neutral chord, without pronounced upward or downward tendencies (Ex. 77a).

Dorian Tonic to Lydian.
The Dorian tonic is the Lydian VI, which is a neutral chord (Ex.77b).

Ex.77: Lydian and Dorian Tonic Triads as Within-Dyad Pivot

Ex. 77a Lydian I to Dorian

Ex. 77b Dorian I to Lydian

Ly.I/Dor.III D:VII⁶ D:I⁶₄ D:V D:IV D:I Dor.I/Ly.VI F:V⁶ F:I⁶ F:III⁶ F:VI F:IV⁶₄ F:V⁶ F:I

Lydian II to Dorian.
The Lydian II is Dorian IV, which is a moderately important step of that mode. It can be a useful pivot, particularly where a more direct modulation is sought (Ex. 78a).

Dorian II to Lydian.
The Dorian II is Lydian VII, which is a fairly neutral step of the mode although it does have a leading tone relation with the tonic (Ex. 78b).

336

Ex.78: Lydian and Dorian II Triads as Within-Dyad Pivot

Lydian III to Dorian.

The Lydian III is the Dorian V, which is important in cadences and should be used with care as pivot (Ex. 79a).

Dorian III to Lydian.

The Dorian III is the Lydian tonic, which is more difficult to use as pivot. If it is used, the inversions might be less awkward (Ex. 79b).

Ex.79: Lydian and Dorian III Triads as Within-Dyad Pivot

Lydian IV to Dorian.

The Lydian IV is the Dorian VI, which is the diminished chord. It is possible to use it but the progressions (and key) are constricted (Ex. 80a).

Dorian IV to Lydian.

The Dorian IV is Lydian II, which is a convenient pivot due to its relative neutrality (Ex. 80b).

Ex.80: Lydian and Dorian IV Triads as Within-Dyad Pivot

Lydian V to Dorian.

The Lydian V is Dorian VII, which is a relatively neutral chord with only a mild tendency to progress to the tonic (Ex. 81a).

Dorian V to Lydian.

The Dorian V is the Lydian III, which is a convenient pivot (Ex. 81b).

Ex.81: Lydian and Dorian V Triads as Within-Dyad Pivot

Lydian VI to Dorian I.
The Lydian VI is Dorian I. This is slightly awkward to use as a pivot unless in inversion (Ex. 82a).

Dorian VI to Lydian.
The Dorian VI is the diminished Lydian IV, which is difficult to use but still possible (Ex. 82b).

Ex.82: Lydian and Dorian VI Triads as Within-Dyad Pivot

Lydian VII to Dorian.
The Lydian VII is Dorian II, which is a relatively neutral chord and useful pivot (Ex. 83a).

Dorian VII to Lydian.

The Dorian VII is Lydian V and a difficult pivot due to its strength against the tonic (Ex. 83b).

Ex.83: Lydian and Dorian VII Triads as Within-Dyad Pivot

Ex. 83a Lydian VII to Dorian   Ex. 83b Dorian VII to Lydian

Ly.VII/ D:VII D:I⁶ D:IV D:V D:I   Dor.VII/ F:I₄⁶ F:II F:VI⁶ F:IV⁶ F:V⁶ F:III⁶ F:I
Dor.II   Ly.V⁶

Between-Dyad Prepared Modulation

Again with between-dyad modulation, the major difficulty is establishing the mode given the existence of the competing relative keys. Between-dyad modulation requires more care in the modern modal system since it can work against the procedures designed to establish and maintain the dyad. Its use requires care also because of its centrifugal effect on the musical form of modal compositions. Generally, a between-dyad modulation has to be made an integral part of a work's structure and sufficient repetition or musical space should be allowed to establish the new dyad. Examples already exist in the within-dyad sections since the same triads are present in each mode (see Table 22).

Lydian Tonic to Mixolydian/Phrygian.

The Lydian tonic is the Mixolydian VII. This is an important step of the mode since it agrees with the tonic. The Lydian I is the Phrygian II, which is a more difficult pivot due to its downward cadential quality.

340

Dorian Tonic to Mixolydian/Phrygian.
The Dorian tonic is the Mixolydian V and Phrygian VII. The Mixolydian V is somewhat more neutral as a pivot than most V chords since it lacks agreement with the tonic. Phrygian VII does play a role in cadences but is still usable.

Lydian II to Mixolydian/Phrygian.
The Lydian II is Mixolydian I, which should be used in inversion as pivot and also Phrygian III, which is a neutral chord.

Dorian II to Mixolydian/Phrygian.
The Dorian II is Mixolydian VI, which is a good choice for pivot. Dorian II is Phrygian I which is more difficult to use as a pivot.

Lydian III to Mixolydian/Phrygian.
The Lydian III is the Mixolydian II and the Phrygian IV. The Mixolydian II is neutral and a good choice for pivot. With respect to Phrygian, it can also be a viable pivot.

Dorian III to Mixolydian/Phrygian.
The Dorian III is the Mixolydian VII, which is important to modal definition but easily used. It is Phrygian II, which is not the best pivot due to its use in the Phrygian cadence.

Lydian IV to Mixolydian/Phrygian.
The diminished Lydian IV is the Mixolydian III, which is key restricted and also awkward as a pivot unless the progression goes to VI. The diminished Phrygian V is a more complex case since it is still the dominant. Its use as a pivot should probably be inversely related to the frequency of its progression to I.

Dorian IV to Mixolydian/Phrygian.
The Dorian IV is Mixolydian I, which is not a convenient pivot. It is also the Phrygian III, which is an easily used pivot.

Lydian V to Mixolydian/Phrygian.
The Lydian V is Mixolydian IV, which is awkward due to its strength in the mode and direct threat to the tonic. It is also Phrygian VI, which is quite usable.

Dorian V to Mixolydian/Phrygian.
The Dorian V is the Mixolydian II a neutral chord and the Phrygian IV, which is important modally but more usable than in Mixolydian.

Lydian VI to Mixolydian/Phrygian.
The Lydian VI is Mixolydian V, which is usable despite being the dominant and Phrygian VII, which is usable although it does have a role in cadences.

Dorian VI to Mixolydian/Phrygian.
The diminished Dorian VI is Mixolydian III and Phrygian V. Therefore, these pivots are key restricted and fairly awkward to use although the Phrygian V has more possibilities.

Lydian VII to Mixolydian/Phrygian.
The Lydian VII is Mixolydian VI, which can be easily used as pivot, as well as Phrygian I which is not the best pivot but can be used in inversion.

Dorian VII to Mixolydian/Phrygian.
The Dorian VII is Mixolydian IV, a difficult to use pivot. It is also Phrygian VI, which is a convenient pivot.

Lydian Tonic to Ionian/Aeolian.
The Lydian tonic is the Ionian IV. This is an important step of the mode, with prominent involvement in cadences and should be used carefully. The Lydian I is the Aeolian VI, which is a convenient pivot.

Dorian Tonic to Ionian/Aeolian.
The Dorian tonic is the Ionian II, a neutral chord and Aeolian IV, somewhat more constrained but still usable.

Lydian II to Ionian/Aeolian.
The Lydian II is Ionian V, which is not a good pivot and Aeolian VII, which is a useful pivot.

Dorian II to Ionian/Aeolian.

The Dorian II is Ionian III, which is generally a good choice for pivot. Dorian II is Aeolian V, which is not a good choice for pivot.

Lydian III to Ionian/Aeolian.

The Lydian III is the Ionian VI and the Aeolian I. Ionian VI is easy to use, but Aeolian I is a less viable pivot.

Dorian III to Ionian/Aeolian.

The Dorian III is the Ionian IV, which is important to the cadence and less easily usable. It is Aeolian VI, which is a useful pivot.

Lydian IV to Ionian/Aeolian.

The diminished Lydian IV is the Ionian VII, which is not a good choice for pivot unless moving to Ionian III. The IV is also Aeolian II, which is somewhat more useable.

Dorian IV to Lydian/Dorian.

The Dorian IV is Ionian V, which is not a convenient pivot. It is the Aeolian VII, which, unlike in the minor scale, is a neutral chord and quite usable.

Lydian V to Ionian/Aeolian.

The Lydian V is Ionian I which is a difficult to use chord. It is also Aeolian III, which is quite usable.

Dorian V to Ionian/Aeolian.

The Dorian V is the neutral Ionian VI and the more awkward Aeolian I.

Lydian VI to Ionian/Aeolian.

The Lydian VI is Ionian II, a neutral chord, and Aeolian IV, which has a role in cadences but is still usable.

Dorian VI to Ionian/Aeolian.

The diminished Dorian VI is Ionian VII, which is not easily usable. It is also Aeolian II, which has more possibilities.

Lydian VII to Ionian/Aeolian.
The Lydian VII is Ionian III, which is quite usable as pivot, as well as Aeolian V, which is a less convenient pivot.

Dorian VII to Ionian/Aeolian.
The Dorian VII is Ionian I, not the best pivot. It is also Aeolian III, which is a convenient pivot.

Appendix 3

The Ionian-Aeolian Dyad

Melodic Character of the Ionian-Aeolian Dyad

As noted previously, this dyad has a relatively even balance between dominant and subdominant influence. The Ionian Mode has the tritone out of the way of melodic cadences since it rests on neither the Final, dominant or subdominant steps. It has ascending half-steps to the 4th and tonic steps. The Aeolian has the tritone positioned between II and VI. The descending half-step to the dominant and non-significant ascending half-steps creates a melodically mild mode with slight downward tendencies.

Cadential Character of the Ionian-Aeolian Dyad

The more effective cadences in both modes of the Ionian-Aeolian dyad are the V - I and IV - I progressions while III - I progressions also work. The Ionian VII - I progression was less often used in the tonal system but can be effective within the modal system. The Aeolian VII - I has less definite character. Both modes have the I, IV and V steps in agreement.

Ionian-Aeolian Parenthetic Harmonies

In Table 13 (Chapter 5), the differing chromatic relations of secondary dominant {V of V} to dominant were displayed in the various modes. The Ionian {V of V} has an altered third, of course, while Aeolian has an altered fifth. However, in the modal system, the parenthetic harmonies go beyond the secondary dominant to apply to all the steps in the same key as the given scale step. The relation of various parenthetic harmonies to the original key and mode necessarily varies as can be seen in Table 23a and b. (Table 23b restates the contents of Table 23a in an Aeolian context for convenience.)

Table 23a: The Ionian (and Aeolian) Keys and their Parenthetic Harmonies (Scales)

Ionian	Aeolian	Aeolian	Ionian	Ionian	Aeolian	-
C/0	d/1♭	e/1♯	F/1♭	G/1♯	a/0	b*
G/1♯	a/0	b/2♯	C/0	D/2♯	e/1♯	f♯*
D/2♯	e/1♯	f/3♯	G/1♯	A/3♯	b/2♯	c♯*
A/3♯	b/2♯	c♯/4♯	D/2♯	E/4♯	f♯/3♯	g♯*
E/4♯	f♯/3♯	g♯/5♯	A/3♯	B/5♯	c♯/4♯	d♯*
B/5♯	c♯/4♯	d♯/6♯	E/4♯	F♯/6♯	g♯/5♯	a♯*
F/1♭	g/2♭	a/0	B♭/2♭	C/0	d/1♭	e*
B♭/2♭	c/3♭	d/1♭	E♭/3♭	F/1♭	g/2♭	a*
E♭/3♭	f/4♭	g/2♭	A♭/4♭	B♭/2♭	c/3♭	d*
A♭/4♭	b♭/5♭	c/3♭	D♭/5♭	E♭/3♭	f/4♭	g*
D♭/5♭	e♭/6♭	f/4♭	G♭/6♯	A♭/4♭	b♭/5♭	c*
G♭/6♭	a♭/5♯	b♭/5♭	C♭/5♯	D♭/5♭	e♭/6♭	f*

Table 23b: The Aeolian (and Ionian) Keys and their Parenthetic Harmonies (Scales)

Aeolian	-	Ionian	Aeolian	Aeolian	Ionian	Ionian
a/0	b*	C/0	d/1♭	e/1♯	F/1♭	G/1♯
e/1♯	f♯*	G/1♯	a/0	b/2♯	C/0	D/2♯
b/2♯	c♯*	D/2♯	e/1♯	f/3♯	G/1♯	A/3♯
f♯/3♯	g♯*	A/3♯	b/2♯	c♯/4♯	D/2♯	E/4♯
c♯/4♯	d♯*	E/4♯	f♯/3♯	g♯/5♯	A/3♯	B/5♯
g♯/5♯	a♯*	B/5♯	c♯/4♯	d♯/6♯	E/4♯	F♯/6♯
d/1♭	e*	F/1♭	g/2♭	a/0	B♭/2♭	C/0
g/2♭	a*	B♭/2♭	c/3♭	d/1♭	E♭/3♭	F/1♭
c/3♭	d*	E♭/3♭	f/4♭	g/2♭	A♭/4♭	B♭/2♭
f/4♭	g*	A♭/4♭	b♭/5♭	c/3♭	D♭/5♭	E♭/3♭
b♭/5♭	c*	D♭/5♭	e♭/6♭	f/4♭	G♭/6♯	A♭/4♭
e♭/6♭	f*	G♭/6♭	a♭/5♯	b♭/5♭	C♭/5♯	D♭/5♭

Looking at Table 23a, we see the Ionian-Aeolian pattern of chromatic notes introduced by parenthetic harmonies. It should be emphasized that the notes are chromatic in relation to C Ionian since they are diatonic to the tonic key formed on that step. This is in contrast to the major-minor system practice of chromatically raising notes in secondary dominant harmony which are foreign to both the primary and secondary keys, e.g. the raised third in the minor chord. Parenthetic harmonies are not provided for the step on the diminished triad (b°) nor on the step of the relative minor A Aeolian since the modern modal system doesn't use a harmonically altered form.

Steps II, III, IV and V have parenthetic harmonies that introduce chromatic alterations into the primary key (C Ionian) However, the particular point of introduction varies in accessibility with normal triadic chords. Only one chromatic change, at most, is introduced with all Ionian-Aeolian parenthetic harmonies. Moving from {II of II} to {VII of II}, the chromatic note is introduced at the fifth on {II of II} (e° chord) and sequentially downward until the change occurs on the seventh of {VII of II}. Similarly, Ionian III is also E Aeolian. The chromatic change occurs on the root of {II of III} (f♯° chord).

Ionian parenthetic harmonies based on IV and V are Ionian in character. For example, the IV of **C** Ionian is **F** Ionian which has one flat. Looking at the Table 23a, we can see that parenthetic harmonies based on {II of IV} (**g** minor chord) would involve chromatic alterations of the third of the chord sequentially down to the fifth of {VII of IV}. The Ionian V is also the tonic for **G** Ionian which has one sharp. A chord built on {II of V} (**a** minor chord) would have no chromatic alteration since **A** Aeolian is the relative minor of **C** Ionian.

Table 23b shows the pattern for the Aeolian key of **A** within the dyad. In this case, the parenthetic harmonies are built on IV, V and VI and VII since II is the diminished triad and III is the relative major **C** Ionian. Since the nature of the parenthetic harmonies is the same and the change is simply with the scale step, we don't need to reiterate the parenthetic relationships.

Modulation in the Ionian-Aeolian Dyad

The two tables below (Tables 24a and 24b) display the set of transposed scales for the Ionian and Aeolian scales respectively. Of course, they are no different than the keys of the major-minor system.

Table 24a: Ionian Scale Keys

C	D	E	F	G	A	B
G	A	B	C	D	E	F♯
D	E	F♯	G	A	B	C♯
A	B	C♯	D	E	F♯	G♯
E	F♯	G♯	A	B	C♯	D♯
B	C♯	D♯	E	F♯	G♯	A♯
F	G	A	B♭	C	D	E
B♭	C	D	E♭	F	G	A
E♭	F	G	A♭	B♭	C	D
A♭	B♭	C	D♭	E♭	F	G
D♭	E♭	F	G♭	A♭	B♭	C
G♭	A♭	B♭	C♭	D♭	E♭	F

Table 24b: Aeolian Scale Keys

A	B	C	D	E	F	G
E	F♯	G	A	B	C	D
B	C♯	D	E	F♯	G	A
F♯	G♯	A	B	C♯	D	E
C♯	D♯	E	F♯	G♯	A	B
G♯	A♯	B	C♯	D♯	E	F♯
D	E	F	G	A	B♭	C
G	A	B♭	C	D	E♭	F
C	D	E♭	F	G	A♭	B♭
F	G	A♭	B♭	C	D♭	E♭
B♭	C	D♭	E♭	F	G♭	A♭
E♭	F	G♭	A♭	B♭	C♭	D♭

The tables display the set of transposable Ionian and Aeolian keys. For the purposes of prepared modulation the next Tables display the pattern of pivot chords (triads) between these modal keys. The main difference from the major-minor system is the lack of chromatic minor chords.

Table 25a: The Key Relations of Ionian Pivot Chords (Within-Mode)

I	II	III	IV	V	VI	VII
C/C,F,G	d/ B♭,C, F	e/C,D,G	F/B♭,C, F	G/C,D,G	a/ C,F,G	b*/C
G/C,D,G	a/C,F,G	b/A,D,G	C/C,F,G	D/A,D,G	e/C,D,G	f♯*/G
D/A,D,G	e/C,D,G	f♯/A,D,E	G/C,D,G	A/A,D,E	b/A,D,G	c♯*/D
A/A,D,E	b/A,D,G	c♯/A,B,E	D/A,D,G	E/A,B,E	f♯/A,D,E	g♯*/A
E/A,B,E	f♯/A,D,E	g♯/B,E,G♭	A/A,D,E	B/B,E,G♭	c♯/A,B,E	d♯*/E
B/B,E,G♭	c♯/A,B,E	d♯/B,D♭,G♭	E/A,B,E	F♯/B,D♭,G♭	g♯/B,E,G♭	a♯*/B
F/B♭,C,F	g/B♭,E♭,F	a/C,F,G	B♭/B♭,E♭,F	C/C,F,G	d/B♭,C,F	e*/F
B♭/B♭,E♭,F	c/A♭,B♭,E♭	d/B♭,C,F	E♭/A♭,B♭,E♭	F/B♭,C,F	g/B♭,E♭,F	a*/B♭
E♭/A♭,B♭,E♭	f/A♭,D♭,E♭	g/B♭,E♭,F	A♭/A♭,D♭,E♭	B♭/B♭,E♭,F	c/A♭,B♭,E♭	d*/E♭
A♭/A♭,D♭,E♭	b♭/A♭,D♭,G♭	c/A♭,B♭,E♭	D♭/A♭,D♭,G♭	E♭/A♭,B♭,E♭	f/A♭,D♭,E♭	g*/A♭
D♭/A♭,D♭,G♭	e♭/ B,D♭,G♭	f/A♭,D♭,E♭	G♭/B,D♭,G♭	A♭/A♭,D♭,E♭	b♭/A♭,D♭,G	c*/D♭
G♭/B,D♭,G♭	a♭ /B,E,G♭	b♭/A♭,D♭,G♭	C♭/B,E,G♭	D♭/A♭,D♭,G♭	e♭/ B,D♭,G♭	f*/G♭

351

Table 25b: The Key Relations of Aeolian Pivot Chords (Within-Mode)

I	II	III	IV	V	VI	VII
a/A,D,E	b*/A	C/A,D,E	d/ A,D,G	e/A,B,E	F/A,D,G	G/A,B,E
e/A,B,E	f♯*/E	G/A,B,E	a/A,D,E	b/B,E,F♯	C/A,D,E	D/B,E,F♯
b/B,E,F♯	c♯*/B	D/B,E,F♯	e/A,B,E	f♯/B,C♯,F♯	G/A,B,E	A/B,C♯,F♯
f♯/B,C♯,F♯	g♯*/F♯	A/B,C♯,F♯	b/B,E,F♯	c♯/C♯,F♯,G♯	D/B,E,F♯	E/C♯,F♯,G♯
c♯/C♯,F♯,G♯	d♯*/C♯	E/C♯,F♯,G♯	f♯/B,C♯,F♯	g♯/C♯,E♭,G♯	A/B,C♯,F♯	B/C♯,E♭,G♯
g♯/C♯,E♭,G♯	a♯*/G♯	B/C♯,E♭,G♯	c♯/C♯,F♯,G♯	d♯/B♭,E♭,G♯	E/C♯,F♯,G♯	F♯/B♭,E♭,G♯
d/A,D,G	e*/D	F/A,D,G	g/C,D,G	a/A,D,E	B♭/C,D,G	C/A,D,E
g/C,D,G	a*/G	B♭/C,D,G	c/C,F,G	d/A,D,G	E♭/C,F,G	F/A,D,G
c/C,F,G	d*/C	E♭/C,F,G	f/B♭,C,F	g/C,D,G	A♭/B♭,C,F	B♭/C,D,G
f/B♭,C,F	g*/F	A♭/B♭,C,F	b♭/B♭,E♭,F	c/C,F,G	D♭/ B♭,E♭,F	E♭/C,F,G
b♭/B♭,E♭,F	g*/B♭	D♭/B♭,E♭,F	e♭/B♭,E♭,G♯	f/B♭,C,F	G♭/B♭,E♭,G♯	A♭/B♭,C,F
e♭/B♭,E♭,G♯	c*/E♭	G♭/B♭,E♭,G♯	a♭ /C♯,E♭,G♯	b♭/B♭,E♭,F	C♭/C♯,E♭,G♯	D♭/B♭,E♭,F

Within-Mode Prepared Modulation

The within-mode prepared modulations in Ionian and Aeolian were touched upon previously, but here we'll present the possibilities more systematically. The use of each scale step in modulation will be presented for closer and more distant keys starting with the tonic chords. The Ionian pivot chords are restricted to keys a major second, major third, perfect fourth, and perfect fifth above the tonic.

Ionian Tonic.

The Ionian tonic (in the first key) can be used as pivot in some cases, but is best not used to modulations to the subdominant key. The tonic chord is shared by the Ionian key a perfect fourth and perfect fifth above. In the case of C Ionian, that would be F:V and G:IV. In Ex. 84a, the progressions from C:I to each chord of F and G that introduces a chromatic change are shown.

Ex.84a: Ionian Tonic Triad as Within-Mode Pivot

C:I F:II   C:I F:IV   C:I F:VII   C:I G:III   C:I G:V   C:I G:VII

Aeolian Tonic.

The Aeolian tonic can be used as pivot chord to the shared Aeolian keys a perfect fourth and perfect fifth above. In the case of **A** Aeolian, that would be **D:V** and **E:IV**. However, modulations to the subdominant key are not favorable since the first key tonic is the second key dominant. In Ex. 84b, the progressions from **A:I** to each chord of **D** and **E** Aeolian that introduces a chromatic change are shown.

Ex.84b: Aeolian Tonic Triad as Within-Mode Pivot

A:I D:II   A:I D:IV   A:I D:VI   A:I E:II   A:I E:V   A:I E:VII

Ionian II.

The Ionian II is a minor chord and due to its neutral relations can be a useful pivot in many cases. The II chord is shared by the key a perfect fourth and minor seventh above. In the case of **C** Ionian, that would be **F:VI** and **B♭:III.** In Ex. 85a, the progressions from **C:II** to each chord of **F** and **B♭** Ionian that introduces a chromatic change are shown.

Ex.85a: Ionian II Triad as Within-Mode Pivot

Aeolian II.

The diminished Aeolian II is not a usable pivot to Aeolian keys.

Ionian III.

The Ionian III is a quite useful pivot. The III chord is shared by the key a major second and perfect fifth above. In the case of **C** Ionian, that would be **D:II** and **G:VI.** In Ex. 86a, the progressions from **C:III** to each chord of **D** and **G** Ionian that introduces a chromatic change are shown.

354

Ex.86a: Ionian III Triad as Within-Mode Pivot

C:III D:I C:III D:III C:III D:V C:III D:VI C:III D:VII C:III G:III C:III G:V C:III G:VII

Aeolian III.

The Aeolian III is a convenient pivot due to its overall neutrality. The III can be used as pivot chord to the shared Aeolian keys a perfect fourth and perfect fifth above. In the case of **A** Aeolian, that would be **D**:VII and **E**:VI. (Remember that Aeolian VII is a major triad unlike in the minor scale.) In Ex. 86b, the progressions from **A**:III to each chord of **D** and **E** Aeolian that introduces a chromatic change are shown.

Ex.86b: Aeolian III Triad as Within-Mode Pivot

A:III D:II A:III D:IV A:III D:VI A:III E:II A:III E:V A:III E:VII

Ionian IV.

The Ionian IV has a destination key interpretation as the tonic or dominant, so its use is questionable. The IV chord is shared by the key a perfect fourth and minor seventh above. In the case of C Ionian, that would be F:I and Bb:V. Note however that C:IV is the tonic for F Ionian. In Ex. 87a, the progressions from C:IV to each chord of F and Bb Ionian that introduces a chromatic change are shown.

Ex.87a: Ionian IV Triad as Within-Mode Pivot

C:IV F:II C:IV F:IV C:IV F:VII C:IV Bb:I C:IV Bb:II C:IV Bb:IV C:IV Bb:VI C:IV Bb:VII

Aeolian IV.

The Aeolian IV has similar issues as the Ionian IV when used as a pivot chord since it becomes the tonic or dominant of the second keys. The IV chord is shared by the key a perfect fourth and minor seventh above. In the case of A Aeolian, that would be D:I and G:V. Note however that A:IV is the tonic of D Aeolian. In Ex. 87b, the progressions from A:IV to each chord of D and G Aeolian that introduces a chromatic change are shown.

Ex.87b: Aeolian IV Triad as Within-Mode Pivot

A:IV D:II A:IV D:IV A:IV D:VI A:IV G:I   A:IV G:II   A:IV G:III   A:IV G:IV A:IV G:VI

Ionian V.

The Ionian V chord is shared by the key a major second and perfect fifth above. Obviously, it is not the V in those keys and its use is not restricted for that reason. However, it may appear to be a deceptive cadence in terms of the first key. In the case of C Ionian, that would be D:IV and G:I. Note that C:V is the tonic in the key of G Ionian. In Ex. 88a, the progressions from C:V to each chord of D and G Ionian that introduces a chromatic change are shown.

Ex.88a: Ionian V Triad as Within-Mode Pivot

C:V   D:I   C:V   D:III C:V   D:V   C:V   D:VI C:V D:VII   C:V   G:III   C: V G:V   C:V G:VII

Aeolian V.

The Aeolian V chord is shared by the key a major second and perfect fifth above. In the case of A Aeolian, that would be B:IV and

357

E:I. Note however that **A:V** is the tonic of **E** Aeolian. In Ex. 88b, the progressions from **A:V** to each chord of **B** and **E** Aeolian that introduces a chromatic change are shown.

Ex.88b: Aeolian V Triad as Within-Mode Pivot

A:V B:I A:V B:II A:V B:III A:V B:V A:V B:VII A:V E:II A:V E:V A:V E:VII

Ionian VI.

The minor Ionian VI can be easily used as pivot. The VI chord is shared by the Ionian key a perfect fourth and perfect fifth above. In the case of **C** Ionian, that would be **F:III** and **G:II** Ionian. In Ex. 89a, the progressions from **C:VI** to each chord of **F** and **G** that introduces a chromatic change are shown.

Ex.89a: Ionian VI Triad as Within-Mode Pivot

C:VI F:II C:VI F:IV C:VI F:VII C:VI G:III C:VI G:V C:VI G:VII

Aeolian VI.

The Aeolian VI is a convenient pivot due to its neutrality. The VI chord is shared by the key a perfect fourth and minor seventh above. In the case of **A** Aeolian, that would be **D:III** and **G:VII**. In Ex. 89b, the progressions from **A:VI** to each chord of **D** and **G** Aeolian that introduces a chromatic change are shown.

Ex.89b: Aeolian VI Triad as Within-Mode Pivot

A:VI D:II A:VI D:IV A:VI D:VI A:VI G:I A:VI G:II A:VI G:III A:VI G:IV A:VI G:VI

Ionian VII.

The diminished Ionian VII is not usable as an Ionian pivot.

Aeolian VII.

The Aeolian VII can be used as pivot. The VII chord is shared by the key a major second and perfect fifth above. In the case of **A** Aeolian, that would be **B:VI** and **E:III**. In Ex. 90, the progressions from **A:VII** to each chord of **B** and **E** Aeolian that introduces a chromatic change are shown.

Ex.90: Aeolian VII Triad as Within-Mode Pivot

A:VII B:I A:VII B:II A:VII B:III A:VII B:V A:VII B:VII A:VII E:II A:VII E:V A:VII E:VII

Within-Dyad Prepared Modulation

Although the possibilities inherent in within-dyad modulation are more than within-mode obviously, the additional keys relevant to pivot chords are all relative keys as noted. Thus, the available progressions don't change. However, their particular role in the modulation may vary since the chords play a different role depending on the mode. For example, the V - VI progression in C Ionian would become a VII - I progression in A Aeolian (see Tables 26a and b).

The tricky part of within-dyad modulation, and between-dyad modulation for that matter, is the differentiation of relative keys in different modes. This is the reason for the extensive examination in previous chapters on characteristic progressions for each of the modes. As was also noted, the establishment of a mode is a lengthier process outside of the Ionian mode since there is nothing as decisive as the V^7 - I progression. Therefore the focus here will be on such modulations to relative keys. The other keys which have overlapping triads can be investigated by the reader since they involve no new procedures.

360

Table 26a: The Relations of Ionian Scale Degrees with the other Modes (Within-Dyad and Between-Dyad Modulation)

Ionian	I	II	III	IV	V	VI	VII
Aeolian	III	IV	V	VI	VII	I	II
Mixolyd.	IV	V	VI	VII	I	II	III
Phrygian	VI	VII	I	II	III	IV	V
Lydian	V	VI	VII	I	II	III	IV
Dorian	VII	I	II	III	IV	V	VI

Table 26b: The Relations of Aeolian Scale Degrees with the other Modes (Within-Dyad and Between-Dyad Modulation)

Aeolian	I	II	III	IV	V	VI	VII
Ionian	VI	VII	I	II	III	IV	V
Mixolyd.	II	III	IV	V	VI	VII	I
Phrygian	IV	V	VI	VII	I	II	III
Lydian	III	IV	V	VI	VII	I	II
Dorian	V	VI	VII	I	II	III	IV

Ionian Tonic to Aeolian.

The Ionian tonic is the Aeolian III, which is a generally neutral chord without pronounced upward or downward tendencies (Ex. 91a).

Aeolian Tonic to Ionian.

The Aeolian tonic is the Ionian VI, which is a neutral chord (Ex. 91b).

Ex.91: Ionian and Aeolian Tonic Triads as Within-Dyad Pivot

Ionian II to Aeolian.

The Ionian II is Aeolian IV, which is an important step of that mode. It can be a useful pivot, particularly where a more direct modulation is sought (Ex. 92a).

Aeolian II to Ionian.

The diminished Aeolian II is Ionian VII, which has a strong cadential relation to I, but can be used in some restricted circumstances (Ex. 92b).

Ex.92: Ionian and Aeolian II Triads as Within-Dyad Pivot

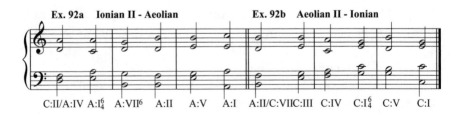

Ionian III to Aeolian.

The Ionian III is the Aeolian V, which is not the best pivot due to its importance as dominant (Ex. 93a).

Aeolian III to Ionian.

The Aeolian III is the Ionian tonic, which is difficult to use as pivot, unless in inversion (Ex. 93b).

Ex.93: Ionian and Aeolian III Triads as Within-Dyad Pivot

Ionian IV to Aeolian.

The Ionian IV is the Aeolian VI, which has some downward tendencies to the Aeolian V (Ex. 94a).

Aeolian IV to Ionian.

The Aeolian IV is Ionian II, which is a convenient pivot due to its neutrality (Ex. 94b).

Ex.94: Ionian and Aeolian IV Triads as Within-Dyad Pivot

Ex. 94a   Ionian IV - Aeolian   Ex. 94b   Aeolian IV - Ionian

C:IV/A:VI   A:III   A:VII⁶   A:I⁶₄   A:V   A:I   A:IV/C:II   C:V⁶₄   C:IV   C:I

Ionian V to Aeolian.

The Ionian V is Aeolian VII, which has only a mild tendency to ascend to the tonic and therefore can be more freely used as a pivot (Ex. 95a).

Aeolian V to Ionian.

The Aeolian V is the Ionian III, which is a convenient pivot (Ex. 95b).

Ex.95: Ionian and Aeolian V Triads as Within-Dyad Pivot

Ex. 95a   Ionian V - Aeolian   Ex. 95b   Aeolian V - Ionian

C:V/A:VII A:I⁶   A:IV⁶   A:V⁶   A:III⁶   A:I   A:V/C:III C:VI   C:II   C:V   C:IV   C:I

Ionian VI to Aeolian.

The Ionian VI is Aeolian I. This is difficult to use as a pivot unless possibly in inversion (Ex. 96a).

Aeolian VI to Ionian.

The Aeolian VI is Ionian IV, which is a key step of the mode and also a mild threat to its tonic. Therefore, this pivot has to be used carefully (Ex. 96b).

Ex.96: Ionian and Aeolian VI Triads as Within-Dyad Pivot

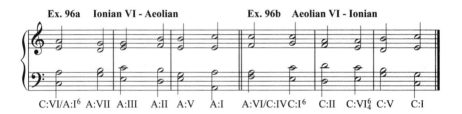

Ionian VII to Aeolian.

The diminished Ionian VII is Aeolian II, which can be used in some circumstances as a pivot (Ex. 97a).

Aeolian VII to Ionian.

The Aeolian VII is Ionian V, which is not a convenient pivot (Ex. 97b).

Ex.97: Ionian and Aeolian VII Triads as Within-Dyad Pivot

Ex. 97a   Ionian VII - Aeolian   Ex. 97b   Aeolian VII - Ionian

C:VII/A:II A:V⁶   A:VI   A:I⁶₄   A:V   A:I   A:VII/   C:III   C:VI⁶   C:IV⁶₄   C:V   C:I
                                              C:V⁶₄

Between-Dyad Prepared Modulation

Far more so than within-dyad prepared modulation, between-dyad prepared modulation has enough different possibilities to fill several chapters describing them. Again the major difficulty is establishing the mode given the existence of the competing relative keys. Between-dyad modulation is the most difficult to accomplish successfully in the modern modal system since it somewhat loosens the procedures designed to establish and maintain the dyad. Its use requires care also because of its centrifugal effect on the musical form of modal compositions. Generally, between-dyad modulation has to be made an integral part of a work's structure and sufficient repetition or musical space should be allowed to establish the new dyad. As displayed in Tables 26a and b, examples are already presented in the within-dyad sample progressions (e.g. Ionian II to Myxolydian corresponds to Phrygian VII to Mixolydian).

Ionian Tonic to Lydian/Dorian.
The Ionian tonic is the Lydian V. This is an important step of the mode, with prominent involvement in cadences and should be used carefully. The Ionian I is the Dorian VII, which is a convenient pivot.

Aeolian Tonic to Lydian/Dorian.
The Aeolian tonic is the Lydian III and Dorian V. The Lydian III is more neutral than Dorian V, with its role in cadences.

Ionian II to Lydian/Dorian.
The Ionian II is Lydian VI, which is a neutral step and Dorian I, which is more awkward to use.

Aeolian II to Lydian/Dorian.
The diminished Aeolian II is Lydian IV, which is generally not a good choice for pivot. Aeolian II is Dorian VI, which could be used in some circumstances, particularly progressing to II.

Ionian III to Lydian/Dorian.
The Ionian III is the Lydian VII and the Dorian II. Both are usable but the Lydian VII has a leading tone relation to I.

Aeolian III to Lydian/Dorian.
The Aeolian III is the Lydian V, which is important to modal cadences and difficult to use. It is also Dorian VII, which is a useful pivot.

Ionian IV to Lydian/Dorian.
The Ionian IV is the Lydian I which is not a good choice for pivot. The IV is also Dorian III, which is a neutral chord.

Aeolian IV to Lydian/Dorian.
The Aeolian IV is Lydian VI, which is a convenient pivot due to its neutrality. It is the Dorian I, which is a less convenient pivot.

Ionian V to Lydian/Dorian.
The Ionian V is Lydian II which is a usable chord and is also Dorian I, which is not easily usable.

Aeolian V to Lydian/Dorian.
The Aeolian V is the Lydian VII and the Dorian II, both of which are usable with some care.

Ionian VI to Lydian/Dorian.
The Ionian VI is Lydian III, a neutral chord, and Dorian II, which has a role in cadences.

Aeolian VI to Lydian/Dorian.
The Aeolian VI is Lydian I which is a difficult step to use. It is also Dorian III, which is a neutral chord.

Ionian VII to Lydian/Dorian.
The diminished Ionian VII is Lydian IV, which cannot be easily used as pivot, as well as Dorian III, which is a convenient pivot.

Aeolian VII to Lydian/Dorian.
The Aeolian VII is Lydian II and a convenient pivot although it does have a role in cadences. It is also Dorian IV, which because of its lack of agreement with the tonic is a more easily used pivot than some other modal subdominants.

Ionian Tonic to Mixolydian/Phrygian.
The Ionian tonic is the Mixolydian IV. This is an important step of the mode, with prominent involvement in cadences and should be used carefully. The Ionian I is the Phrygian VI, which is a convenient pivot.

Aeolian Tonic to Mixolydian/Phrygian.
The Aeolian tonic is the Mixolydian II, a neutral chord and Phrygian IV, which is a prominent step but usable.

Ionian II to Mixolydian/Phrygian.
The Ionian II is Mixolydian V, which is more usable than most other dominants and Phrygian VII, which is important in cadences but can be used carefully.

Aeolian II to Mixolydian/Phrygian.
The diminished Aeolian II is Mixolydian III, which is generally not a good choice for pivot. Aeolian II is Phrygian V which is similarly difficult to use as pivot.

Ionian III to Mixolydian/Phrygian.
The Ionian III is the Mixolydian VI, quite usable, and the Phrygian tonic, difficult to use as a pivot.

368

Aeolian III to Mixolydian/Phrygian.

The Aeolian III is the Mixolydian IV, which is important to the cadence and not easily usable. It is also Phrygian VI, which is a useful pivot.

Ionian IV to Mixolydian/Phrygian.

The Ionian IV is the Mixolydian VII, which is a prominent step but usable if care is taken. The IV is also Phrygian II, which is a difficult to use due to its use in the cadence.

Aeolian IV to Lydian/Dorian.

The Aeolian IV is Mixolydian V, which is a usable pivot if care is taken. It is the Phrygian VII, which also must be used carefully as pivot.

Ionian V to Mixolydian/Phrygian.

The Ionian V is Mixolydian I, which is difficult to use. It is also Phrygian III, which is quite usable.

Aeolian V to Mixolydian/Phrygian.

The Aeolian V is the Mixolydian VI which is a neutral chord and quite useable. It is also the Phrygian I, which is difficult to use.

Ionian VI to Mixolydian/Phrygian.

The Ionian VI is Mixolydian II, a neutral chord, and Phrygian IV, which has an important role in cadences.

Aeolian VI to Mixolydian/Phrygian.

The Aeolian VI is Mixolydian VII, which can be used if care is taken. It is also Phrygian II, which is a difficult chord as pivot.

Ionian VII to Mixolydian/Phrygian.

The diminished Ionian VII is Mixolydian III, as well as Phrygian V, which are usable under certain circumstances as pivot.

Aeolian VII to Mixolydian/Phrygian.

The Aeolian VII is Mixolydian I, a more difficult choice as pivot. It is also Phrygian III, which is easily used.

Appendix 4
Root Position Triad Progressions
to the Other Triads and Seventh Chords

Appendix 4

Appendix 4

Appendix 4

Appendix 4

APPENDIX 4

Appendix 4

APPENDIX 5
PARENTHETIC HARMONIES BY MODAL KEY

Ionian - Aeolian Dyad Parenthetic Harmonies

Ionian	C	d	e	F	G	a	b*	C	O
Parenthetic Key									
Aeolian	d	e*	F	g	a	B♭	C	d	1♭
		II of II	III of II	IV of II	V of II	VI of II	VII of II		
Altered note	6th	5th♭	4th	3rd	2nd	root	7th		
Aeolian	e	f#*	G	a	b	C	D	e	1#
		II of III	III of III	IV of III	V of III	VI of III	VII of III		
Altered note	2nd	root	7th	6th	5th	4th#	3rd		
Ionian	F	g	a	B♭	C	d	e*	F	1♭
		II of IV	III of IV	IV of IV	V of IV	VI of IV	VII of IV		
Altered note	4th	3rd	2nd	root	7th	6th	5th♭		
Ionian	G	a	b	C	D	e	f#※	G	1#
		II of V	III of V	IV of V	V of V	VI of V	VII of V		
Altered note	7th	6th	5th	4th#	3rd	2nd	root		

Aeolian	a	b*	C	d	e	F	G	a	O
Parenthetic Key									
Aeolian	d	e*	F	g	a	B♭	C	d	1♭
		II of IV	III of IV	IV of IV	V of IV	VI of IV	VII of IV		
Altered note	6th	5th♭	4th	3rd	2nd	root	7th		
Aeolian	e	f#*	G	a	b	C	D	e	1#
		II of V	III of V	IV of V	V of V	VI of V	VII of V		
Altered note	2nd	root	7th	6th	5th	4th#	3rd		
Ionian	F	g	a	B♭	C	d	e*	F	1♭
		II of VI	III of VI	IV of VI	V of VI	VI of VI	VII of VI		
Altered note	4th	3rd	2nd	root	7th	6th	5th♭		
Ionian	G	a	b	C	D	e	f#*	G	1#
		II of VII	III of VII	IV of VII	V of VII	VI of VII	VII of VII		
Altered note	7th	6th	5th	4th#	3rd	2nd	root		

Ionian	G	a	b	C	D	e	f#*	G	1#
Parenthetic Key									
Aeolian	a	b*	C	d	e	F	G	a	O
		II of II	III of II	IV of II	V of II	VI of II	VII of II		
Altered note	6th	5th♭	4th	3rd	2nd	root	7th		
Aeolian	b	c#*	D	e	f#	G	A	b	2#
		II of III	III of III	IV of III	V of III	VI of III	VII of III		
Altered note	2nd	root	7th	6th	5th	4th#	3rd		
Ionian	C	d	e	F	G	a	b*	C	O
		II of IV	III of IV	IV of IV	V of IV	VI of IV	VII of IV		
Altered note	4th	3rd	2nd	root	7th	6th	5th♭		
Ionian	D	e	f#	G	A	b	c#*	D	2#
		II of V	III of V	IV of V	V of V	VI of V	VII of V		
Altered note	7th	6th	5th	4th#	3rd	2nd	root		

Aeolian	e	f#*	G	a	b	C	D	e	1#
Parenthetic Key									
Aeolian	a	b*	C	d	e	F	G	a	O
		II of IV	III of IV	IV of IV	V of IV	VI of IV	VII of IV		
Altered note	6th	5th♭	4th	3rd	2nd	root	7th		
Aeolian	b	c#*	D	e	f#	G	A	b	2#
		II of V	III of V	IV of V	V of V	VI of V	VII of V		
Altered note	2nd	root	7th	6th	5th	4th#	3rd		
Ionian	C	d	e	F	G	a	b*	C	O
		II of VI	III of VI	IV of VI	V of VI	VI of VI	VII of VI		
Altered note	4th	3rd	2nd	root	7th	6th	5th♭		
Ionian	D	e	f#	G	A	b	c#*	D	2#
		II of VII	III of VII	IV of VII	V of VII	VI of VII	VII of VII		
Altered note	7th	6th	5th	4th#	3rd	2nd	root		

380

Ionian	D	e	f#	G	A	b	c#*	D	2#
Parenthetic Key									
Aeolian	e	f#*	G	a	b	C	D	e	1#
		II of II	III of II	IV of II	V of II	VI of II	VII of II		
Altered note	6th	5th♭	4th	3rd	2nd	root	7th		
Aeolian	f#	g#*	A	b	c#	D	E	f#	3#
		II of III	III of III	IV of III	V of III	VI of III	VII of III		
Altered note	2nd	root	7th	6th	5th	4th#	3rd		
Ionian	G	a	b	C	D	e	f#*	G	1#
		II of IV	III of IV	IV of IV	V of IV	VI of IV	VII of IV		
Altered note	4th	3rd	2nd	root	7th	6th	5th♭		
Ionian	A	b	c#	D	E	f#	g#*	A	3#
		II of V	III of V	IV of V	V of V	VI of V	VII of V		
Altered note	7th	6th	5th	4th#	3rd	2nd	root		

Aeolian	b	c#*	D	e	f#	G	A	b	2#
Parenthetic Key									
Aeolian	e	f#*	G	a	b	C	D	e	1#
		II of IV	III of IV	IV of IV	V of IV	VI of IV	VII of IV		
Altered note	6th	5th♭	4th	3rd	2nd	root	7th		
Aeolian	f#	g#*	A	b	c#	D	E	f#	3#
		II of V	III of V	IV of V	V of V	VI of V	VII of V		
Altered note	2nd	root	7th	6th	5th	4th#	3rd		
Ionian	G	a	b	C	D	e	f#*	G	1#
		II of VI	III of VI	IV of VI	V of VI	VI of VI	VII of VI		
Altered note	4th	3rd	2nd	root	7th	6th	5th♭		
Ionian	A	b	c#	D	E	f#	g#*	A	3#
		II of VII	III of VII	IV of VII	V of VII	VI of VII	VII of VII		
Altered note	7th	6th	5th	4th#	3rd	2nd	root		

Ionian	A	b	c#	D	E	f#	g#*	A	3#
Parenthetic Key									
Aeolian	b	c#*	D	e	f#	G	A	b	2#
		II of II	III of II	IV of II	V of II	VI of II	VII of II		
Altered note	6th	5th♭	4th	3rd	2nd	root	7th		
Aeolian	c#	d#*	E	f#	g#	A	B	c#	4#
		II of III	III of III	IV of III	V of III	VI of III	VII of III		
Altered note	2nd	root	7th	6th	5th	4th#	3rd		
Ionian	D	e	f#	G	A	b	c#*	D	2#
		II of IV	III of IV	IV of IV	V of IV	VI of IV	VII of IV		
Altered note	4th	3rd	2nd	root	7th	6th	5th♭		
Ionian	E	f#	g#	A	B	c#	d#*	E	4#
		II of V	III of V	IV of V	V of V	VI of V	VII of V		
Altered note	7th	6th	5th	4th#	3rd	2nd	root		

Aeolian	f#	g#*	A	b	c#	D	E	f#	3#
Parenthetic Key									
Aeolian	b	c#*	D	e	f#	G	A	b	2#
		II of IV	III of IV	IV of IV	V of IV	VI of IV	VII of IV		
Altered note	6th	5th♭	4th	3rd	2nd	root	7th		
Aeolian	c#	d#*	E	f#	g#	A	B	c#	4#
		II of V	III of V	IV of V	V of V	VI of V	VII of V		
Altered note	2nd	root	7th	6th	5th	4th#	3rd		
Ionian	D	e	f#	G	A	b	c#*	D	2#
		II of VI	III of VI	IV of VI	V of VI	VI of VI	VII of VI		
Altered note	4th	3rd	2nd	root	7th	6th	5th♭		
Ionian	E	f#	g#	A	B	c#	d#*	E	4#
		II of VII	III of VII	IV of VII	V of VII	VI of VII	VII of VII		
Altered note	7th	6th	5th	4th#	3rd	2nd	root		

Ionian	E	f#	g#	A	B	c#	d#×	E	4#
Parenthetic Key									
Aeolian	f#	g#*	A	b	c#	D	E	f#	3#
		II of II	III of II	IV of II	V of II	VI of II	VII of II		
Altered note	6th	5th♭	4th	3rd	2nd	root	7th		
Aeolian	g#	a#*	B	c#	d#	E	F#	g#	5#
		II of III	III of III	IV of III	V of III	VI of III	VII of III		
Altered note	2nd	root	7th	6th	5th	4th#	3rd		
Ionian	A	b	c#	D	E	f#	g#*	A	3#
		II of IV	III of IV	IV of IV	V of IV	VI of IV	VII of IV		
Altered note	4th	3rd	2nd	root	7th	6th	5th♭		
Ionian	B	c#	d#	E	F#	g#	a#*	B	5#
		II of V	III of V	IV of V	V of V	VI of V	VII of V		
Altered note	7th	6th	5th	4th#	3rd	2nd	root		

Aeolian	c#	d#*	E	f#	g#	A	B	c#	4#
Parenthetic Key									
Aeolian	f#	g#*	A	b	c#	D	E	f#	3#
		II of IV	III of IV	IV of IV	V of IV	VI of IV	VII of IV		
Altered note	6th	5th♭	4th	3rd	2nd	root	7th		
Aeolian	g#	a#×	B	c#	d#	E	F#	g#	5#
		II of V	III of V	IV of V	V of V	VI of V	VII of V		
Altered note	2nd	root	7th	6th	5th	4th#	3rd		
Ionian	A	b	c#	D	E	f#	g#*	A	3#
		II of VI	III of VI	IV of VI	V of VI	VI of VI	VII of VI		
Altered note	4th	3rd	2nd	root	7th	6th	5th♭		
Ionian	B	c#	d#	E	F#	g#	a#*	B	5#
		II of VII	III of VII	IV of VII	V of VII	VI of VII	VII of VII		
Altered note	7th	6th	5th	4th#	3rd	2nd	root		

383

Ionian	B	c#	d#	E	F#	g#	a#*	B	5#
Parenthetic Key									
Aeolian	c#	d#*	E	f#	g#	A	B	c#	4#
		II of II	III of II	IV of II	V of II	VI of II	VII of II		
Altered note	6th	5th♭	4th	3rd	2nd	root	7th		
Aeolian	d#	e#*	F#	g#	a#	B	C#	d#	6#
		II of III	III of III	IV of III	V of III	VI of III	VII of III		
Altered note	2nd	root	7th	6th	5th	4th#	3rd		
Ionian	E	f#	g#	A	B	c#	d#*	E	4#
		II of IV	III of IV	IV of IV	V of IV	VI of IV	VII of IV		
Altered note	4th	3rd	2nd	root	7th	6th	5th♭		
Ionian	F#	g#	a#	B	C#	d#	e#✳	F#	6#
		II of V	III of V	IV of V	V of V	VI of V	VII of V		
Altered note	7th	6th	5th	4th#	3rd	2nd	root		

Aeolian	g#	a#✳	B	c#	d#	E	F#	g#	5#
Parenthetic Key									
Aeolian	c#	d#*	E	f#	g#	A	B	c#	4#
		II of IV	III of IV	IV of IV	V of IV	VI of IV	VII of IV		
Altered note	6th	5th♭	4th	3rd	2nd	root	7th		
Aeolian	d#	e#*	F#	g#	a#	B	C#	d#	6♭/6#
		II of V	III of V	IV of V	V of V	VI of V	VII of V		
Altered note	2nd	root	7th	6th	5th	4th#	3rd		
Ionian	E	f#	g#	A	B	c#	d#*	E	4#
		II of VI	III of VI	IV of VI	V of VI	VI of VI	VII of VI		
Altered note	4th	3rd	2nd	root	7th	6th	5th♭		
Ionian	F#/G♭	g#	a#	B	C#	d#	e#✳	F#	6#/6♭
		II of VII	III of VII	IV of VII	V of VII	VI of VII	VII of VII		
Altered note	7th	6th	5th	4th#	3rd	2nd	root		

Ionian	F♯/G♭	g♯	a♯	B	C♯	d♯	e♯×	F♯	6♯/6♭
Parenthetic Key									
Aeolian	g♯	a♯×	B	c♯	d♯	E	F♯	g♯	5♯
		II of II	III of II	IV of II	V of II	VI of II	VII of II		
Altered note	6th	5th♭	4th	3rd	2nd	root	7th		
Aeolian	b♭	c*	D♭	e♭	f	G♭	A♭	b♭	5♭/7♯
		II of III	III of III	IV of III	V of III	VI of III	VII of III		
Altered note	2nd	root	7th	6th	5th	4th♯	3rd		
Ionian	B	c♯	d♯	E	F♯	g♯	a♯*	B	5♯
		II of IV	III of IV	IV of IV	V of IV	VI of IV	VII of IV		
Altered note	4th	3rd	2nd	root	7th	6th	5th♭		
Ionian	D♭	e♭	f	G♭	A♭	b♭	c*	D♭	5♭/7♯
		II of V	III of V	IV of V	V of V	VI of V	VII of V		
Altered note	7th	6th	5th	4th♯	3rd	2nd	root		

Aeolian	e♭/d♯	f*	G♭	a♭	b♭	C♭	D♭	e♭	6♭/6♯
Parenthetic Key									
Aeolian	g♯/a♭	a♯×	B	c♯	d♯	E	F♯	g♯	5♯/7♭
		II of IV	III of IV	IV of IV	V of IV	VI of IV	VII of IV		
Altered note	6th	5th♭	4th	3rd	2nd	root	7th		
Aeolian	b♭	c*	D♭	e♭	f	G♭	A♭	b♭	5♭/7♯
		II of V	III of V	IV of V	V of V	VI of V	VII of V		
Altered note	2nd	root	7th	6th	5th	4th♯	3rd		
Ionian	B	c♯	d♯	E	F♯	g♯	a♯*	B	5♯/7♭
		II of VI	III of VI	IV of VI	V of VI	VI of VI	VII of VI		
Altered note	4th	3rd	2nd	root	7th	6th	5th♭		
Ionian	D♭	e♭	f	G♭	A♭	b♭	c*	D♭	5♭/7♯
		II of VII	III of VII	IV of VII	V of VII	VI of VII	VII of VII		
Altered note	7th	6th	5th	4th♯	3rd	2nd	root		

385

Ionian	F	g	a	B♭	C	d	e*	F	1♭
Parenthetic Key									
Aeolian	g	a*	B♭	c	d	E♭	F	g	2♭
		II of II	III of II	IV of II	V of II	VI of II	VII of II		
Altered note	6th	5th♭	4th	3rd	2nd	root	7th		
Aeolian	a	b*	C	d	e	F	G	a	O
		II of III	III of III	IV of III	V of III	VI of III	VII of III		
Altered note	2nd	root	7th	6th	5th	4th♯	3rd		
Ionian	B♭	c	d	E♭	F	g	a*	B♭	2♭
		II of IV	III of IV	IV of IV	V of IV	VI of IV	VII of IV		
Altered note	4th	3rd	2nd	root	7th	6th	5th♭		
Ionian	C	d	e	F	G	a	b*	C	O
		II of V	III of V	IV of V	V of V	VI of V	VII of V		
Altered note	7th	6th	5th	4th♯	3rd	2nd	root		

Aeolian	d	e*	F	g	a	B♭	C	d	1♭
Parenthetic Key									
Aeolian	g	a*	B♭	c	d	E♭	F	g	2♭
		II of IV	III of IV	IV of IV	V of IV	VI of IV	VII of IV		
Altered note	6th	5th♭	4th	3rd	2nd	root	7th		
Aeolian	a	b*	C	d	e	F	G	a	O
		II of V	III of V	IV of V	V of V	VI of V	VII of V		
Altered note	2nd	root	7th	6th	5th	4th♯	3rd		
Ionian	B♭	c	d	E♭	F	g	a*	B♭	2♭
		II of VI	III of VI	IV of VI	V of VI	VI of VI	VII of VI		
Altered note	4th	3rd	2nd	root	7th	6th	5th♭		
Ionian	C	d	e	F	G	a	b*	C	O
		II of VII	III of VII	IV of VII	V of VII	VI of VII	VII of VII		
Altered note	7th	6th	5th	4th♯	3rd	2nd	root		

386

Ionian	B♭	c	d	E♭	F	g	a*	B♭	2♭
Parenthetic Key									
Aeolian	c	d*	E♭	f	g	A♭	B♭	c	3♭
			II of II	III of II	IV of II	V of II	VI of II	VII of II		
Altered note	6th	5th♭	4th	3rd	2nd	root	7th		
Aeolian	d	e*	F	g	a	B♭	C	d	1♭
			II of III	III of III	IV of III	V of III	VI of III	VII of III		
Altered note	2nd	root	7th	6th	5th	4th♯	3rd		
Ionian	E♭	f*	g	A♭	B♭	c	d*	E♭	3♭
			II of IV	III of IV	IV of IV	V of IV	VI of IV	VII of IV		
Altered note	4th	3rd	2nd	root	7th	6th	5th♭		
Ionian	F	g	a	B♭	C	d	e*	F	1♭
			II of V	III of V	IV of V	V of V	VI of V	VII of V		
Altered note	7th	6th	5th	4th♯	3rd	2nd	root		

Aeolian	g	a*	B♭	c	d	E♭	F	g	2♭
Parenthetic Key									
Aeolian	c	d*	E♭	f	g	A♭	B♭	c	3♭
			II of IV	III of IV	IV of IV	V of IV	VI of IV	VII of IV		
Altered note	6th	5th♭	4th	3rd	2nd	root	7th		
Aeolian	d	e*	F	g	a	B♭	C	d	1♭
			II of V	III of V	IV of V	V of V	VI of V	VII of V		
Altered note	2nd	root	7th	6th	5th	4th♯	3rd		
Ionian	E♭	f*	g	A♭	B♭	c	d*	E♭	3♭
			II of VI	III of VI	IV of VI	V of VI	VI of VI	VII of VI		
Altered note	4th	3rd	2nd	root	7th	6th	5th♭		
Ionian	F	g	a	B♭	C	d	e*	F	1♭
			II of VII	III of VII	IV of VII	V of VII	VI of VII	VII of VII		
Altered note	7th	6th	5th	4th♯	3rd	2nd	root		

Ionian	E♭	f	g	A♭	B♭	c	d*	E♭	3♭
Parenthetic Key									
Aeolian	f	g*	A♭	b♭	c	D♭	E♭	f	4♭
		II of II	III of II	IV of II	V of II	VI of II	VII of II		
Altered note	6th	5th♭	4th	3rd	2nd	root	7th		
Aeolian	g	a*	B♭	c	d	E♭	F	g	2♭
		II of III	III of III	IV of III	V of III	VI of III	VII of III		
Altered note	2nd	root	7th	6th	5th	4th♯	3rd		
Ionian	A♭	b♭	c	D♭	E♭	f	g*	A♭	4♭
		II of IV	III of IV	IV of IV	V of IV	VI of IV	VII of IV		
Altered note	4th	3rd	2nd	root	7th	6th	5th♭		
Ionian	B♭	c	d	E♭	F	g	a*	B♭	2♭
		II of V	III of V	IV of V	V of V	VI of V	VII of V		
Altered note	7th	6th	5th	4th♯	3rd	2nd	root		

Aeolian	c	d*	E♭	f	g	A♭	B♭	c	3♭
Parenthetic Key									
Aeolian	f	g*	A♭	b♭	c	D♭	E♭	f	4♭
		II of IV	III of IV	IV of IV	V of IV	VI of IV	VII of IV		
Altered note	6th	5th♭	4th	3rd	2nd	root	7th		
Aeolian	g	a*	B♭	c	d	E♭	F	g	2♭
		II of V	III of V	IV of V	V of V	VI of V	VII of V		
Altered note	2nd	root	7th	6th	5th	4th♯	3rd		
Ionian	A♭	b♭	c	D♭	E♭	f	g*	A♭	4♭
		II of VI	III of VI	IV of VI	V of VI	VI of VI	VII of VI		
Altered note	4th	3rd	2nd	root	7th	6th	5th♭		
Ionian	B♭	c	d	E♭	F	g	a*	B♭	2♭
		II of VII	III of VII	IV of VII	V of VII	VI of VII	VII of VII		
Altered note	7th	6th	5th	4th♯	3rd	2nd	root		

Ionian	A♭	b♭	c	D♭	E♭	f	g*	A♭	4♭
Parenthetic Key									
Aeolian	b♭	c*	D♭	e♭	f	G♭	A♭	b♭	5♭
		II of II	III of II	IV of II	V of II	VI of II	VII of II		
Altered note	6th	5th♭	4th	3rd	2nd	root	7th		
Aeolian	c	d*	E♭	f	g	A♭	B♭	c	3♭
		II of III	III of III	IV of III	V of III	VI of III	VII of III		
Altered note	2nd	root	7th	6th	5th	4th♯	3rd		
Ionian	D♭	e♭	f	G♭	A♭	b♭	c*	D♭	5♭
		II of IV	III of IV	IV of IV	V of IV	VI of IV	VII of IV		
Altered note	4th	3rd	2nd	root	7th	6th	5th♭		
Ionian	E♭	f	g	A♭	B♭	c	d*	E♭	3♭
		II of V	III of V	IV of V	V of V	VI of V	VII of V		
Altered note	7th	6th	5th	4th♯	3rd	2nd	root		

Aeolian	f	g*	A♭	b♭	c	D♭	E♭	f	4♭
Parenthetic Key									
Aeolian	b♭	c*	D♭	e♭	f	G♭	A♭	b♭	5♭/7♯
		II of IV	III of IV	IV of IV	V of IV	VI of IV	VII of IV		
Altered note	6th	5th♭	4th	3rd	2nd	root	7th		
Aeolian	c	d*	E♭	f	g	A♭	B♭	c	3♭
		II of V	III of V	IV of V	V of V	VI of V	VII of V		
Altered note	2nd	root	7th	6th	5th	4th♯	3rd		
Ionian	D♭	e♭	f	G♭	A♭	b♭	c*	D♭	5♭/7♯
		II of VI	III of VI	IV of VI	V of VI	VI of VI	VII of VI		
Altered note	4th	3rd	2nd	root	7th	6th	5th♭		
Ionian	E♭	f	g	A♭	B♭	c	d*	E♭	3♭
		II of VII	III of VII	IV of VII	V of VII	VI of VII	VII of VII		
Altered note	7th	6th	5th	4th♯	3rd	2nd	root		

Ionian	Db	eb	f	Gb	Ab	bb	c*	Db	5b
Parenthetic Key									
Aeolian	eb	f*	Gb	ab	bb	Cb	Db	eb	6b/6#
		II of II	III of II	IV of II	V of II	VI of II	VII of II		
Altered note	6th	5thb	4th	3rd	2nd	root	7th		
Aeolian	f	g*	Ab	bb	c	Db	Eb	f	4b
		II of III	III of III	IV of III	V of III	VI of III	VII of III		
Altered note	2nd	root	7th	6th	5th	4th#	3rd		
Ionian	Gb	ab	bb	Cb	Db	eb	f*	Gb	6b/6#
		II of IV	III of IV	IV of IV	V of IV	VI of IV	VII of IV		
Altered note	4th	3rd	2nd	root	7th	6th	5thb		
Ionian	Ab	bb	c	Db	Eb	f	g*	Ab	4b
		II of V	III of V	IV of V	V of V	VI of V	VII of V		
Altered note	7th	6th	5th	4th#	3rd	2nd	root		

Aeolian	bb	c*	Db	eb	f	Gb	Ab	bb	5b/7#
Parenthetic Key									
Aeolian	eb/d#	f*	Gb	ab	bb	Cb	Db	eb	6b/6#
		II of IV	III of IV	IV of IV	V of IV	VI of IV	VII of IV		
Altered note	6th	5thb	4th	3rd	2nd	root	7th		
Aeolian	f	g*	Ab	bb	c	Db	Eb	f	4b
		II of V	III of V	IV of V	V of V	VI of V	VII of V		
Altered note	2nd	root	7th	6th	5th	4th#	3rd		
Ionian	Gb	ab	bb	Cb	Db	eb	f*	Gb	6b/6#
		II of VI	III of VI	IV of VI	V of VI	VI of VI	VII of VI		
Altered note	4th	3rd	2nd	root	7th	6th	5thb		
Ionian	Ab	bb	c	Db	Eb	f	g*	Ab	4b
		II of VII	III of VII	IV of VII	V of VII	VI of VII	VII of VII		
Altered note	7th	6th	5th	4th#	3rd	2nd	root		

390

Lydian - Dorian Dyad Parenthetic Harmonies

Lydian	F	G	a	b*	C	d	e	F	O
Parenthetic Key									
Lydian	G	A	b	c#*	D	e	f#	G	2#
		II of II	III of II	IV of II	V of II	VI of II	VII of II		
Altered note	4th#/7th	3rd/6th	2nd/5th	root/4th	3rd/7th	2nd/6th	root/5th		
Dorian	a	b	C	D	e	f#*	G	a	1#
		II of III	III of III	IV of III	V of III	VI of III	VII of III		
Altered note	6th	5th	4th#	3rd	2nd	root	7th		
Lydian	C	D	e	f#*	G	a	b	C	1#
		II of V	III of V	IV of V	V of V	VI of V	VII of V		
Altered note	4th#	3rd	2nd	root	7th	6th	5th		
Dorian	e	f#	G	A	b	c#*	D	e	2#
		II of VII	III of VII	IV of VII	V of VII	VI of VII	VII of VII		
Altered note	2nd/6th	root/5th	4th#/7th	3rd/6th	2nd/5th	root/4th	3rd/7th		

Dorian	d	e	F	G	a	b*	C	d	O
Parenthetic Key									
Dorian	e	f#	G	A	b	c#*	D	e	2#
		II of II	III of II	IV of II	V of II	VI of II	VII of II		
Altered note	2nd/6th	root/5th	4th#/7th	3rd/6th	2nd/5th	root/4th	3rd/7th		
Lydian	G	A	b	c#*	D	e	f#	G	2#
		II of IV	III of IV	IV of IV	V of IV	VI of IV	VII of IV		
Altered note	4th#/7th	3rd/6th	2nd/5th	root/4th	3rd/7th	2nd/6th	root/5th		
Dorian	a	b	C	D	e	f#*	G	a	1#
		II of V	III of V	IV of V	V of V	VI of V	VII of V		
Altered note	6th	5th	4th#	3rd	2nd	root	7th		
Lydian	C	D	e	f#*	G	a	b	C	1#
		II of VII	III of VII	IV of VII	V of VII	VI of VII	VII of VII		
Altered note	4th#	3rd	2nd	root	7th	6th	5th		

Lydian	C	D	e	f#*	G	a	b	C	1#
Parenthetic Key									
Lydian	D	E	f#	g#*	A	b	c#	D	3#
		II of II	III of II	IV of II	V of II	VI of II	VII of II		
Altered note	4th#/7th	3rd/6th	2nd/5th	root/4th#	3rd/7th	2nd/6th	root/5th		
Dorian	e	f#	G	A	b	c#*	D	e	2#
		II of III	III of III	IV of III	V of III	VI of III	VII of III		
Altered note	6th	5th	4th#	3rd	2nd	root	7th		
Lydian	G	A	b	c#*	D	e	f#	G	2#
		II of V	III of V	IV of V	V of V	VI of V	VII of V		
Altered note	4th#	3rd	2nd	root	7th	6th	5th		
Dorian	b	c#	D	E	f#	g#*	A	b	3#
		II of VII	III of VII	IV of VII	V of VII	VI of VII	VII of VII		
Altered note	2nd/6th	root/5th	4th#/7th	3rd/6th	2nd/5th	root/4th	3rd/7th		

Dorian	a	b	C	D	e	f#*	G	a	1#
Parenthetic Key									
Dorian	b	c#	D	E	f#	g#*	A	b	3#
		II of II	III of II	IV of II	V of II	VI of II	VII of II		
Altered note	2nd/6th	root/5th	4th#/7th	3rd/6th	2nd/5th	root/4th	3rd/7th		
Lydian	D	E	f#	g#*	A	b	c#	D	3#
		II of IV	III of IV	IV of IV	V of IV	VI of IV	VII of IV		
Altered note	4th#/7th	3rd/6th	2nd/5th	root/4th	3rd/7th	2nd/6th	root/5th		
Dorian	e	f#	G	A	b	c#*	D	e	2#
		II of V	III of V	IV of V	V of V	VI of V	VII of V		
Altered note	6th	5th	4th#	3rd	2nd	root	7th		
Lydian	G	A	b	c#*	D	e	f#	G	2#
		II of VII	III of VII	IV of VII	V of VII	VI of VII	VII of VII		
Altered note	4th#	3rd	2nd	root	7th	6th	5th		

Lydian	G	A	b	c#*	D	e	f#	G	2#
Parenthetic Key									
Lydian	A	B	c#	d#*	E	f#	g#	A	4#
		II of II	III of II	IV of II	V of II	VI of II	VII of II		
Altered note	4th#/7th	3rd/6th	2nd/5th	root/4th	3rd/7th	2nd/6th	root/5th		
Dorian	b	c#	D	E	f#	g#*	A	b	3#
		II of III	III of III	IV of III	V of III	VI of III	VII of III		
Altered note	6th	5th	4th#	3rd	2nd	root	7th		
Lydian	D	E	f#	g#*	A	b	c#	D	3#
		II of V	III of V	IV of V	V of V	VI of V	VII of V		
Altered note	4th#	3rd	2nd	root	7th	6th	5th		
Dorian	f#	g#	A	B	c#	d#*	E	f#	4#
		II of VII	III of VII	IV of VII	V of VII	VI of VII	VII of VII		
Altered note	2nd/6th	root/5th	4th#/7th	3rd/6th	2nd/5th	root/4th	3rd/7th		

Dorian	e	f#	G	A	b	c#*	D	e	2#
Parenthetic Key									
Dorian	f#	g#	A	B	c#	d#*	E	f#	4#
		II of II	III of II	IV of II	V of II	VI of II	VII of II		
Altered note	2nd/6th	root/5th	4th#/7th	3rd/6th	2nd/5th	root/4th	3rd/7th		
Lydian	A	B	c#	d#*	E	f#	g#	A	4#
		II of IV	III of IV	IV of IV	V of IV	VI of IV	VII of IV		
Altered note	4th#/7th	3rd/6th	2nd/5th	root/4th	3rd/7th	2nd/6th	root/5th		
Dorian	b	c#	D	E	f#	g#*	A	b	3#
		II of V	III of V	IV of V	V of V	VI of V	VII of V		
Altered note	6th	5th	4th#	3rd	2nd	root	7th		
Lydian	D	E	f#	g#*	A	b	c#	D	3#
		II of VII	III of VII	IV of VII	V of VII	VI of VII	VII of VII		
Altered note	4th#	3rd	2nd	root	7th	6th	5th		

393

Lydian	D	E	f#	g#*	A	b	c#	D	3#
Parenthetic Key									
Lydian	E	F#	g#	a#*	B	c#	d#	E	5#
		II of II	III of II	IV of II	V of II	VI of II	VII of II		
Altered note	4th#/7th	3rd/6th	2nd/5th	root/4th	3rd/7th	2nd/6th	root/5th		
Dorian	f#	g#	A	B	c#	d#*	E	f#	4#
		II of III	III of III	IV of III	V of III	VI of III	VII of III		
Altered note	6th	5th	4th#	3rd	2nd	root	7th		
Lydian	A	B	c#	d#*	E	f#	g#	A	4#
		II of V	III of V	IV of V	V of V	VI of V	VII of V		
Altered note	4th#	3rd	2nd	root	7th	6th	5th		
Dorian	c#	d#	E	F#	g#	a#*	B	c#	5#
		II of VII	III of VII	IV of VII	V of VII	VI of VII	VII of VII		
Altered note	2nd/6th	root/5th	4th#/7th	3rd/6th	2nd/5th	root/4th	3rd/7th		

Dorian	b	c#	D	E	f#	g#*	A	b	3#
Parenthetic Key									
Dorian	c#	d#	E	F#	g#	a#*	B	c#	5#
		II of II	III of II	IV of II	V of II	VI of II	VII of II		
Altered note	2nd/6th	root/5th	4th#/7th	3rd/6th	2nd/5th	root/4th	3rd/7th		
Lydian	E	F#	g#	a#*	B	c#	d#	E	5#
		II of IV	III of IV	IV of IV	V of IV	VI of IV	VII of IV		
Altered note	4th#/7th	3rd/6th	2nd/5th	root/4th	3rd/7th	2nd/6th	root/5th		
Dorian	f#	g#	A	B	c#	d#*	E	f#	4#
		II of V	III of V	IV of V	V of V	VI of V	VII of V		
Altered note	6th	5th	4th#	3rd	2nd	root	7th		
Lydian	A	B	c#	d#*	E	f#	g#	A	4#
		II of VII	III of VII	IV of VII	V of VII	VI of VII	VII of VII		
Altered note	4th#	3rd	2nd	root	7th	6th	5th		

Lydian	A	B	c♯	d♯*	E	f♯	g♯	A	4♯
Parenthetic Key									
Lydian	B	C♯	d♯	e♯*	F♯	g♯	a♯	B	6♯/6♭
		II of II	III of II	IV of II	V of II	VI of II	VII of II		
Altered note	4th♯/7th	3rd/6th	2nd/5th	root/4th	3rd/7th	2nd/6th	root/5th		
Dorian	c♯	d♯	E	F♯	g♯	a♯*	B	c♯	5♯
		II of III	III of III	IV of III	V of III	VI of III	VII of III		
Altered note	6th	5th	4th♯	3rd	2nd	root	7th		
Lydian	E	F♯	g♯	a♯*	B	c♯	d♯	E	5♯
		II of V	III of V	IV of V	V of V	VI of V	VII of V		
Altered note	4th♯	3rd	2nd	root	7th	6th	5th		
Dorian	g♯	a♯	B	C♯	d♯	e♯*	F♯	g♯	6♯/6♭
		II of VII	III of VII	IV of VII	V of VII	VI of VII	VII of VII		
Altered note	2nd/6th	root/5th	4th♯/7th	3rd/6th	2nd/5th	root/4th	3rd/7th		

Dorian	f♯	g♯	A	B	c♯	d♯*	E	f♯	4♯
Parenthetic Key									
Dorian	g♯	a♯	B	C♯	d♯	e♯*	F♯	g♯	6♯/6♭
		II of II	III of II	IV of II	V of II	VI of II	VII of II		
Altered note	2nd/6th	root/5th	4th♯/7th	3rd/6th	2nd/5th	root/4th	3rd/7th		
Lydian	B	C♯	d♯	e♯*	F♯	g♯	a♯	B	6♯/6♭
		II of IV	III of IV	IV of IV	V of IV	VI of IV	VII of IV		
Altered note	4th♯/7th	3rd/6th	2nd/5th	root/4th	3rd/7th	2nd/6th	root/5th		
Dorian	c♯	d♯	E	F♯	g♯	a♯*	B	c♯	5♯
		II of V	III of V	IV of V	V of V	VI of V	VII of V		
Altered note	6th	5th	4th♯	3rd	2nd	root	7th		
Lydian	E	F♯	g♯	a♯*	B	c♯	d♯	E	5♯
		II of VII	III of VII	IV of VII	V of VII	VI of VII	VII of VII		
Altered note	4th♯	3rd	2nd	root	7th	6th	5th		

Lydian	E	F#	g#	a#*	B	c#	d#	E	5#
Parenthetic Key									
Lydian	Gb/F#	Ab	bb	c*	Db	eb	f	Gb	5b/7#
		II of II	III of II	IV of II	V of II	VI of II	VII of II		
Altered note	4th#/7th	3rd/6th	2nd/5th	root/4th	3rd/7th	2nd/6th	root/5th		
Dorian	g#	a#	B	C#	d#	e#*	F#	g#	6#/6b
		II of III	III of III	IV of III	V of III	VI of III	VII of III		
Altered note	6th	5th	4th#	3rd	2nd	root	7th		
Lydian	B	C#	d#	e#*	F#	g#	a#	B	6#/6b
		II of V	III of V	IV of V	V of V	VI of V	VII of V		
Altered note	4th#	3rd	2nd	root	7th	6th	5th		
Dorian	eb/d#	f	Gb	Ab	bb	c*	Db	eb	5b/7#
		II of VII	III of VII	IV of VII	V of VII	VI of VII	VII of VII		
Altered note	2nd/6th	root/5th	4th#/7th	3rd/6th	2nd/5th	root/4th	3rd/7th		

Dorian	c#	d#	E	F#	g#	a#*	B	c#	5#
Parenthetic Key									
Dorian	eb/d#	f	Gb	Ab	bb	c*	Db	eb	5b/7#
		II of II	III of II	IV of II	V of II	VI of II	VII of II		
Altered note	2nd/6th	root/5th	4th#/7th	3rd/6th	2nd/5th	root/4th	3rd/7th		
Lydian	Gb/F#	Ab	bb	c*	Db	eb	f	Gb	5b/7#
		II of IV	III of IV	IV of IV	V of IV	VI of IV	VII of IV		
Altered note	4th#/7th	3rd/6th	2nd/5th	root/4th	3rd/7th	2nd/6th	root/5th		
Dorian	g#	a#	B	C#	d#	e#*	F#	g#	6#/6b
		II of V	III of V	IV of V	V of V	VI of V	VII of V		
Altered note	6th	5th	4th#	3rd	2nd	root	7th		
Lydian	B	C#	d#	e#*	F#	g#	a#	B	6#/6b
		II of VII	III of VII	IV of VII	V of VII	VI of VII	VII of VII		
Altered note	4th#	3rd	2nd	root	7th	6th	5th		

396

Lydian	B	C#	d#	e#*	F#	g#	a#	B	6#/6♭
Parenthetic Key									
Lydian	D♭	E♭	f	g*	A♭	b♭	c	D♭	4♭
		II of II	III of II	IV of II	V of II	VI of II	VII of II		
Altered note	4th♯/7th	3rd/6th	2nd/5th	root/4th	3rd/7th	2nd/6th	root/5th		
Dorian	e♭/d♯	f	G♭	A♭	b♭	c*	D♭	e♭	5♭/7♯
		II of III	III of III	IV of III	V of III	VI of III	VII of III		
Altered note	6th	5th	4th♯	3rd	2nd	root	7th		
Lydian	G♭/F♯	A♭	b♭	c*	D♭	e♭	f	G♭	5♭/7♯
		II of V	III of V	IV of V	V of V	VI of V	VII of V		
Altered note	4th♯	3rd	2nd	root	7th	6th	5th		
Dorian	b♭	c	D♭	E♭	f	g*	A♭	b♭	4♭
		II of VII	III of VII	IV of VII	V of VII	VI of VII	VII of VII		
Altered note	2nd/6th	root/5th	4th♯/7th	3rd/6th	2nd/5th	root/4th	3rd/7th		

Dorian	g♯	a♯	B	C#	d#	e#*	F#	g♯	6#/6♭
Parenthetic Key									
Dorian	b♭	c	D♭	E♭	f	g*	A♭	b♭	4♭
		II of II	III of II	IV of II	V of II	VI of II	VII of II		
Altered note	2nd/6th	root/5th	4th♯/7th	3rd/6th	2nd/5th	root/4th	3rd/7th		
Lydian	D♭	E♭	f	g*	A♭	b♭	c	D♭	4♭
		II of IV	III of IV	IV of IV	V of IV	VI of IV	VII of IV		
Altered note	4th♯/7th	3rd/6th	2nd/5th	root/4th	3rd/7th	2nd/6th	root/5th		
Dorian	e♭/d♯	f	G♭	A♭	b♭	c*	D♭	e♭	5♭/7♯
		II of V	III of V	IV of V	V of V	VI of V	VII of V		
Altered note	6th	5th	4th♯	3rd	2nd	root	7th		
Lydian	G♭/F♯	A♭	b♭	c*	D♭	e♭	f	G♭	5♭/7♯
		II of VII	III of VII	IV of VII	V of VII	VI of VII	VII of VII		
Altered note	4th♯	3rd	2nd	root	7th	6th	5th		

397

Lydian	Bb	C	d	e*	F	g	a	Bb	1b
Parenthetic Key									
Lydian	C	D	e	f#*	G	a	b	C	1#
		II of II	III of II	IV of II	V of II	VI of II	VII of II		
Altered note	4th#/7th	3rd/6th	2nd/5th	root/4th	3rd/7th	2nd/6th	root/5th		
Dorian	d	e	F	G	a	b*	C	d	O
		II of III	III of III	IV of III	V of III	VI of III	VII of III		
Altered note	6th	5th	4th#	3rd	2nd	root	7th		
Lydian	F	G	a	b*	C	d	e	F	O
		II of V	III of V	IV of V	V of V	VI of V	VII of V		
Altered note	4th#	3rd	2nd	root	7th	6th	5th		
Dorian	a	b	C	D	e	f#*	G	a	1#
		II of VII	III of VII	IV of VII	V of VII	VI of VII	VII of VII		
Altered note	2nd/6th	root/5th	4th#/7th	3rd/6th	2nd/5th	root/4th	3rd/7th		

Dorian	g	a	Bb	C	d	e*	F	g	1b
Parenthetic Key									
Dorian	a	b	C	D	e	f#*	G	a	1#
		II of II	III of II	IV of II	V of II	VI of II	VII of II		
Altered note	2nd/6th	root/5th	4th#/7th	3rd/6th	2nd/5th	root/4th	3rd/7th		
Lydian	C	D	e	f#*	G	a	b	C	1#
		II of IV	III of IV	IV of IV	V of IV	VI of IV	VII of IV		
Altered note	4th#/7th	3rd/6th	2nd/5th	root/4th	3rd/7th	2nd/6th	root/5th		
Dorian	d	e	F	G	a	b*	C	d	O
		II of V	III of V	IV of V	V of V	VI of V	VII of V		
Altered note	6th	5th	4th#	3rd	2nd	root	7th		
Lydian	F	G	a	b*	C	d	e	F	O
		II of VII	III of VII	IV of VII	V of VII	VI of VII	VII of VII		
Altered note	4th#	3rd	2nd	root	7th	6th	5th		

398

Lydian	Eb	F	g	a*	Bb	c	d	Eb	2b
Parenthetic Key									
Lydian	F	G	a	b*	C	d	e	F	O
		II of II	III of II	IV of II	V of II	VI of II	VII of II		
Altered note	4th♯/7th	3rd/6th	2nd/5th	root/4th	3rd/7th	2nd/6th	root/5th		
Dorian	g	a	Bb	C	d	e*	F	g	1b
		II of III	III of III	IV of III	V of III	VI of III	VII of III		
Altered note	6th	5th	4th♯	3rd	2nd	root	7th		
Lydian	Bb	C	d	e*	F	g	a	Bb	1b
		II of V	III of V	IV of V	V of V	VI of V	VII of V		
Altered note	4th♯	3rd	2nd	root	7th	6th	5th		
Dorian	d	e	F	G	a	b*	C	d	O
		II of VII	III of VII	IV of VII	V of VII	VI of VII	VII of VII		
Altered note	2nd/6th	root/5th	4th♯/7th	3rd/6th	2nd/5th	root/4th	3rd/7th		

Dorian	c	d	Eb	F	g	a*	Bb	c	2b
Parenthetic Key									
Dorian	d	e	F	G	a	b*	C	d	O
		II of II	III of II	IV of II	V of II	VI of II	VII of II		
Altered note	2nd/6th	root/5th	4th♯/7th	3rd/6th	2nd/5th	root/4th	3rd/7th		
Lydian	F	G	a	b*	C	d	e	F	O
		II of IV	III of IV	IV of IV	V of IV	VI of IV	VII of IV		
Altered note		3rd/6th	2nd/5th	root/4th	3rd/7th	2nd/6th	root/5th		
Dorian	g	a	Bb	C	d	e*	F	g	1b
		II of V	III of V	IV of V	V of V	VI of V	VII of V		
Altered note	6th	5th	4th♯	3rd	2nd	root	7th		
Lydian	Bb	C	d	e*	F	g	a	Bb	1b
		II of VII	III of VII	IV of VII	V of VII	VI of VII	VII of VII		
Altered note	4th♯	3rd	2nd	root	7th	6th	5th		

399

Lydian	Ab	Bb	c	d*	Eb	f	g	Ab	3b
Parenthetic Key									
Lydian	Bb	C	d	e*	F	g	a	Bb	1b
		II of II	III of II	IV of II	V of II	VI of II	VII of II		
Altered note	4th#/7th	3rd/6th	2nd/5th	root/4th	3rd/7th	2nd/6th	root/5th		
Dorian	c	d	Eb	F	g	a*	Bb	c	2b
		II of III	III of III	IV of III	V of III	VI of III	VII of III		
Altered note	6th	5th	4th#	3rd	2nd	root	7th		
Lydian	Eb	F	g	a*	Bb	c	d	Eb	2b
		II of V	III of V	IV of V	V of V	VI of V	VII of V		
Altered note	4th#	3rd	2nd	root	7th	6th	5th		
Dorian	g	a	Bb	C	d	e*	F	g	1b
		II of VII	III of VII	IV of VII	V of VII	VI of VII	VII of VII		
Altered note	2nd/6th	root/5th	4th#/7th	3rd/6th	2nd/5th	root/4th	3rd/7th		

Dorian	f	g	Ab	Bb	c	d*	Eb	f	3b
Parenthetic Key									
Dorian	g	a	Bb	C	d	e*	F	g	1b
		II of II	III of II	IV of II	V of II	VI of II	VII of II		
Altered note	2nd/6th	root/5th	4th#/7th	3rd/6th	2nd/5th	root/4th	3rd/7th		
Lydian	Bb	C	d	e*	F	g	a	Bb	1b
		II of IV	III of IV	IV of IV	V of IV	VI of IV	VII of IV		
Altered note	4th#/7th	3rd/6th	2nd/5th	root/4th	3rd/7th	2nd/6th	root/5th		
Dorian	c	d	Eb	F	g	a*	Bb	c	2b
		II of V	III of V	IV of V	V of V	VI of V	VII of V		
Altered note	6th	5th	4th#	3rd	2nd	root	7th		
Lydian	Eb	F	g	a*	Bb	c	d	Eb	2b
		II of VII	III of VII	IV of VII	V of VII	VI of VII	VII of VII		
Altered note	4th#	3rd	2nd	root	7th	6th	5th		

400

Lydian	D♭	E♭	f	g*	A♭	b♭	c	D♭	4♭
Parenthetic Key									
<u>Lydian</u>	E♭	F	g	a*	B♭	c	d	E♭	2♭
		II of II	III of II	IV of II	V of II	VI of II	VII of II		
Altered note	4th♯/7th	3rd/6th	2nd/5th	root/4th	3rd/7th	2nd/6th	root/5th		
<u>Dorian</u>	f	g	A♭	B♭	c	d*	E♭	f	3♭
		II of III	III of III	IV of III	V of III	VI of III	VII of III		
Altered note	6th	5th	4th♯	3rd	2nd	root	7th		
<u>Lydian</u>	A♭	B♭	c	d*	E♭	f	g	A♭	3♭
		II of V	III of V	IV of V	V of V	VI of V	VII of V		
Altered note	4th♯	3rd	2nd	root	7th	6th	5th		
<u>Dorian</u>	c	d	E♭	F	g	a*	B♭	c	2♭
		II of VII	III of VII	IV of VII	V of VII	VI of VII	VII of VII		
Altered note	2nd/6th	root/5th	4th♯/7th	3rd/6th	2nd/5th	root/4th	3rd/7th		

Dorian	b♭	c	D♭	E♭	f	g*	A♭	b♭	4♭
Parenthetic Key									
<u>Dorian</u>	c	d	E♭	F	g	a*	B♭	c	2♭
		II of II	III of II	IV of II	V of II	VI of II	VII of II		
Altered note	2nd/6th	root/5th	4th♯/7th	3rd/6th	2nd/5th	root/4th	3rd/7th		
<u>Lydian</u>	E♭	F	g	a*	B♭	c	d	E♭	2♭
		II of IV	III of IV	IV of IV	V of IV	VI of IV	VII of IV		
Altered note	4th♯/7th	3rd/6th	2nd/5th	root/4th	3rd/7th	2nd/6th	root/5th		
<u>Dorian</u>	f	g	A♭	B♭	c	d*	E♭	f	3♭
		II of V	III of V	IV of V	V of V	VI of V	VII of V		
Altered note	6th	5th	4th♯	3rd	2nd	root	7th		
<u>Lydian</u>	A♭	B♭	c	d*	E♭	f	g	A♭	3♭
		II of VII	III of VII	IV of VII	V of VII	VI of VII	VII of VII		
Altered note	4th♯	3rd	2nd	root	7th	6th	5th		

Lydian	G♭	A♭	b♭	c*	D♭	e♭	f	G♭	5♭/7♯
Parenthetic Key									
Lydian	A♭	B♭	c	d*	E♭	f	g	A♭	3♭
		II of II	III of II	IV of II	V of II	VI of II	VII of II		
Altered note	4th♯/7th	3rd/6th	2nd/5th	root/4th	3rd/7th	2nd/6th	root/5th		
Dorian	b♭	c	D♭	E♭	f	g*	A♭	b♭	4♭
		II of III	III of III	IV of III	V of III	VI of III	VII of III		
Altered note	6th	5th	4th♯	3rd	2nd	root	7th		
Lydian	D♭	E♭	f	g*	A♭	b♭	c	D♭	4♭
		II of V	III of V	IV of V	V of V	VI of V	VII of V		
Altered note	4th♯	3rd	2nd	root	7th	6th	5th		
Dorian	f	g	A♭	B♭	c	d*	E♭	f	3♭
		II of VII	III of VII	IV of VII	V of VII	VI of VII	VII of VII		
Altered note	2nd/6th	root/5th	4th♯/7th	3rd/6th	2nd/5th	root/4th	3rd/7th		

Dorian	e♭/d♯	f	G♭	A♭	b♭	c*	D♭	e♭	5♭/7♯
Parenthetic Key									
Dorian	f	g	A♭	B♭	c	d*	E♭	f	3♭
		II of II	III of II	IV of II	V of II	VI of II	VII of II		
Altered note		root/5th	4th♯/7th	3rd/6th	2nd/5th	root/4th	3rd/7th		
Lydian	A♭	B♭	c	d*	E♭	f	g	A♭	3♭
		II of IV	III of IV	IV of IV	V of IV	VI of IV	VII of IV		
Altered note	4th♯/7th	3rd/6th	2nd/5th	root/4th	3rd/7th	2nd/6th	root/5th		
Dorian	b♭	c	D♭	E♭	f	g*	A♭	b♭	4♭
		II of V	III of V	IV of V	V of V	VI of V	VII of V		
Altered note	6th	5th	4th♯	3rd	2nd	root	7th		
Lydian	D♭	E♭	f	g*	A♭	b♭	c	D♭	4♭
		II of VII	III of VII	IV of VII	V of VII	VI of VII	VII of VII		
Altered note	4th♯	3rd	2nd	root	7th	6th	5th		

402

Mixolydian - Phrygian Dyad Parenthetic Harmonies

Mixolydian	G	a	b*	C	d	e	F	G	O
Parenthetic Key									
Phrygian	a	Bb	C	d	e*	F	g	a	1b
		II of II	III of II	IV of II	V of II	VI of II	VII of II		
Altered note	2nd	root	7th	6th	5thb	4th	3rd		
Mixolydian	C	d	e*	F	g	a	Bb	C	1b
		II of IV	III of IV	IV of IV	V of IV	VI of IV	VII of IV		
Altered note	7th	6th	5thb	4th	3rd	2nd	root		
Phrygian	d	Eb	F	g	a*	Bb	c	d	2b
		II of V	III of V	IV of V	V of V	VI of V	VII of V		
Altered note	2nd/6th	root/5th	4th/7th	3rd/6th	2nd/5thb	root/4th	3rd/7th		
Mixolydian	F	g	a*	Bb	c	d	Eb	F	2b
		II of VII	III of VII	IV of VII	V of VII	VI of VII	VII of VII		
Altered note	4th/7th	3rd/6th	2nd/5thb	root/4th	3rd/7th	2nd/6th	root/5th		

Phrygian	e	F	G	a	b*	C	d	e	O
Parenthetic Key									
Mixolydian	F	g	a*	Bb	c	d	Eb	F	2b
		II of II	III of II	IV of II	V of II	VI of II	VII of II		
Altered note	4th/7th	3rd/6th	2nd/5thb	root/4th	3rd/7th	2nd/6th	root/5th		
Phrygian	a	Bb	C	d	e*	F	g	a	1b
		II of IV	III of IV	IV of IV	V of IV	VI of IV	VII of IV		
Altered note	2nd	root	7th	6th	5thb	4th	3rd		
Mixolydian	C	d	e*	F	g	a	Bb	C	1b
		II of VI	III of VI	IV of VI	V of VI	VI of VI	VII of VI		
Altered note	7th	6th	5thb	4th	3rd	2nd	root		
Phrygian	d	Eb	F	g	a*	Bb	c	d	2b
		II of VII	III of VII	IV of VII	V of VII	VI of VII	VII of VII		
Altered note	2nd/6th	root/5th	4th/7th	3rd/6th	2nd/5thb	root/4th	3rd/7th		

403

Mixolydian	D	e	f♯*	G	a	b	C	D	1♯
Parenthetic Key									
Phrygian	e	F	G	a	b*	C	d	e	O
		II of II	III of II	IV of II	V of II	VI of II	VII of II		
Altered note	2nd	root	7th	6th	5th♭	4th	3rd		
Mixolydian	G	a	b*	C	d	e	F	G	O
		II of IV	III of IV	IV of IV	V of IV	VI of IV	VII of IV		
Altered note	7th	6th	5th♭	4th	3rd	2nd	root		
Phrygian	a	B♭	C	d	e*	F	g	a	1♭
		II of V	III of V	IV of V	V of V	VI of V	VII of V		
Altered note	2nd/6th	root/5th	4th/7th	3rd/6th	2nd/5th♭	root/4th	3rd/7th		
Mixolydian	C	d	e*	F	g	a	B♭	C	1♭
		II of VII	III of VII	IV of VII	V of VII	VI of VII	VII of VII		
Altered note	4th/7th	3rd/6th	2nd/5th♭	root/4th	3rd/7th	2nd/6th	root/5th		

Phrygian	b	C	D	e	f♯※	G	a	b	1♯
Parenthetic Key									
Mixolydian	C	d	e*	F	g	a	B♭	C	1♭
		II of II	III of II	IV of II	V of II	VI of II	VII of II		
Altered note	4th/7th	3rd/6th	2nd/5th♭	root/4th	3rd/7th	2nd/6th	root/5th		
Phrygian	e	F	G	a	b*	C	d	e	O
		II of IV	III of IV	IV of IV	V of IV	VI of IV	VII of IV		
Altered note	2nd	root	7th	6th	5th♭	4th	3rd		
Mixolydian	G	a	b*	C	d	e	F	G	O
		II of VI	III of VI	IV of VI	V of VI	VI of VI	VII of VI		
Altered note	7th	6th	5th♭	4th	3rd	2nd	root		
Phrygian	a	B♭	C	d	e*	F	g	a	1♭
		II of VII	III of VII	IV of VII	V of VII	VI of VII	VII of VII		
Altered note	2nd/6th	root/5th	4th/7th	3rd/6th	2nd/5th♭	root/4th	3rd/7th		

Mixolydian	A	b	c#*	D	e	f#	G	A	2#
Parenthetic Key									
Phrygian	b	C	D	e	f#*	G	a	b	1#
		II of II	III of II	IV of II	V of II	VI of II	VII of II		
Altered note	2nd	root	7th	6th	5thb	4th	3rd		
Mixolydian	D	e	f#*	G	a	b	C	D	1#
		II of IV	III of IV	IV of IV	V of IV	VI of IV	VII of IV		
Altered note	7th	6th	5thb	4th	3rd	2nd	root		
Phrygian	e	F	G	a	b*	C	d	e	O
		II of V	III of V	IV of V	V of V	VI of V	VII of V		
Altered note	2nd/6th	root/5th	4th/7th	3rd/6th	2nd/5thb	root/4th	3rd/7th		
Mixolydian	G	a	b*	C	d	e	F	G	O
		II of VII	III of VII	IV of VII	V of VII	VI of VII	VII of VII		
Altered note	4th/7th	3rd/6th	2nd/5thb	root/4th	3rd/7th	2nd/6th	root/5th		

Phrygian	f#	G	A	b	c#*	D	e	f#	2#
Parenthetic Key									
Mixolydian	G	a	b*	C	d	e	F	G	O
		II of II	III of II	IV of II	V of II	VI of II	VII of II		
Altered note	4th/7th	3rd/6th	2nd/5thb	root/4th	3rd/7th	2nd/6th	root/5th		
Phrygian	b	C	D	e	f#*	G	a	b	1#
		II of IV	III of IV	IV of IV	V of IV	VI of IV	VII of IV		
Altered note	2nd	root	7th	6th	5thb	4th	3rd		
Mixolydian	D	e	f#*	G	a	b	C	D	1#
		II of VI	III of VI	IV of VI	V of VI	VI of VI	VII of VI		
Altered note	7th	6th	5thb	4th	3rd	2nd	root		
Phrygian	e	F	G	a	b*	C	d	e	O
		II of VII	III of VII	IV of VII	V of VII	VI of VII	VII of VII		
Altered note	2nd/6th	root/5th	4th/7th	3rd/6th	2nd/5thb	root/4th	3rd/7th		

Mixolydian	E	f#	g#*	A	b	c#	D	E	3#
Parenthetic Key									
Phrygian	f#	G	A	b	c#*	D	e	f#	2#
		II of II	III of II	IV of II	V of II	VI of II	VII of II		
Altered note	2nd	root	7th	6th	5th♭	4th	3rd		
Mixolydian	A	b	c#*	D	e	f#	G	A	2#
		II of IV	III of IV	IV of IV	V of IV	VI of IV	VII of IV		
Altered note	7th	6th	5th♭	4th	3rd	2nd	root		
Phrygian	b	C	D	e	f#*	G	a	b	1#
		II of V	III of V	IV of V	V of V	VI of V	VII of V		
Altered note	2nd/6th	root/5th	4th/7th	3rd/6th	2nd/5th♭	root/4th	3rd/7th		
Mixolydian	D	e	f#*	G	a	b	C	D	1#
		II of VII	III of VII	IV of VII	V of VII	VI of VII	VII of VII		
Altered note	4th/7th	3rd/6th	2nd/5th♭	root/4th	3rd/7th	2nd/6th	root/5th		

Phrygian	c#	D	E	f#	g#*	A	b	c#	3#
Parenthetic Key									
Mixolydian	D	e	f#*	G	a	b	C	D	1#
		II of II	III of II	IV of II	V of II	VI of II	VII of II		
Altered note	4th/7th	3rd/6th	2nd/5th♭	root/4th	3rd/7th	2nd/6th	root/5th		
Phrygian	f#	G	A	b	c#*	D	e	f#	2#
		II of IV	III of IV	IV of IV	V of IV	VI of IV	VII of IV		
Altered note	2nd	root	7th	6th	5th♭	4th	3rd		
Mixolydian	A	b	c#*	D	e	f#	G	A	2#
		II of VI	III of VI	IV of VI	V of VI	VI of VI	VII of VI		
Altered note	7th	6th	5th♭	4th	3rd	2nd	root		
Phrygian	b	C	D	e	f#*	G	a	b	1#
		II of VII	III of VII	IV of VII	V of VII	VI of VII	VII of VII		
Altered note	2nd/6th	root/5th	4th/7th	3rd/6th	2nd/5th♭	root/4th	3rd/7th		

406

Mixolydian	B	c#	d#*	E	f#	g#	A	B	4#
Parenthetic Key									
Phrygian	c#	D	E	f#	g#*	A	b	c#	3#
		II of II	III of II	IV of II	V of II	VI of II	VII of II		
Altered note	2nd	root	7th	6th	5th♭	4th	3rd		
Mixolydian	E	f#	g#*	A	b	c#	D	E	3#
		II of IV	III of IV	IV of IV	V of IV	VI of IV	VII of IV		
Altered note	7th	6th	5th♭	4th	3rd	2nd	root		
Phrygian	f#	G	A	b	c#*	D	e	f#	2#
		II of V	III of V	IV of V	V of V	VI of V	VII of V		
Altered note	2nd/6th	root/5th	4th/7th	3rd/6th	2nd/5th♭	root/4th	3rd/7th		
Mixolydian	A	b	c#*	D	e	f#	G	A	2#
		II of VII	III of VII	IV of VII	V of VII	VI of VII	VII of VII		
Altered note	4th/7th	3rd/6th	2nd/5th♭	root/4th	3rd/7th	2nd/6th	root/5th		

Phrygian	g#	A	B	c#	d#*	E	f#	g#	4#
Parenthetic Key									
Mixolydian	A	b	c#*	D	e	f#	G	A	2#
		II of II	III of II	IV of II	V of II	VI of II	VII of II		
Altered note	4th/7th	3rd/6th	2nd/5th♭	root/4th	3rd/7th	2nd/6th	root/5th		
Phrygian	c#	D	E	f#	g#*	A	b	c#	3#
		II of IV	III of IV	IV of IV	V of IV	VI of IV	VII of IV		
Altered note	2nd	root	7th	6th	5th♭	4th	3rd		
Mixolydian	E	f#	g#*	A	b	c#	D	E	3#
		II of VI	III of VI	IV of VI	V of VI	VI of VI	VII of VI		
Altered note	7th	6th	5th♭	4th	3rd	2nd	root		
Phrygian	f#	G	A	b	c#*	D	e	f#	2#
		II of VII	III of VII	IV of VII	V of VII	VI of VII	VII of VII		
Altered note	2nd/6th	root/5th	4th/7th	3rd/6th	2nd/5th♭	root/4th	3rd/7th		

Mixolydian	F♯	g♯	a♯*	B	c♯	d♯	E	F♯	5♯/7♭
Parenthetic Key									
Phrygian	g♯	A	B	c♯	d♯*	E	f♯	g♯	4♯
		II of II	III of II	IV of II	V of II	VI of II	VII of II		
Altered note	2nd	root	7th	6th	5th♭	4th	3rd		
Mixolydian	B	c♯	d♯*	E	f♯	g♯	A	B	4♯
		II of IV	III of IV	IV of IV	V of IV	VI of IV	VII of IV		
Altered note	7th	6th	5th♭	4th	3rd	2nd	root		
Phrygian	c♯	D	E	f♯	g♯*	A	b	c♯	3♯
		II of V	III of V	IV of V	V of V	VI of V	VII of V		
Altered note	2nd/6th	root/5th	4th/7th	3rd/6th	2nd/5th♭	root/4th	3rd/7th		
Mixolydian	E	f♯	g♯*	A	b	c♯	D	E	3♯
		II of VII	III of VII	IV of VII	V of VII	VI of VII	VII of VII		
Altered note	4th/7th	3rd/6th	2nd/5th♭	root/4th	3rd/7th	2nd/6th	root/5th		

Phrygian	d♯	E	F♯	g♯	a♯*	B	c♯	d♯	5♯/7♭
Parenthetic Key									
Mixolydian	E	f♯	g♯*	A	b	c♯	D	E	3♯
		II of II	III of II	IV of II	V of II	VI of II	VII of II		
Altered note	4th/7th	3rd/6th	2nd/5th♭	root/4th	3rd/7th	2nd/6th	root/5th		
Phrygian	g♯	A	B	c♯	d♯*	E	f♯	g♯	4♯
		II of IV	III of IV	IV of IV	V of IV	VI of IV	VII of IV		
Altered note	2nd	root	7th	6th	5th♭	4th	3rd		
Mixolydian	B	c♯	d♯*	E	f♯	g♯	A	B	4♯
		II of VI	III of VI	IV of VI	V of VI	VI of VI	VII of VI		
Altered note	7th	6th	5th♭	4th	3rd	2nd	root		
Phrygian	c♯	D	E	f♯	g♯*	A	b	c♯	3♯
		II of VII	III of VII	IV of VII	V of VII	VI of VII	VII of VII		
Altered note	2nd/6th	root/5th	4th/7th	3rd/6th	2nd/5th♭	root/4th	3rd/7th		

408

Mixolydian	C	d	e*	F	g	a	B♭	C	1♭
Parenthetic Key									
Phrygian	d	E♭	F	g	a*	B♭	c	d	2♭
		II of II	III of II	IV of II	V of II	VI of II	VII of II		
Altered note	2nd	root	7th	6th	5th♭	4th	3rd		
Mixolydian	F	g	a*	B♭	c	d	E♭	F	2♭
		II of IV	III of IV	IV of IV	V of IV	VI of IV	VII of IV		
Altered note	7th	6th	5th♭	4th	3rd	2nd	root		
Phrygian	g	A♭	B♭	c	d*	E♭	f	g	3♭
		II of V	III of V	IV of V	V of V	VI of V	VII of V		
Altered note	2nd/6th	root/5th	4th/7th	3rd/6th	2nd/5th♭	root/4th	3rd/7th		
Mixolydian	B♭	c	d*	E♭	f	g	A♭	B♭	3♭
		II of VII	III of VII	IV of VII	V of VII	VI of VII	VII of VII		
Altered note	4th/7th	3rd/6th	2nd/5th♭	root/4th	3rd/7th	2nd/6th	root/5th		

Phrygian	a	B♭	C	d	e*	F	g	a	1♭
Parenthetic Key									
Mixolydian	B♭	c	d*	E♭	f	g	A♭	B♭	3♭
		II of II	III of II	IV of II	V of II	VI of II	VII of II		
Altered note	4th/7th	3rd/6th	2nd/5th♭	root/4th	3rd/7th	2nd/6th	root/5th		
Phrygian	d	E♭	F	g	a*	B♭	c	d	2♭
		II of IV	III of IV	IV of IV	V of IV	VI of IV	VII of IV		
Altered note	2nd	root	7th	6th	5th♭	4th	3rd		
Mixolydian	F	g	a*	B♭	c	d	E♭	F	2♭
		II of VI	III of VI	IV of VI	V of VI	VI of VI	VII of VI		
Altered note	7th	6th	5th♭	4th	3rd	2nd	root		
Phrygian	g	A♭	B♭	c	d*	E♭	f	g	3♭
		II of VII	III of VII	IV of VII	V of VII	VI of VII	VII of VII		
Altered note	2nd/6th	root/5th	4th/7th	3rd/6th	2nd/5th♭	root/4th	3rd/7th		

409

Mixolydian	F	g	a*	Bb	c	d	Eb	F	2b
Parenthetic Key									
Phrygian	g	Ab	Bb	c	d*	Eb	f	g	3b
		II of II	III of II	IV of II	V of II	VI of II	VII of II		
Altered note	2nd	root	7th	6th	5thb	4th	3rd		
Mixolydian	Bb	c	d*	Eb	f	g	Ab	Bb	3b
		II of IV	III of IV	IV of IV	V of IV	VI of IV	VII of IV		
Altered note	7th	6th	5thb	4th	3rd	2nd	root		
Phrygian	c	Db	Eb	f	g*	Ab	bb	c	4b
		II of V	III of V	IV of V	V of V	VI of V	VII of V		
Altered note	2nd/6th	root/5th	4th/7th	3rd/6th	2nd/5thb	root/4th	3rd/7th		
Mixolydian	Eb	f	g*	Ab	bb	c	Db	Eb	4b
		II of VII	III of VII	IV of VII	V of VII	VI of VII	VII of VII		
Altered note	4th/7th	3rd/6th	2nd/5thb	root/4th	3rd/7th	2nd/6th	root/5th		

Phrygian	d	Eb	F	g	a*	Bb	c	d	2b
Parenthetic Key									
Mixolydian	Eb	f	g*	Ab	bb	c	Db	Eb	4b
		II of II	III of II	IV of II	V of II	VI of II	VII of II		
Altered note	4th/7th	3rd/6th	2nd/5thb	root/4th	3rd/7th	2nd/6th	root/5th		
Phrygian	g	Ab	Bb	c	d*	Eb	f	g	3b
		II of IV	III of IV	IV of IV	V of IV	VI of IV	VII of IV		
Altered note	2nd	root	7th	6th	5thb	4th	3rd		
Mixolydian	Bb	c	d*	Eb	f	g	Ab	Bb	3b
		II of VI	III of VI	IV of VI	V of VI	VI of VI	VII of VI		
Altered note	7th	6th	5thb	4th	3rd	2nd	root		
Phrygian	c	Db	Eb	f	g*	Ab	bb	c	4b
		II of VII	III of VII	IV of VII	V of VII	VI of VII	VII of VII		
Altered note	2nd/6th	root/5th	4th/7th	3rd/6th	2nd/5thb	root/4th	3rd/7th		

410

Mixolydian	B♭	c	d*	E♭	f	g	A♭	B♭	3♭
Parenthetic Key									
Phrygian	c	D♭	E♭	f	g*	A♭	b♭	c	4♭
		II of II	III of II	IV of II	V of II	VI of II	VII of II		
Altered note	2nd	root	7th	6th	5th♭	4th	3rd		
Mixolydian	E♭	f	g*	A♭	b♭	c	D♭	E♭	4♭
		II of IV	III of IV	IV of IV	V of IV	VI of IV	VII of IV		
Altered note	7th	6th	5th♭	4th	3rd	2nd	root		
Phrygian	f	G♭	A♭	b♭	c*	D♭	e♭	f	5♭
		II of V	III of V	IV of V	V of V	VI of V	VII of V		
Altered note	2nd/6th	root/5th	4th/7th	3rd/6th	2nd/5th♭	root/4th	3rd/7th		
Mixolydian	A♭	b♭	c*	D♭	e♭	f	G♭	A♭	5♭
		II of VII	III of VII	IV of VII	V of VII	VI of VII	VII of VII		
Altered note	4th/7th	3rd/6th	2nd/5th♭	root/4th	3rd/7th	2nd/6th	root/5th		

Phrygian	g	A♭	B♭	c	d*	E♭	f	g	3♭
Parenthetic Key									
Mixolydian	A♭	b♭	c*	D♭	e♭	f	G♭	A♭	5♭
		II of II	III of II	IV of II	V of II	VI of II	VII of II		
Altered note	4th/7th	3rd/6th	2nd/5th♭	root/4th	3rd/7th	2nd/6th	root/5th		
Phrygian	c	D♭	E♭	f	g*	A♭	b♭	c	4♭
		II of IV	III of IV	IV of IV	V of IV	VI of IV	VII of IV		
Altered note	2nd	root	7th	6th	5th♭	4th	3rd		
Mixolydian	E♭	f	g*	A♭	b♭	c	D♭	E♭	4♭
		II of VI	III of VI	IV of VI	V of VI	VI of VI	VII of VI		
Altered note	7th	6th	5th♭	4th	3rd	2nd	root		
Phrygian	f	G♭	A♭	b♭	c*	D♭	e♭	f	5♭
		II of VII	III of VII	IV of VII	V of VII	VI of VII	VII of VII		
Altered note	2nd/6th	root/5th	4th/7th	3rd/6th	2nd/5th♭	root/4th	3rd/7th		

Mixolydian	E♭	f	g*	A♭	b♭	c	D♭	E♭	4♭
Parenthetic Key									
Phrygian	f	G♭	A♭	b♭	c*	D♭	e♭	f	5♭
		II of II	III of II	IV of II	V of II	VI of II	VII of II		
Altered note	2nd	root	7th	6th	5th♭	4th	3rd		
Mixolydian	A♭	b♭	c*	D♭	e♭	f	G♭	A♭	5♭
		II of IV	III of IV	IV of IV	V of IV	VI of IV	VII of IV		
Altered note	7th	6th	5th♭	4th	3rd	2nd	root		
Phrygian	b♭	C♭	D♭	e♭	f*	G♭	a♭	b♭	6♭
		II of V	III of V	IV of V	V of V	VI of V	VII of V		
Altered note	2nd/6th	root/5th	4th/7th	3rd/6th	2nd/5th♭	root/4th	3rd/7th		
Mixolydian	D♭	e♭	f*	G♭	a♭	b♭	C♭	D♭	6♭
		II of VII	III of VII	IV of VII	V of VII	VI of VII	VII of VII		
Altered note	4th/7th	3rd/6th	2nd/5th♭	root/4th	3rd/7th	2nd/6th	root/5th		

Phrygian	c	D♭	E♭	f	g*	A♭	b♭	c	4♭
Parenthetic Key									
Mixolydian	D♭	e♭	f*	G♭	a♭	b♭	C♭	D♭	6♭
		II of II	III of II	IV of II	V of II	VI of II	VII of II		
Altered note	4th/7th	3rd/6th	2nd/5th♭	root/4th	3rd/7th	2nd/6th	root/5th		
Phrygian	f	G♭	A♭	b♭	c*	D♭	e♭	f	5♭
		II of IV	III of IV	IV of IV	V of IV	VI of IV	VII of IV		
Altered note	2nd	root	7th	6th	5th♭	4th	3rd		
Mixolydian	A♭	b♭	c*	D♭	e♭	f	G♭	A♭	5♭
		II of VI	III of VI	IV of VI	V of VI	VI of VI	VII of VI		
Altered note	7th	6th	5th♭	4th	3rd	2nd	root		
Phrygian	b♭	C♭	D♭	e♭	f*	G♭	a♭	b♭	6♭
		II of VII	III of VII	IV of VII	V of VII	VI of VII	VII of VII		
Altered note	2nd/6th	root/5th	4th/7th	3rd/6th	2nd/5th♭	root/4th	3rd/7th		

Mixolydian	A♭	b♭	c*	D♭	e♭	f	G♭	A♭	5#/7♭
Parenthetic Key									
Phrygian	b♭/a#	C♭	D♭	e♭	f*	G♭	a♭	b♭	6♭/6#
		II of II	III of II	IV of II	V of II	VI of II	VII of II		
Altered note	2nd	root	7th	6th	5th♭	4th	3rd		
Mixolydian	D♭/C#	e♭	f*	G♭	a♭	b♭	C♭	D♭	6♭/6#
		II of IV	III of IV	IV of IV	V of IV	VI of IV	VII of IV		
Altered note	7th	6th	5th♭	4th	3rd	2nd	root		
Phrygian	d#	E	F#	g#	a#*	B	c#	d#	5#/7♭
		II of V	III of V	IV of V	V of V	VI of V	VII of V		
Altered note	2nd/6th	root/5th	4th/7th	3rd/6th	2nd/5th♭	root/4th	3rd/7th		
Mixolydian	F#	g#	a#*	B	c#	d#	E	F#	5#/7♭
		II of VII	III of VII	IV of VII	V of VII	VI of VII	VII of VII		
Altered note	4th/7th	3rd/6th	2nd/5th♭	root/4th	3rd/7th	2nd/6th	root/5th		

Phrygian	f	G♭	A♭	b♭	c*	D♭	e♭	f	5♭
Parenthetic Key									
Mixolydian	F#	g#	a#*	B	c#	d#	E	F#	5#/7♭
		II of II	III of II	IV of II	V of II	VI of II	VII of II		
Altered note	4th/7th	3rd/6th	2nd/5th♭	root/4th	3rd/7th	2nd/6th	root/5th		
Phrygian	b♭	C♭	D♭	e♭	f*	G♭	a♭	b♭	6♭/6#
		II of IV	III of IV	IV of IV	V of IV	VI of IV	VII of IV		
Altered note	2nd	root	7th	6th	5th♭	4th	3rd		
Mixolydian	D♭	e♭	f*	G♭	a♭	b♭	C♭	D♭	6♭/6#
		II of VI	III of VI	IV of VI	V of VI	VI of VI	VII of VI		
Altered note	7th	6th	5th♭	4th	3rd	2nd	root		
Phrygian	d#	E	F#	g#	a#*	B	c#	d#	5#/7♭
		II of VII	III of VII	IV of VII	V of VII	VI of VII	VII of VII		
Altered note	2nd/6th	root/5th	4th/7th	3rd/6th	2nd/5th♭	root/4th	3rd/7th		

Mixolydian	D♭	e♭	f*	G♭	a♭	b♭	C♭	D♭	6♭
Parenthetic Key									
Phrygian	d#	E	F#	g#	a#*	B	c#	d#	5#/7♭
			II of II	III of II	IV of II	V of II	VI of II	VII of II	
Altered note	2nd	root	7th	6th	5th♭	4th	3rd		
Mixolydian	F#	g#	a#*	B	c#	d#	E	F#	5#/7♭
			II of IV	III of IV	IV of IV	V of IV	VI of IV	VII of IV	
Altered note	7th	6th	5th♭	4th	3rd	2nd	root		
Phrygian	g#	A	B	c#	d#*	E	f#	g#	4#
			II of V	III of V	IV of V	V of V	VI of V	VII of V	
Altered note	2nd/6th	root/5th	4th/7th	3rd/6th	2nd/5th♭	root/4th	3rd/7th		
Mixolydian	B/C♭	c#	d#*	E	f#	g#	A	B	4#
			II of VII	III of VII	IV of VII	V of VII	VI of VII	VII of VII	
Altered note	4th/7th	3rd/6th	2nd/5th♭	root/4th	3rd/7th	2nd/6th	root/5th		

Phrygian	b♭	C♭	D♭	e♭	f*	G♭	a♭	b♭	6♭
Parenthetic Key									
Mixolydian	B/C♭	c#	d#*	E	f#	g#	A	B	4#
			II of II	III of II	IV of II	V of II	VI of II	VII of II	
Altered note	4th/7th	3rd/6th	2nd/5th♭	root/4th	3rd/7th	2nd/6th	root/5th		
Phrygian	d#	E	F#	g#	a#*	B	c#	d#	5#/7♭
			II of IV	III of IV	IV of IV	V of IV	VI of IV	VII of IV	
Altered note	2nd	root	7th	6th	5th♭	4th	3rd		
Mixolydian	F#	g#	a#*	B	c#	d#	E	F#	5#/7♭
			II of VI	III of VI	IV of VI	V of VI	VI of VI	VII of VI	
Altered note	7th	6th	5th♭	4th	3rd	2nd	root		
Phrygian	g#	A	B	c#	d#*	E	f#	g#	4#
			II of VII	III of VII	IV of VII	V of VII	VI of VII	VII of VII	
Altered note	2nd/6th	root/5th	4th/7th	3rd/6th	2nd/5th♭	root/4th	3rd/7th		

414

Index